D1154426

THE BAND'S MUSIC

THE BAND'S MUSIC

BY

RICHARD FRANKO GOLDMAN

ASSOCIATE CONDUCTOR, GOLDMAN BAND
FORMER SPECIAL FELLOW IN FINE ARTS, COLUMBIA UNIVERSITY

PITMAN PUBLISHING CORPORATION

NEW YORK 1938

COPYRIGHT, 1938, BY
PITMAN PUBLISHING CORPORATION

All rights reserved. No part of this book may be reproduced in any form without the written permission of the publisher.

CM
788
G619

FIRST EDITION

ASSOCIATED COMPANIES

SIR ISAAC PITMAN & SONS, LTD.
Pitman House, Parker Street, Kingsway, London, W.C.2

THE PITMAN PRESS, Bath

PITMAN HOUSE, Little Collins Street, Melbourne

SIR ISAAC PITMAN & SONS (Canada), Ltd.
(Incorporating the Commercial Text Book Company)
Pitman House, 381-383 Church Street, Toronto

PRINTED IN THE UNITED STATES OF AMERICA

PREFACE

THIS BOOK ENDEAVORS to provide a set of reasonably useful program notes for the repertory of the present day American concert band. The numbers listed are for the most part—indeed almost exclusively—transcriptions of works written originally for orchestra or pianoforte. They are of unequal value, therefore, not only as music, but also as adaptations. No attempt has been made in this book to compare or tabulate the differences which exist among various editions, but only insofar as possible to list the names of the publishing houses after the title of each composition. These lists have been made from an exhaustive survey of the catalogues of leading publishers in America and England.

So far as the compositions themselves are concerned, there has likewise been no attempt to observe a critical attitude. In an impartial guide to the band repertory, preferences must be temporarily laid aside. For that reason, the note on the Fugue in A minor of J. S. Bach is no longer than that on the "1812" Overture. Indeed it may be here observed that it is more difficult to write about music which is sufficient unto itself than it is to write about items which depend for their appeal on the pictures they are supposed to evoke. The works listed embrace as much of standard or "classical" music as has been arranged for band, together with a number of representative contemporary works. These works, for better or for worse, constitute the present band repertory. If any deserving compositions are not listed the author asks the reader to believe that the omissions were caused by inadvertence rather than by malice. A number of once popular compositions are

10 Jan 41 Br T 2865

now out of print; these have not been included in this book for obvious reasons.

The notes have been designed less for reference than for actual use in printed programs. They represent an attempt to present, concisely, relevant historical and musical facts about compositions played by bands. In the cases of most composers, brief biographical sketches will be found, together with separate short items for each of the individual compositions. Rather than repeat facts of the composer's life with each of these, the author has left it to the user of the book to combine the biographical with the musical material; he has, however, endeavored to present his material in such a form as to facilitate this combination where it is necessary.

With the major composers a slightly larger form of the same treatment has been adopted. The biographies of these composers, however, are obviously not intended to be exhaustive. They simply present salient items in a form suitable for inclusion in a short program note. They lend themselves readily to further condensation and to combination with the material given under the headings of the compositions.

In the cases of composers of less importance, especially those who are known to band audiences by a single work each, no attempt has been made to include separate biographical sketches. The biographical material has been combined with the note on the composition. Such notes may, if desired, be used without change on a program; the publisher and author will, of course, be duly gratified if acknowledgment of the use is made.

Many composers, such as Offenbach and Suppé, wrote countless dozens of light works which are or have been arranged for band. Most of these works are comic-opera overtures or potpourris which have long and perhaps justly been forgotten. Such works have not been included in this volume, since they will be of little practical interest. The more enduring compositions of the same composers have, however, been included.

The reader will find that there are a very few compositions which are listed, but for which no notes are given. It is to be hoped that the reader will find the reason apparent. In most cases these compositions are short characteristic pieces with titles descriptive enough to serve (for a person of any imagination) in lieu of notes.

To make these notes more generally serviceable, and to cover much of the pertinent material which they necessarily avoid, the author has included in this volume a number of introductory essays. These form an integral part of the volume; it is to be hoped that they will be found both provocative and informative, and that they will provide some sort of framework upon which the program notes themselves may be fitted.

Mr. Grainger's foreword is a contribution which should be read, and preferably memorized, by any person seriously interested in bands or band music. The author cannot possibly express his indebtedness to Mr. Grainger, not only for his interest in this volume, but also for the stimulation of his ideas and for the many lines of thought and research he has suggested.

Grateful acknowledgments are due numerous composers and bandmasters who have favored the author with first-hand information about themselves and their works. As nearly as possible, this information has been presented to the reader in the exact form in which the author received it.

Thanks are also due to the many music publishers mentioned in this volume, and to many representatives of their firms, for music and information put at the author's disposal. Were it not for the whole-hearted co-operation of these publishers, this book would be perhaps still merely on the way.

Parts of the essay on *Original Wind-Instrument Music* first appeared in the *Musical Courier* of December 26, 1931. The enlarged essay is here reprinted with the kind permission of the editor and publisher of that magazine. For further help in research, and for much additional knowledge in the field covered by that essay, the author is indebted to Dr. C. S. Smith of the New York Public Library and to Dr. Hans David of New York University. Needless to say, here again Mr. Grainger has shed much light.

Not least, the author is immeasurably indebted to Dr. Edwin Franko Goldman, at whose suggestion this volume was undertaken, and without whose co-operation it could not possibly have been completed.

Richard Franko Goldman

1938

FOREWORD

THIS BOOK OF RICHARD FRANKO GOLDMAN'S will be a boon not only to band leaders and bandsmen of all kinds, but equally to all music-lovers interested in wind instruments and their music. It fills a long-felt want in unfolding a complete panorama of all the music available for band and wind ensembles, while its copious program-notes and biographical information about outstanding composers provide priceless material to those conductors who want to enrich their band programs with esthetically and emotionally vital data.

The book opens up a fine working knowledge of musical history to any culturally inquisitive band student who lights upon it; the whole history of the band and its development is laid bare in masterly fashion. Especially informative are the author's accounts of the political, sociological and psychological stirs that called the modern concert band into being. Mr. Goldman sees all facts surrounding the band of today and of the past with the eye of a mental marksman, and the merciless yet graceful sarcasm of his pen when dealing with band abuses will not be missed by those with a relish for artistic justice.

Approaching band problems from the constructive, benevolent and life-giving viewpoint of his great father (who is no less than the patron saint of the modern American concert band), Richard Goldman enjoys a singularly inspired vision of the band, and a precise insight into the musical morality incumbent upon band leaders and others responsible for bands. His awareness of these artistic duties has stood him in good stead when compiling his exhaustive lists of the music available for band and wind ensembles, and if conductors of bands and other wind groups will pursue the roads to knowledge charted in this volume they may steer their organizations clear of the fatal mistakes that have beset the symphony orchestra as a popularizer of the world's best music.

For some reason or other music, as it is practised in our concert halls, is the most backward of the arts. We would regard as an ignoramus a professor of literature who taught his students nothing about Homer, Confucius, The Arabian Nights, The Anglo-Saxon Chronicle, The Tale of Genji, The Icelandic Sagas, and who imparted to them no familiarity with the highlights of current literature. A student of architecture would seem a freak if he had never heard of the temples of Egypt, Greece, India and Cambodia, and of the cathedrals of Europe, or if he were unaware of American skyscrapers and of the distinctive contemporary architecture of Holland and Finland. Yet in our musical life laymen and professionals alike admit unblushingly their almost complete ignorance of the great musical creative giants of the 12th, 13th, 14th, 15th, 16th and 17th centuries (men as great as Bach, Beethoven, Wagner, César Franck), and are equally unashamed of their unfamiliarity with most of the greatest compositions of our own century—masterpieces such as "The Mass of Life" by the Englishman Frederick Delius, "Voluspaa," by the Norwegian David Monrad Johansen, the "Evolutionary Quintet," by the American Arthur Fickenscher, "Five Orchestral Pieces," by the Austrian Jew Arnold Schoenberg.

Our audiences are familiar with European music from 1700 to 1900, but before and after that period (which in the opinion of some studious musicians is one of the weakest periods in musical history) their knowledge does not normally extend.

What would we think of the theatre if it presented practically no plays written before 1700 (no Shakespeare, no

Euripides) or after 1900 (no Eugene O'Neill, no Bernard Shaw)? The 500 years of decipherable music that precedes Bach is at least as lovely and important as all post-Bach music, and in the opinion of many well-informed and "classically"-trained music-lovers, the 20th has already proven itself a century, so far, singularly rich in music of spiritual content and soulful beauty. Yet these old and new musical treasures are, and remain, unperformed in our midst.

Broad-minded musicians would have been deeply grateful to the symphony orchestras if they, in their own concerts and in the festivals they dominate, had played a man's part in lifting the veil of ignorance that separates us from the older and newer masterworks of tone. But this chance has been lost. One slender excuse for the symphony orchestra may be made: strictly symphonic orchestration hardly existed before 1700 and is, since about 1900, no longer, it would seem, the normal vehicle for the younger composers of today. This may perhaps explain the indifference of symphony conductors toward compositions that lie outside the conventionally known period, but it does not absolve symphony orchestras from the obligation to present older and newer masterworks that are scored for combinations of instruments that lie contained in the mammoth make-up of the symphony orchestra.

Since little of note was written direct for band during the 18th and 19th centuries (so that the band, in dealing with the compositional output of these centuries, has to be content with arrangements from other mediums), it is to be hoped that the band—already such a wide-spread and many-sided influence in our musical life—will not repeat the mistakes of the symphony orchestra, nor band conductors emulate the ignorance of symphony orchestra conductors. This book should prove a vital agent in banishing such ignorance. In its pages the reader may read of much of the important music written during the Middle Ages and the Renaissance for chamber music combinations of wind instruments by themselves or in conjunction with a voice or voices.

Experimentation will prove to band leaders and band arrangers that much of this earlier music arranges more easily and more effectively for band—with less dissipation of its original character—than does much of the highly string-minded music of the 18th and 19th centuries. Many of these early pieces of music (alive as the day they were written, and performable by small solo groups of wind instruments or by larger band groups such as the saxophone family, the clarinet family, the complete reed band, the brass band) are ideal for giving soloistic chamber-music opportunities to the more skillful band members, and for bringing tonal variety into band programs—just as similar tonal relief is introduced into Suites such as Grieg's "Peer Gynt," Gabriel Fauré's "Pélléas and Mélisande," Bizet's "L'Arlésienne," and Tchaikovsky's "Nutcracker," by sandwiching movements for part of the orchestra (string orchestra, etc.) between movements for the complete orchestra.

Many of these early chamber works for wind may be consulted in Arnold Schering's "Geschichte der Musik in Beispielen" (Musical History in Musical Examples), so often referred to by Mr. Goldman. Those who wish to hear with ears to what heights of euphony these older wind combinations can rise, should listen to some of the gramophone records of the "L'Anthologie Sonore" series,* notably to the double-sided record of Franco-Belgian music, on which such combinations as flute, trombone, other instruments and voice make ravishing tonal blends in romances by Dufay (ca. 1400-1474), Isaac (15th Century) and Ockeghem (ca. 1434-1496).

The most cursory study of the Schering History and of the other informative volumes cited by Mr. Goldman will

* Available from The Gramophone Shop, New York City.

tend to dissipate such untenable current notions as the following—all of which have a deterrent and discouraging influence upon forward-looking band leaders anxious to further musical enlightenment by way of the band:

1. that Haydn "was the father of chamber music,"
2. that chamber music is mainly for strings,
3. that the music of "the great polyphonic period" was primarily for unaccompanied voices,
4. that there was no clear line of demarcation between vocal and instrumental music prior to about 1600.

By perusing the books alluded to by Mr. Goldman the reader will soon discover that the greatest flowering of European chamber music lies before, rather than after, Bach.* Think of the vast mass of music composed for recorders alone!† We need only look at Dufay's exquisite "La Bernardina" (which, by the way, sounds better on wind instruments than on strings) to realize how thoroughly a purely instrumental style of writing—unthinkable for voices—was developed by the time of its publication. (Venice, 1503.)

It is true that most of the older examples of chamber music are for unspecified instruments; but there is no reason to imagine that strings were favored above wind. An examination of old drawings, pictures, sculptures, etc., depicting musical rehearsals and performances will foster a contrary opinion.

Such authoritative students of old music as Arnold Dolmetsch and Dom Anselm Hughes, O.S.B., assure us that the older vocal music was oftenest accompanied by instruments (originally in unison with the voices, no doubt) and the fact that church choirs in the Middle Ages were equipped with portative and positive organs (of the size of the reed

* Read, in this connection, Robert Donington's light-shedding brochure, "The Work and Ideas of Arnold Dolmetsch," procurable from The Dolmetsch Foundation, West Street, Haslemere, Surrey, England.

† Flute à bec; flauto dolce.

organs of today) shows that wind color, as much as string color, was considered a normal tonal background to vocal music.

Thus we are fully justified in accompanying with wind instruments such models of the vocal aria (surely never since surpassed!) as "Anima mea liquefacta est,"* by Lionel Power (English, ca. 1500), "Le jour s'endort,"* by Guillaume Dufay (Netherlands, 15th Cent.) and "O Schönes Weib,"* by Heinrich Finck (German, ca. 1500).

Highly illuminating are Mr. Goldman's lists of music for fanfare or brass band (ranging from Josquin des Près, 1450-1521, to Florent Schmitt, contemporary), and for chorus with wind accompaniment. From the latter class I will mention one masterpiece that, alone, is transcendental enough to alter our conception of musical history and of the artistic possibilities of the wind band: "O Salutaris Hostia," for alto and tenor voices and brass instruments, by the Fleming, Adrian Willaert, published in Venice shortly after 1500.

One is tempted to say that Willaert is deeper and grander than Bach (just as Bach, in his turn, is deeper and grander than Haydn) and that this piece for voices and wind instruments overtops in noble grandeur and solemnity everything known to us for chorus and orchestra by our favorite masters, whoever they be: Bach, Handel, Hadyn, Mozart, Beethoven, Wagner, Franck, Brahms, Delius, Sparre Olsen, etc. Be that as it may, such uplifting music as this (suitable for performance with massed wind instruments†), together with the delectable morsels for wind chamber music touched upon above, and balanced with life-lit compositions for band by living composers (such as Stravinski's Concerto for piano and wind instruments, Hindemith's "Blasmusik," Ernst Toch's

* All these are in Schering.

† Consider also that sensationally effective Mass by Guillaume de Machault (French 1300-1377) for chorus and brass, covering four gramophone records in the fourth volume of "L'Anthologie Sonore."

"Spiel" for wind instruments, Henry Cowell's "Celtic Set") justifies the giving of musical festivals for which the band forms the instrumental nucleus. Such undertakings would extend considerably the radius of band activity, would give the band an enhanced esthetic standing in the community, and would open up to impressionable band-players new vistas of the extent and sublimity of classical music from 1200 to our day.

This book of Richard Franko Goldman's, listing impartially as it does, wind music of all types and periods—thus making band conductors aware both of the immense role played by wind instruments down the earlier centuries of European music and of the renewed interest in the band taken by the most outstanding composers of today—should go far towards establishing that viewpoint, without which even the continually expanding band activities of today will remain artistically fruitless: the realization that the band has esthetic possibilities and responsibilities every bit as high as those of the symphony orchestra.

Percy Grainger

October 13, 1937

"Spiel" for wind instruments, Henry Cowell's "Celtic Set") justifies the giving of musical festivals for which the band forms the instrumental nucleus. Such undertakings would extend considerably the radius of band activity, would give the band an enhanced esthetic standing in the community, and would open up to impressionable band-players new vistas of the extent and sublimity of classical music from 1200 to our day.

This book of Richard Franko Goldman's, listing impartially as it does, wind music of all types and periods—thus making band conductors aware both of the immense role played by wind instruments down the earlier centuries of European music and of the renewed interest in the band taken by the most outstanding composers of today—should go far towards establishing that viewpoint, without which even the continually expanding band activities of today will remain artistically fruitless: the realization that the band has esthetic possibilities and responsibilities every bit as high as those of the symphony orchestra.

Percy Grainger

October 13, 1937.

CONTENTS

PART ONE
INTRODUCTORY

The Band and the Public

ONCE upon a time, and not so long ago at that, band concerts consisted principally of bits of fluff. Overtures by Auber, Rossini, Hérold and other brighteners of the nineteenth century helped give "solidity" to the programs; but the sauce was generally more abundant than the meat. I have before me as I write, a program of a band concert in Central Park; it bears the date of August, 1871. I am, frankly, just as glad as not that I arrived a bit too late for the concert, for here is what it included:

1. Grand March "Don Bucefalo"
2. Overture, "The Merry Wives of Windsor" ....Nicolai
3. Air, "I Think of Thee" ....Abt
4. Galop, "The Wild Hunt" ....Budik
5. Grand Selection, "The Elixir of Love" ....Donizetti
6. Waltz, "Hesperian Sounds" ....Gungl
7. Quartet, "Sancta Mater" ....Rossini
8. Galop, "The Racer" ....Faust
9. Overture, "Semiramide" ....Rossini
10. Waltz ....Strauss
11. Air, "Departed Days" ....Loomis
12. March

One can, without being too complacent, put alongside of this a Central Park program of 1938. The comparison is interesting if one is interested in the development of the band repertory, in the music the band plays. Sixty years ago, it must be remembered, a selection from Gounod was excitingly contemporary, a selection from Wagner dangerously revolutionary, and a selection from Bach about as startling as a selection from Adam de la Hale would be today. (We have not yet quite reached the limits of sophistication!) The

Bach selection, be it added, would more than likely have fallen on deaf benches.

Today bands play Bach, and audiences, even if they do not care for the music, are at least courteous enough to applaud enthusiastically, and sometimes to demand an encore. This, of course, proves more about audiences than it does about bands, but it is important for precisely that reason. It cannot be too strongly emphasized that the development of band music depends largely on the development of audiences. The band repertory can never too greatly outstrip contemporary taste, although bandmasters undoubtedly exert a considerable influence on that taste. The phenomenon goes two ways: bandmasters can "educate" or form the musical intelligence of the public, but the public still can, and does, dictate what the band shall play.

The growth of the band repertory is, therefore, in a large sense the growth of an appreciative public. The factors contributing to this in recent years are many: there are, to begin with, the radio, the awakening of the national "culture-consciousness" under the stimulations both of leisure and of propaganda, and the installation of music in the schools.

The results, in many fields, are interesting and sometimes amusing, but except insofar as they affect bands, must form the material for another study. On the technical side, we have an entirely different matter with which we must deal; the development of the band itself as a medium of musical expression. These two factors, the technical evolution of the band and the musical evolution of the audience, are inseparable. A historical retrospect which makes any pretension to validity must, too, include a number of things which may seem at first sight irrelevant.

We must remember that the band has a definite tradition arising out of the military. From the time of the bands which accompanied Edward III to battle, to the early town bands of

Germany, the oboe bands of Louis XIV and the Napoleonic army bands, wind-instrument combinations have had their musical functions subordinated to what may be termed their moral, civic, or martial duties. A survey of the original literature will show that much honest music was written for wind instruments, but with the exception of marches, little for bands. The concert band did not begin to take shape until the nineteenth century, although its prototype was fully evolved in the eighteenth, as is evidenced by the compositions of Mozart for open-air performance. Technical limitations, the imperfections of wind instruments, had their part in restraining the development of a band literature.

The French Revolution may be said to have actually prepared the way for the growth of band music, although the connection may not be apparent on the surface. Nevertheless, the impulse toward a democratization of the arts was a notable concomitant of the political and social changes of the period. A musical body capable of performing in the open air, where large crowds of people could gather and listen, was an obviously desirable thing; the military bands were soon somewhat augmented for the purpose. It is at this time that we find the first large compositions for wind band: the three symphonies of Gossec. I have no doubt whatsoever that a diligent research would reveal a great number of compositions for wind band dating from the years 1789-1815. Others besides Gossec must have written works like that composer's hymns for band, inspired by fervent republicanism and dedicated to Liberty, Equality and Fraternity.

With the general spread of the social changes brought about by the industrial revolution, the demand for a "popularized" music inevitably grew; and it was met throughout Europe by the military band. Whatever the form of government in a given country, there was created by the shift in the basic structure of society a new public, congregated in cities.

Just as the string quartet was an appropriate musical medium for the salon of a nobleman, so was the enlarged nineteenth century orchestra or band the obvious means of giving musical satisfaction to the larger numbers of the newly franchised middle class. The orchestra developed along lines with which we are familiar; it became the organization appropriate to the large concert-hall. The band became, as it were, an institution for the overflow, for those whose limited material resources excluded them from the orchestra concerts (which, incidentally, built up a clientele just as proud in its way as the nobility), or whose inability to enjoy the increasingly complicated compositions of the musical vanguard led them to demand a more simple and immediate form of musical entertainment.

The instrumental composition of the band had to be perfected in order to keep up with the growing demands on it. Had the band remained a purely military organization it is doubtful whether the elaboration of its instrumentation would have proceeded at so rapid a pace. It is true that Wieprecht made his great reforms for the Prussian regimental bands, but it is also true that those bands were frequently engaged in performances of a non-military character. The interplay of influence—the band on the audience and the audience on the band—holds true even for the development of the band's instrumentation.

The music played by bands in the nineteenth century was, of course, to a great extent determined by the public taste. The repertory consisted chiefly of transcriptions of light-opera overtures (since hallowed by time and nothing more), salon-pieces, dances and under the heading of "Original Works for Band" . . . marches or polkas.

The outdoor concert itself imposed certain limitations on the extension of the band repertory into fields more elevated than those represented by light-opera overtures, marches and polkas. There is, in the abstract, no reason why music in the open air should not be as good as music in a stuffy room, but there are several practical reasons. Open-air concerts take place, as a rule, not in amphitheatres or stadia, but in public squares and parks, on promenades and in front of cafés. The audience remains in a state of greater or less instability; it goes or comes, converses or eats. Its concentration, in other words, is not entirely on the music. For such an audience, the type of music evidently prescribed is that in which half of the notes may be unheard without an appreciable disruption of the artistic experience involved. There is nothing inappropriate in this; if dinner music is deserved by diners, so band music is the reflection of the needs and desires of the people who listen to it.

It seems to me that no appreciable change in the calibre of the band repertory can be recorded until the institution of what we might call "fenced-in" band concerts: concerts given in a place where the movement of the audience is restricted, and where one can assume that at least part of the audience's attention will be on the music itself. And this in turn, it will be remembered, can only take place if there is an audience willing to be "fenced-in." One cannot seat people by force and make them listen to a band concert or any other sort of a concert. Once there is such an audience, however, it becomes evident that a slightly more substantial type of music may be performed. This, again, leads us to another problem which is of the greatest consequence.

Since until recent years the large majority of bands played to the semi-perambulatory type of audience described above, it follows that the greatest amount of band music was published to suit their needs. One can hardly blame publishers for printing what will sell; but as a result the bandmaster wishing to give a formal concert found that he had to have special arrangements made. The bandmasters who have had the greatest influence in developing the band repertory have done precisely that, not only in this country but similarly in Europe. In America, Gilmore, then Sousa, and then Goldman have had to face this problem, and little by little their pioneering work has taken root.

One cannot separate this development, however, from the development of the audience and the technical improvement of the band itself. Assuming for the moment the existence of an audience demanding a somewhat more serious music than that provided by the average band, it is evident that the same serious music must be played in a satisfactory manner. I maintain, although I foresee opposition, that the technical improvement of the band is as much due to increased audience pressure as it is to the consciences of individual bandmasters.

But where did the more serious audience come from? It is a comparatively recent development and again the factors behind it are many. The more general diffusion of education is certainly one; the existence of symphony orchestras is another. Long before radio, general education and the tours of orchestras had created a desire for better music. If, in a small city, boasting no orchestra of its own, a touring orchestra should succeed in arousing a curiosity about the music it performed, or if the schools had succeeded in prompting a cultural skepticism, the city's band would sooner or later feel the effects. And the continuing interaction of the elements involved would produce the forward movement that is, by the people concerned, held desirable.

In these times the most thoroughly progressive forces are unquestionably the American Bandmasters' Association and the National School Band Association. The American Bandmasters' Association, by engaging the active professional bandmasters in a common program, has been able to impose its generally admirable decisions on its own members and has enlisted the co-operation of music publishers. For this the publishers deserve their full share of praise. Were it not for the school bands, however, the reforms advocated by the A. B. A. would be in a large sense unrealizable. Publishers would certainly not bring out new arrangements for the benefit of the few professional bands which concertize regularly and command large audiences. But credit must be given the professional bands, particularly the Goldman Band, Frank Simon's Band and the Service Bands, for their readiness to answer the demand for good music and for using their prestige to bring still better things to the public's attention. In the matter of enlarging the band repertory by means of special arrangements, and in encouraging composers to contribute serious works to it, Dr. Goldman has taken special advantage of the unique position which he enjoys; his activity in this respect has been a vitalizing influence on the band movement. More than four hundred works, either totally new or in new transcriptions, have had their first hearings at his concerts. This figure does not include marches.

The development of school and college bands has in some ways an even greater importance for the future of band music. The remarkable work that has been and is being done by men like A. R. McAllister, Dr. A. A. Harding, J. S. Maddy, Ernest Williams, William Revelli, G. C. Bainum and others is almost a guarantee that school band music is on a sound musical and practical basis. The school bands are making future audiences as well as players. Not all of the youngsters who have learned to play an instrument well will follow music as a profession, but all of them will, it is safe to say, be interested in music for the rest of their lives. They will form the nucleus of a public which will demand of bands even better things than bands are doing now. For that reason it is most important that they be taught good music from the start. It is largely on their taste and education that the direction of the extension of the band repertory will depend.

The Development of the Band Repertory

MOST of the music played by bands is transcribed from orchestral or pianoforte music. Since this is the case, it follows that the selection of music to be so transcribed is a matter of great importance. The extent to which this selection is determined by the band's public and by the traditional relations between it and the band I have attempted to suggest in the previous essay. The part played by bandmasters and publishers is largely dependent on those considerations. One cannot, of course, discount pioneering and initiative on the part of individuals; one must remember, however, that a "pioneer" is one who is the first to express some fundamental trend which is a necessary and inevitable social expression. Unless this is so, the "pioneer" is considered not as such, but as an eccentric. History alone is able to decide which of the two a man has been.

Bandmasters, arrangers and publishers have the entire field of written music from which to choose, since there is little music which could not conceivably be transcribed for band. The band's own repertory, of works written specifically for it, is not even a drop in the bucket by comparison. And since deceased masters are hardly likely to make further contributions, the past may be disregarded in a discussion of enlarging the band's particular literature. This can be done only by contemporary composers, and they (I speak of front-rank composers) will be attracted to writing for band when they feel confident of being able to command audiences willing to listen to their music. They have already done so, it is true; but it is also unfortunately true that some of the most valuable original band compositions of recent years remain in manuscript.

In any case, even if we momentarily become so optimistic as to presuppose a mad scramble by Messrs. Sibelius, Stravinsky and other leading composers of the day suddenly to enrich the band repertory, we should still have to rely on transcriptions for the greater part of our band programs. The immense resources of musical literature can be enjoyed by bands only through that process. The question therefore remains: What is to be transcribed?

The argument against transcription itself, sometimes advanced by the band's ill-wishers, may be disposed of quite briefly. Composers themselves have not only authorized transcriptions, but have often been guilty of making them themselves. Readers of the following notes on original wind-instrument music will see that the most ancient tradition in instrumentation was to avoid it altogether, that is, to avoid specification of certain instruments. Music up to and through the time of Bach was written for whatever instruments were available rather than for special instruments chosen because of their "color" values. There can be little question, in the case of Bach, that had he had modern instruments he would have used them. And, in fact, when we play *The Well-Tempered Clavichord* or the sonatas of Mozart on a modern pianoforte we are, *ipso facto,* winking at a transcription.

A glance through this book will show approximately what has been transcribed, at least for the use of American bands. It will be noticed that Suppé overbalances Handel, that there is more Massenet than Mozart, more Rossini than Bach, and it will be remembered, too, that the larger part of the band's repertory—marches, potpourris, characteristic pieces and so forth—is not included, since this volume is limited more or less to "standard" music. The obvious conclusion is that serious music in the band repertory is considerably outweighed by light music.

Since the primary purpose of the band is to entertain, rather than to educate or to elevate, no one will question the propriety of light music on band programs. In other words, the increased demand of band audiences for "good music" does not mean that bands can make a sudden and definite break with their pasts. Band audiences will have to arrive at a radically different conception of what is entertaining before that can happen, and even assuming the possibility of such a change it is obvious that it would be gradual. Today general agreement can probably be reached on the tenet that the inclusion of "relief from the heavy numbers" is indispensable on a band program. In theory, likewise, there will probably be agreement that there is such a thing as discrimination in this "relief," that there are qualitative distinctions to be made in light music as well as in ponderous music. In practice, however, this principle is often forgotten. Contrast is an eminently desirable thing, but a band concert need not be turned into a vaudeville show for the sake of it.

What is more important from the standpoint of those seriously interested in "raising the standards of bands and band music" is the quality of the "relief from the light numbers." This "relief" necessarily takes the form of what is considered "good music." The rather unfortunate aspect of this distinction is the attitude which it implies: that "good music" is utterly incapable of entertaining anyone, or that it is a bitter medicine which, for the good of the patient, must be mixed with sarsaparilla.

One may assume that for the worthy purpose of "improving" the band repertory, more and more transcriptions of "good music" are in order. But the prevailing opinion as to what is good music (or entertaining music) is determined on a wide-spread social plane, and varies enormously from one period to another. There are no canons of taste which are unchangeable and irreplaceable. For seventy-five years after Bach's death his music was neglected, although it was admired during his lifetime. Our great-grandchildren may regard Bach's music in a light quite different from our own. Gyrowetz was once considered on a par with Mozart, and Eberl with Beethoven; Mendelssohn, once the darling of musicians and critics, was, until the re-shifting of opinion in recent years, despised as a sentimentalist and a Victorian. But today even Victorian furniture is having a renascence!

It must be acknowledged that the band is somewhat slow to reflect changes in taste. Tchaikovsky and Wagner have become fixtures in the band repertory, but only many years after they had been enthusiastically adopted by the vanguard of musical thought and receptiveness, and in fact only by the time that certain circles had already begun to react against them. The lagging response to be noted in band music is neither unhealthy nor reprehensible; it is due to a number of factors which cannot be separated from the existence of bands. One of these, and a rather important one, is the fact that few works by contemporaries (I do not speak of twentieth-century contemporaries who write nineteenth-century music) are composed directly for band. In general one waits to see whether a work will be accepted or not by orchestra audiences or by critics, and only when it is accepted decides to take a chance on a band transcription. The decision will always be guided by a guess or a certainty that the larger audience commanded by the band will be prepared and willing to listen to it.

Bach, to choose an example, is much more of a newcomer to the band repertory than either Tchaikovsky or Wagner. Bandmen need not blush for the fact that transcriptions of Bach's music for band were indicated and made possible by previous revival of interest in Bach through the media of the orchestra, the organ and the chorus. Did any one band or group of bands play for an audience of more developed musical responsiveness, this condition would not necessarily hold true. But until there arrives a band which plays for an audience comparable to that, say, of the Boston Symphony, it will continue to be a factor in the determination of what is to be transcribed for wind combinations. Bach's music today is apparently growing in popularity among bandmen and their audiences, a phenomenon that is often indicated as an example of the improvement of the band's musical status. But, and this is a big *but,* if one begins to discuss this development from the standpoint of "improvement," one sets up certain critical standards which are, for all that there may be general agreement on them, definitely open to discussion. One should remember the circumstances which make the "improvement," more safely called "development," possible.

Certain tendencies in musical taste today are sufficiently well marked to cast their shadows before them on the band movement. We are on fairly safe ground if we say that the last several years have seen a more general admiration of the music of Bach and Handel, a greater interest in the music of the sixteenth and seventeenth centuries, a reaction against romanticism. It should be made clear, however, from a historical and cultural standpoint, that these tendencies, except for the first-named, have not yet found expression in the band field. The band, conditioned as it is by its mass audience, will be almost the last medium to reflect them. And, needless to add, those bands which have thus far done most of the "pioneering" in Bach and other music old and new, will be the first to take up any further new tendencies.

The analogy is the old one of the pebble thrown in a pool: the circles spread concentrically, becoming larger, until they reach the shore, after which they turn back on themselves. One need only be reminded, as illustration, that Wagner in his day was greeted with suspicion and defamation by the larger part of the public. The vanguard of the period, however (the coterie around Liszt at Weimar), took up the crusade for Wagner's music. Wagner was doing exactly what they would have been doing had they been as talented as he; in other words, he was expressing what they, and a large number of others, felt and wanted to express: the full riot of romanticism. Bit by bit, sympathy for Wagner spread. It was inevitable that people should accept his ideas, for they were the ideas of a whole period rather than those of an isolated individual. It is just as inevitable that the immediacy and the full sum of Wagnerism should be on the wane today. We can enjoy Wagner's music, but we can no longer fully accept Wagner's ideas of art. There is really no good reason why a normal twentieth-century person should swallow all of the mythological nonsense that evidently meant so much to Wagner himself. There is no such thing as a definitive art-form; Wagner's music-drama, which he considered definitive, was definitive for his era, perhaps, but certainly no more.

In any case it would be just as well to remember that Wagner and Liszt do not represent the vanguard of musical thought in 1938. Tastes of periods change; before we are old and decrepit swing music may be considered quaint, Stravinsky's music archaic. The conclusion, insofar as band transcription is involved, is that it can do no more than reflect these changes. Specifically, one might hazard a guess that within the coming years there will be transcribed for bands a good deal more Bach, less program-music, possibly more fifteenth-, sixteenth-, seventeenth- and twentieth-century music. One might even say that barring certain side-trackings, the prediction is less of a guess than a certainty.

The conservatism of the band, that is, the lagging of its response to new movements and trends in music, is something which can be diminished only by the circulation and extension of a thoroughly overhauled music education. The attitude of the nineteenth century toward art is certainly not compatible with a twentieth-century attitude toward everything else, yet it still prevails, for the most part, in schools, colleges and conservatories. The teacher of music history and appreciation, if he is to do anything except repeat mouldy platitudes, must first of all clear the air of his classroom and prepare the student for an objective and open-minded approach to music itself; the objection seems to be that this is too simple to be pedagogical.

It has been my experience, in attempting to foster the musical development of students, that many who have remarkable talents for the playing of an instrument have never actually listened to music. That is to say, enjoyment or appreciation of the values of music (deprived of literary, emotional or pictorial associations) remains an impossibility for them. For some the primary function of music is "to tell a story"; for others music always remains, as Santayana put it, "a drowsy reverie interrupted by nervous thrills." The first idea, that of music as the bastard of literature, comes from a fundamentally incorrect education; the second, greatly preferable, from no education at all. (It is generally to be remarked that the literary tastes of the music-tells-a-story group leave something to be desired.) I have found that a brief course in the music of Mozart and Haydn is the best remedy; it is surprising and gratifying to see how rapidly even the youngest students, exposed to such music, begin to wake up and to be stimulated to an interest in and curiosity about all music.

The problem is important if one has concerns about the future of the band repertory. Actual enjoyment and appreciation—or better yet, understanding—of music will do more than anything else to create a demand for better band music. It must be an enjoyment of music based on music itself and not on extraneous associations of music. I have refrained from referring to the number of works by Bach now published for band as an indication of the "improvement" of the band repertory because I believe that statement in such terms sets a bad precedent. It is tantamount to saying that a work is great because it is by Bach; and while conceivably there are some who will say that everything of Bach is great, the position is difficult to maintain for many other composers. A band cannot be judged by how much Bach or Beethoven it plays, any more than it can be judged by how loud or fast it plays. Yet this method of judging a composition by the name of its composer is a phenomenon which is rather wide-spread and which is by no means confined to bands. It should, of course, be obvious that Bach's fame does not rest on the well-known Bourrée, nor does Beethoven's on *The Praise of God in Nature.* The addition of the latter to a band's repertory cannot seriously be termed an "improvement"; were it not by Beethoven it is safe to say that it would have long since been forgotten.

In the band field, with its peculiar dependence on transcription, there has arisen what seems to me a misguided idea which stems directly from the preceding considerations. That is the practice of making "simplified" versions of accepted "classics" for the use of young bands. There are a good many publications on the pattern of "Beethoven's Fifth Symphony (Excerpts from)," or "Theme from Unfinished Symphony . . . Franz Schubert." These, I believe, do more harm than good from the standpoint of music education and the development of taste. By taking away the setting of a theme or melody, by knocking down the structure of its context, by completely upsetting the balance and design of the whole composition, one is hardly providing a sound introduction to honest music. The melody of the first movement of the "Unfinished" is, assuredly, a good melody; but it is not the only good melody there is, and I would even go so far as to say that Mr. X or Mr. Y, if suitably encouraged, might manage to produce one not too far inferior. What makes the musical value, what sustains the musical interest of the "Unfinished" is what Schubert does with the melody—and that is precisely what is eliminated from the "simplified" arrangement. Were this not true, we should have to defend the position that Mr. Sigmund Romberg's version of the melody in his operetta is quite as good as the symphony itself. The *reductio ad absurdum* of the process of simplification is to imagine a "simplified arrangement" of a Bach fugue, or to ponder the musical value of a morsel entitled "Theme from Bach Fugue in A minor." Rather than use the name of a "great" composer, the arranger might do far better to compose a little masterpiece of his own. Students would profit more from hearing elaborate music in its original form played by others, and by playing it themselves when they have reached adequate proficiency.

The remedy for such minor evils unquestionably lies in education, but in education from the ground up, in education based on a direct approach to the abstractions of form and the realities of sound on which music is based. I feel confident that such a direction has already been undertaken, and hopeful that it will continue to spread, with admirable effect on the status of American music in general, and on the improvement of bands in particular.

Original Wind-Instrument Music
A Brief Historical Essay

The more one studies the history of wind-instrument music, the more one is impressed by the extraordinary wealth and variety of the known literature. The modern bandsman, or student of ensemble music, has a rich and almost untouched field from which to draw.

Wind instruments, of course, have an ancestry at least as ancient and honorable as that of the strings. It is incorrect to think of our present wind instruments as having been evolved from new types suddenly discovered during the Middle Ages. Rather there has been a steady development from primitive times, somewhat broken and irregular it is true, but nevertheless discernible. Our studies can begin, however, only with the earliest written material which has been preserved and is available, and with such music as can be played on modern instruments.

By the fourteenth century there were in common use the direct prototypes of most of the instruments with which we are now familiar. Little of the music they played has been preserved; the important music of the period was vocal, and the development of the polyphonic style which culminated in the achievements of the Netherlands school was the principal feature of musical activity. We do know, however, that the instrumental music of the fourteenth, fifteenth and sixteenth centuries to a great extent paralleled the vocal music, and we also know that instruments were often used in conjunction with the voices. In various Psalters of the sixteenth century and earlier, it is stated that the music may be either sung or played; that this was the common practice is further demonstrated in the thousands of polyphonic compositions which have come down to us, in which no indication, whether vocal or instrumental, is given as to the distribution of parts for performance.

That there was differentiation as well as parallelism in the vocal and instrumental styles is proven less by the existence of written records than by the internal evidence of many compositions which can easily be consulted. A number of works reproduced in Arnold Schering's *Geschichte der Musik in Beispielen* * (*History of Music in Examples*) lead one inevitably to this conclusion.

A number of limitations somewhat conditioned the technique of writing for wind instruments in this period. The undeveloped instruments were many in number, falling into various groups most of which included the complete range from soprano to bass. Many of these groups were mutually exclusive in the sense that to tune them harmoniously was practically an impossibility. From that difficulty there developed in consequence a tendency to write for choirs of similar or related instruments, a practice not wholly changed by experiment until the time of Bach and Rameau, and reflected to this day in the familiar string quartet. This principle was likewise, on the esthetic side, a carry-over into the instrumental field of the vocal style, the *a cappella* chorus of human voices being the purest possible example of music performed by a group of related instruments. "Color," such as we know it in modern orchestration, is comparatively new, and is the result of a conception of music altogether foreign to the early composers. The student of painting will be familiar with this difference in conceptions under the guise of "line" and "color," and will recall that the history of painting in the Italian Renaissance exhibits the identical change that we see

---

* Published by Breitkopf & Härtel.

in music. Giotto and Rubens find their counterparts in Josquin Des Près and Wagner.

Examples of music with indicated instrumentation for wind are extremely rare in the period from 1350-1600. Dr. Hans David states that the first compositions we can trace which were definitely composed for wind instruments are probably two *Arie di Battaglia per Instrumenti da Fiato* (*Battle Airs for Wind Instruments*), written by Andrea Gabrieli and Annibale Padoano, and published in 1580. Schering gives examples of earlier date, but the instrumental indications are difficult to verify. In any case we know that many of the canzonas, motets, canons, sinfonias and other works of the Netherlandish masters were performed by combinations of wind instruments as well as by voices or by stringed instruments. And since the style and traditions of the Netherlanders were carried to Venice by Adrian Willaert, we expect to find the same usages carried on by Giovanni Gabrieli and other composers of the Italian school.

To establish another foundation of the wind-instrument tradition—it is necessary to refer to a practice dating far back into the Middle Ages. This was the retention, especially by the German towns, of wind players in towers for the purpose of keeping watch and announcing the hours. These towermen (*thuermer*) played at specified times, and performed various civic offices. In time they formed small groups of six or eight and played processional music, dance music, and the accompaniments for church chorales. According to J. A. Kappey (*History of Military Music*),* their duties became more arduous after the Reformation (early 16th century), when they had to remind the people to pray, by performing chorales on trombones and *zinken* (wooden instruments played with a cup mouthpiece) three times a day. It

* Published by Boosey and Co. 1894.

was not long before they reached a semi-official status as town bands, and began to combine other instruments with the two just mentioned.

Until the middle of the seventeenth century, these bands of *thuermer* were, perhaps, the most important exponents of wind-instrument music. The court orchestras, however, were likewise mainly wind; the trumpet, considered the aristocrat of ancient instruments, being reserved for the use of these organizations and for the nobility in general. The band of Henry VIII consisted of three lutes, three rebecs, a harp, two viols, fourteen trumpets, ten trombones, four drums, two tambourines and a bagpipe. That of Queen Elizabeth contained six trombones and a number of trumpets given variously at ten to sixteen, as well as two flutes, a bagpipe, drums and a few stringed instruments. There is a record of a fête given by François I in 1518, during which a Pavane was performed by "three *buccinas* (prototype of the French horn), different sorts of wooden flutes, and two brass instruments in the Milanese fashion." But such combinations as the last, aside from court music, were rare in any case, and presumably were used only for state functions of a more or less social nature.

Those who have attended the Bach festivals at Bethlehem or other places are familiar with the tower men who play chorales on trombones. I have pointed out that the pleasing effect of such instruments in playing four-part music was appreciated at a very early date. J. B. Weckerlin quotes a book published at Berlin in 1784 by C. C. Rolle, in which it is stated that in church ceremonies of the seventeenth century the singing was accompanied by cornets (*zinken*) and trombones, but that trumpets were reserved for great solemnities. Likewise that "those who play simple chorales from towers, also have sonatas composed for them, which they play together to all the inhabitants of the town." Such written records testify amply to the prevalent use of wind instruments, even though we have so little of the music with instrumental indications explicitly given. Kappey reprints, among other specimens, the town marches of Bamberg (fourteenth century) and Worms (fifteenth century) and a *Basse Danse* by an unknown composer, published at Paris in 1530. Many examples should be brought to light by further diligent research.

In direct relation to the activities of the *thuermer* was the practice of using wind instruments in connection with the organ and with the choir. Here we are dealing with a field rich in examples which have been preserved, especially from the early seventeenth century. There are a great number of chorales for organ and trombones by such typical composers of the period as Rosenmüller, Franck, Hammerschmidt and Schütz. Nor could such compositions as the "Sonata" from the *Kirchen- und Tafel-Musik* of Andreas Hammerschmidt (1612-1675) have been rare. That sonata calls for two alto voices (unison), two trumpets and four trombones. It may be compared to Henrich Schütz's famous Lament, *Absalon, mi fili,* for bass voice and four trombones, published in 1629.

While in the North, wind-instrument music was progressing along such lines, composers in Italy and the South were proceeding in their own manner. We have already seen that Adrien (or Adrian) Willaert, perhaps the greatest of the followers of Josquin des Près, traveled to Italy about the beginning of the sixteenth century and was instrumental in creating the Venetian school. Schering gives a number of examples of the music of this period in Venice, including some scored for wind instruments. Willaert himself is represented by a truly magnificent work, the *O Salutaris Hostia* for voices and brass, which provides a sort of connecting link between the musical usages (insofar as instrumentation and use of media is concerned) of the Northern and Southern schools.

The theoreticians of the Venetian school, Zacconi and Zarlino, devote ample consideration to the wind instruments. The trombone especially was in great use; it is said that a choir of trombones was used in Venice at the celebration of such important civic ceremonies as the annual wedding of the Doge to the Adriatic. The use of the trumpet was evidently more restricted. From the data available, however, it is reasonable to assume that many of the instrumental compositions of Gabrieli, Frescobaldi, Claudio Merulo and others were regularly performed by choirs of trombones and other wind instruments.

Dr. David provides me with the following note on this period: "The Venetian masters particularly liked music for several groups of singers or instruments in *cori spezzati*, or differentiated choirs. Giovanni Gabrieli, nephew of Andrea Gabrieli, started the practice of writing differently for different instruments. Among his compositions we find a Canzona for 2 Cornets, 2 Violins and 2 Trombones which may be considered one of the finest early attempts at modern orchestration. In his instrumental music this composer went so far as to write a Sonata in 22 parts, divided into 5 choirs. This music may have been played in San Marco as well as on the Piazza before the Cathedral or at festivals of the Republic. Its style is of extreme liveliness. Giovanni Gabrieli generally used small motifs, in the invention of which he was of almost unbelievable fertility. These motifs were carried through all the choirs he introduces, or through all voices of one of them, or between a few parts only. The compositions generally are short, taking from two to eight minutes for performance. They are constructed with the finest sense of balance and with an astonishingly rich variety of mood and stylistic character.

"Gabrieli comparatively seldom gave complete indications of the instruments to take the single parts, but there are several exceptions. (These are listed below. *R.F.G.*) Gabrieli published these compositions partly in his *Sacrae Symphoniae* (1597), and partly in his *Canzoni e Sonate* (1615). The first collection includes vocal pieces as well as instrumental; the second presents instrumental music only.

"The difference between the *Canzoni* and the *Sonate* is that the former are closer to the vocal music from which their name is derived (French *chanson,* song). The *Sonate* have more gravity. It has been conjectured that the *Canzoni* generally were intended for strings rather than for wind instruments, while the *Sonate* were intended for the latter. The *Sonate* have a very buoyant style which makes them excellent material for performance with wind instruments alone."

In addition to the works of Gabrieli, there are extant such works as the two canzoni of Florentino Maschera (1593) for wind instruments, and dozens of other compositions for unspecified instruments by even more illustrious representatives of the school. Frescobaldi published in 1620-1637 two books of canzoni "a 1-4 voci per sonare e per cantare con ogni sorte d'istrumento" (songs in 1-4 voices to play or to sing with any sort of instruments). Peri, in his *Euridice* (1600), wrote a sinfonia for flutes alone. Monteverde included an intrada for brass instruments in his *Orfeo;* he also composed a great number of madrigals for one to six voices to sing with various instruments. Such items are found in great abundance, and there is no reason to suppose that the usage of the time called for any such thing as a preponderance of stringed instruments.

Outside of Italy, and a little later in the seventeenth century, the growth of formal "military music" may be said to have begun. In France, Louis XIV had established bands of oboes to perform marches and signal calls. When Lully

(1633-1687) became court musician, the king asked him to compose and arrange music for these bands. Lully was well fitted for this work, for he understood the oboe thoroughly and had used it constantly in his operas. Among the numbers which Lully arranged for the King's oboes are the famous *Marche des Mousquetaires du Roi de France* and the *Marche des Dragons du Roi*. Many of these pieces are quite pleasing, and have more than historical value.

Most of these pieces by Lully were re-arranged and collected by André Philidor, father of the famous chess player and composer of opera. Weckerlin, in his curious book *Nouveau Musiciana* (Paris, 1890) cites in addition a volume entitled *Pièces de Trompettes et Timballes, à 2, 3 et 4 Parties: 1er Livre, par M. Philidor l'Aisné, etc.*,* published by Christophe Ballard at Paris in 1685. This collection contains fifty-two pieces, ranging from fanfares and dance pieces to canons and chaconnes. According to Weckerlin many of these are very well-developed and worth performing.

The year 1670 saw the publication of an important collection at Leipzig. This was the *Hora Decima Musicorum Lipsiensium—zum Abblasen um 10 Uhr Vormittage in Leipzig*,† composed by Johann Pezelius or Pezel. This volume contained suites and sonatas, mostly in five parts, for cornets (*zinken*) and trombones. Schering reproduces a tower-sonata from this volume. In 1685 Pezel published at Frankfort another volume, entitled *Fünfstimmige Blasende Musik* (*Five-part Music for Wind Instruments*), containing intradas, sarabandes and other dances and miscellaneous pieces. These pieces are interesting as definite evidence that the tower-players had by that time definitely outgrown their simple

* "Pieces for Trumpets and Tympani, in 2, 3 and 4 parts, 1st Book, by Mr. Philidor the Elder, etc." It is interesting to note that, despite the title, there are two pieces in 5 parts and one in 6.

† Translatable as *Ten O'clock in Leipzig's Music—to be performed at 10:00 o'clock A. M. in Leipzig.*

functions, and had combined into groups which performed music for public dances, parades and other civic events. Many of these pieces by Pezel have intrinsic musical value; the two collections as a whole, being the first volumes given exclusively to wind instruments, have immense historical interest.

From the beginning of the eighteenth century the history of wind-instrument music must be divided into two channels; wind chamber music (in a large sense) and military or band music. The history of the former, being that of the actual music written for wind combinations, is our main interest; the history of the latter, being largely the history of wind instrumentation, has little place here. But it is necessary to outline the development of the military band, as the background for the work of various later composers.

The clarinet and horn came into use around 1700, and thus give the period considerable importance. The instrumentation of the early military band, patterned after the small town bands, was developed in Germany. A fairly typical group at the beginning of the eighteenth century included two flutes, two oboes, two horns, two trumpets, two bassoons and a trombone. The first military band score which includes clarinet is given by Kappey as that of the march *Prinz Anton,* dated 1720. Little further progress was made during the century, except for the introduction of cymbals and triangles and various small drums. These were popularized in Europe by the vogue of the Turkish Janissary bands during the first half of the century. Later, the French Revolution and the Napoleonic wars gave the greatest impetus in history to the military band. Music, like everything else, was "popularized," paraded, played in the open air. Bands grew to include thirty-six performers in the time of Napoleon I; and from that time on the progress has been steady. The contributions of Wieprecht, and his triumph in 1838, are so well known, as are the achievements of Gilmore and his successors, that they require no comment at this point. The modern wind band requires a history of its own.

We must return to the previous century and to the wind music itself. The great composers of the time, Bach, Handel, Purcell and the Italian school, did only an insignificant amount of writing purely for wind; not until Haydn and Mozart do we have highly developed wind chamber music. The progress between the time of Pezelius and Philidor and that of Haydn and Mozart is a familiar story; but insofar as wind music is in question, the latter men had not only the rich tradition of their great predecessors, but also the advantage of better instruments, and of the experiment and development of military bands before and during their own lifetimes.

It seems odd that the wind chamber music of Haydn and Mozart has fallen into comparative neglect, for much of it is very fine. Haydn composed a great many divertimenti and other ensemble pieces for winds, the works called *Feldpartien,* and three trios for flutes. Haydn's music for wind instruments is light and pleasant, not very great music, perhaps—but rather superior to most of the light music played by bands today. With a few slight modifications to suit modern instruments, and perhaps some judicious doubling of parts, these little pieces of "Papa" Haydn would make an addition to any repertory.

With Mozart we reach the highest peak of wind music until our own century. Few composers have understood the wind instruments, and particularly the reeds, better than he. His compositions for wind combinations are not so many in number, but they are far more developed than anything before his time. In the complete Köchel catalogue there are listed, among other works for wind: three serenades, ten divertimenti, two concerti for flute, one for bassoon, four for horn, one for clarinet; two flute quartets, one oboe quartet, a quintet for pianoforte, oboe, clarinet, horn and bassoon; and various pieces for flute, oboe, clarinet, basset-horn and bassoon, individually and in combination. Some of the concerti are, of course, famous, as are the clarinet quintet and the first serenade for wind instruments (K. 361). This serenade is scored for two oboes, two clarinets, two basset-horns, four hunting horns, two bassoons and contra-bassoon. It consists of five movements, with an introduction to the first. It may be considered one of Mozart's greatest chamber-music works. Aside from its gaiety and charm, it is instrumentally well balanced and sonorous. Interesting too, are some of the divertimenti, written for from six to eleven instruments. Six of these are for two oboes, two horns, two bassoons; two are for two oboes, two clarinets, two English horns, two French horns, and two bassoons; and two are for two flutes, five trumpets, and four drums. There are from four to ten pieces in each of these. The fourth divertimento is typical, being in four movements, in concise sonata form. There is not a great deal to single out in such a work, for everyone is familiar with the Mozart string quartets, and this is very similar in melodic outline and contrapuntal treatment. It is, however, perfectly conceived for the powers and sonorities of the wind choirs.

Beethoven wrote a number of works for wind instruments, all of which are cited in the list below. Most of them are perfectly playable today, and are worth the effort. Needless to say, the marches and other numbers for band are not on a level with the symphonies for musical interest or grandeur, nor are the ensemble pieces comparable to the later string quartets for intensity. They are, however, by no means negligible. The three *equales* for trombones have an interesting history. Beethoven composed them in 1812 for All Souls' Day. Two of the *equales* were performed at Beethoven's funeral on March 29, 1827, the four trombones alternating with a choir of sixteen voices singing the words of the *Miserere* specially arranged by Seyfried.

A curious work, apparently issued with Beethoven's approval, is a full band arrangement of the famous "Battle Symphony" (*Wellington's Sieg*). Beethoven composed this program-symphony in 1812. It was published, for orchestra, in 1816; the band arrangement, of which the only known copy is at the New York Public Library, was printed in the same year. The conclusion is inescapable that Beethoven knew about it, and it is even within the bounds of possibility that the arrangement was made by himself. The *Nocturne in C for Wind Instruments and Turkish Band,* by Spohr, a contemporary of Beethoven, is interesting as an illustration of the influence of the Janissary Bands on European music. It is said that Richard Strauss has had the work successfully revived in recent years.

The Weber works for band are said to be poor, but Weber's *Concerti* and *Concertino for Clarinet* need no introduction. Other works of the period are given later; the appended list of compositions for wind instruments is, I believe, the most complete available catalogue of such music. It will be seen that the amount of composition for bands or wind instruments alone is altogether insignificant in the nineteenth century. The reasons for this evident lack of interest are not hard to discover. The nineteenth century was first and foremost the age of the romantic composers, the age of "emotional" and "dramatic" music. The string orchestra, with added touches, was the ideal vehicle to convey such music. The conception of orchestral coloring to a large extent supplanted the old conception of choirs. Reed and wind instruments were used for their "color values." It is unquestionable that the popularity of descriptive adjectives applied to instruments (the "plaintive" oboe, the "noble" clarinet, the "martial" trumpet, the "mellow" bassoon, etc.) reached a special peak during this period. The effects of this essentially romantic approach have not yet completely disappeared in contemporary writing, although the leaders of present-day composition have shown the way.

The nineteenth century did produce a number of sonatas and concertos for various wind instruments, notably clarinet or horn. These works are of unequal interest; many of them appeal to virtuosi for their technical elaborateness, others because they fill gaps in the repertory. The amount of concerted chamber music for wind instruments, with or without piano, is appreciably smaller; much of it, from the standpoint of musical interest, may be altogether ignored. (See following listing.) Works for band are rare; with few exceptions the nineteenth-century works by composers of established reputation are marches which suffer enormously in comparison with Sousa's. The notable works, which have some claim to revival, are the Mendelssohn *Overture in C* and the strange *Funeral and Triumphal Symphony* of Berlioz. These, with possibly the *Nocturne* by Spohr, might make interesting additions to the band repertory.

The twentieth century has seen a strong renewal of interest in writing for wind instruments; the reed instruments in particular have been the objects of much thoughtful attention. In general this interest and attention have not tended toward a search for rarer and more exciting color effects, but rather toward a re-discovery of a genuine wind-type of line. Whereas much of nineteenth-century orchestral music was evidently conceived for string orchestra with added color (as decoration, one might say), through the Russians and through such composers as Grieg a more direct and idiomatic use of wind instruments came to later composers as an already explored possibility. Mr. Grainger points out the wind-character of much of Grieg's music, the possible traces of bagpipe influence, and asks whether that is not a starting point for much of later instrumental feeling. Mr. Grainger himself, under the influence of Grieg, began as early as 1902 a series of experiments in reed instrumentation from this standpoint. His *First Hill-Song* (1902) was scored for 2 piccolos, 6 oboes, 6 English horns, 6 bassoons and contra-bassoon; the *Second Hill-Song* (1907) was scored for piccolo, 2 flutes, English horn, 2 bassoons, contra-bassoon, bass clarinet, 4 saxophones, 2 trumpets and horns.

The rediscovery of wind-instrument writing which is esthetically as well as technically idiomatic is quite clear if one refers to such modern scores as Stravinsky's *Sacre du Printemps*, Honegger's *King David* or Gustav Holst's *Suites for Band*. These works of Stravinsky and Honegger are predominantly wind-instrument scores, though they are designated as orchestral. Stravinsky's *Symphonie des Psaumes* actually shows a radical elimination of strings. Many more of the most interesting scores written recently show the same tendency; all abound in real wind-instrument phrases, and point to the ever-growing desire of composers to realize the boundless possibilities within the reed and brass choirs.

With this interest, and with the efforts being made to stimulate and reward original composition for the developed wind band, there should be a steady and healthy growth of the band repertory. To attain the artistic level envisaged by the most competent and constructive bandmasters, the band must eliminate much from its present repertory; but the replacement of this with the best of the old and the best of the new is a prospect which should give joy to anyone who really believes in band music.

ORIGINAL WIND-INSTRUMENT MUSIC

(The list below is not presented as a definitive list, but rather includes a cross-section of wind-instrument music which may be interesting musically or historically. The listings of the works of composers such as Mozart and Beethoven are, however, as complete as careful research can make them, as are the portions of the list dealing with comparatively modern works. No works for less than four wind instruments are included, unless they are of special interest and easily available.)

I. 1400-1700

A. Music Written for Specified Wind Instruments

Robert Parsons died 1569	Fantasia for 6 Trumpets
De Macque ca. 1555-1613	Toccata for 4 Trumpets
Giovanni Gabrieli 1557-1612	Canzon in Echo 6 Trombones, 4 Cornets
	Sonata à 14, in 3 Choirs 10 Trombones, 4 Cornets
	Sonata à 15, in 3 Choirs 12 Trombones, 2 Cornets, Violin
	Sonata Pian e Forte, à 8, in 2 Choirs 6 Trombones, Cornet, Violin (Republished by Peters, for 8 Trombones.)
	Canzon for 8 Trombones
Tiburzio Massaini d. ca. 1608	Canzon for 16 Trombones
Claudio Monteverde 1567-1643	Intrada from *Orfeo* 5 Trumpets (3 Trumpets, 2 Trombones)

Michael Praetorius 1571-1621	Passamezzo for 6 Trumpets
J. H. Schein 1586-1630	Suites from the *Banchetto Musicale* (Suite No. 22, for 4 Horns, reprinted by Breitkopf & Härtel.)
Samuel Scheidt 1587-1654	Canzon for 4 Cornets Courante 2 Clarini (high Trumpets), 3 Trombones
Biagio Marini 1597-1665	Canzoni for 4 Trombones, 2 Cornets
M. Weckmann 1621-1674	Sonata Violin, Cornetino, Trombone, Bassoon and Basso Continuo
J. H. Schmelzer 1623-1687 (The *Arie* were written in 1667 for the wedding of Leopold I of Austria.)	From *Arie per il Balletto a Cavallo:* Corrente à 6, For Trumpets and Tympani Follia and Sarabande, ditto Sonatas à 7 2 Cornets, 2 Clarini, 3 Trombones
Nicholas Hasse ca. 1658	Polish Dances 2 Trumpets and Basso Continuo
J.-B. Lully 1633-1687	Marches and Airs Written for the Court Band of Louis XIV Scored for Oboes (Discant, Alto, Tenor and Bass) and Drums. These pieces collected by André Philidor, the Elder. One example given in Kappey, *History of Military Music.* Three re-edited by L. Chomel and published by Buffet-Crampon, Paris.
Johann Pezel ca. 1670	*Hora Decima Musicorum Lipsiensium—zum Abblasen um 10 Uhr Vormittage in Leipzig* Containing Sonatas, etc., for Cornets and Trombones. Published at Leipzig, 1670. *Intraten à 4, nehmlich mit einem*

		Cornett und 3 Trombonen (4-part Intradas for 1 Cornet and 3 Trombones.) Published in 1683.
		Fünfstimmige Blasende Musik (v.s.) Frankfort, 1685
		18 Selected Pieces and 2 Sonatas reprinted by Breitkopf & Härtel.
André Philidor	1647-1730	*Pièces de Trompettes et Timballes, etc.* Published by C. Ballard at Paris, 1685. This collection includes 52 pieces, mostly in 4 parts, but contains several in 2 or 3 parts, 2 in 5 parts and 1 in 6 parts. One example given in Weckerlin, *Nouveau Musiciana.* (Paris, 1890)
Daniel Speer	ca. 1685	2 Airs for 6 Trumpets or Cornets 2 Airs for 2 Cornets and 3 Trombones 1 Air for 4 Trombones 2 Airs for 1 Cornet and 3 Trombones
J. P. Krieger	1649-1725	*Lustige Feldmusik* (Joyous Outdoor Music) for Oboes and Bassoons
J. C. Pez	1664-1716	Sonatas, etc., for 2 Flutes or Oboes with Basso Continuo. One reprinted in Nagel's Music Archives (AMP).
J. G. Reiche	1667-1734	*24 Neue Quatricinia—vornehmlich auff den Rathhäusern oder Thürmen mit Fleiss gestellet* (Tower-Sonatas for 1 Cornet and 3 Trombones.) Original Volume published at Leipzig in 1696. One *Quatricinium* or 4-part Sonata, reprinted by Breitkopf & Härtel.
Ph. Wieland	ca. 1700	Overture for 2 Oboes, Taille, Bassoon

J.-J. Mouret	1682-1738	47 Divertissements, including Fanfares for Trumpets, Oboes and Tympani

Many of These Works to be Found in D.D.T. and D.D.T.O.
(See bibliographical note.)

B. Music Known to Have Been Played on Specified Wind Instruments, Although the Instrumentation is Not Printed

Antonius Romanus	?	Motet for 2 Trumpets and 2 Trombones. Composed for the Induction of Tommaso Mocenigo as Doge of Venice, 1413. Reprinted by Schering, *Geschichte der Musik in Beispielen.* (Breitkopf & Härtel)
Orlandus Lassus	1532-1594	Motet à 7, in 2 Choirs, entitled *Providebam Dominum* Played at a Wedding in 1568 by Lassus himself, with 5 Cornets and 2 Alto Trombones.

C. Music Written for Wind Instruments—Exact Instruments Not Specified

Josquin des Près	1450-1521	*Vive le Roy,* 4-part Canon
Unknown Composer		Chorale, *Christ Ist Erstanden* For 4 Wind Instruments. Mainz, 1503. Cited in Schering.
Johann Kugelmann	d. 1542	Chorale, *Nun Lob' Mein Seel' Den Herrn* For 5 Wind Instruments. Augsburg, 1540. Cited by Schering. (Kugelmann was Prussian Court Trumpeter.)
Johann Walther	1496-1570	Canon for 3 Wind Instruments 1542. Cited by Schering.

D. Reprints Lacking Documentation for Original Instrumentation

Florentio Maschera ca. 1593	2 Canzoni for Wind Instruments (Breitkopf & Härtel)
Giovanni Gabrieli 1557-1612	Sonata for Wind Instruments (Breitkopf & Härtel)
Henry Purcell 1658-1695	Voluntary For 3 Trumpets, 3 Trombones, Tympani, Side Drum and Organ. Arranged by Sir Henry Wood. (London: Murdock & Murdock)

E. Reprints of Music Written for Any Kind of Instruments

Th. Stolzer 1450-1526	Fantasias à 5 (Schott)
Adrien Willaert 1480-1562	Ricercari à 3 (Schott)
G. P. Palestrina 1524-1594	Ricercari à 4 (Schott)
Giovanni Gabrieli 1557-1612	Canzoni à 4 (Schott)
Girolamo Frescobaldi 1583-1643	Canzoni à 2 (Schott)

F. A List of Music Arranged for Band or Wind Ensembles by Percy Grainger

Anonymous 13th Cent.	*The Annunciation Carol*
G. de Machault 1300-1377	Ballade (No. 17)
Josquin des Près 1450-1521	*La Bernardina* Royal Fanfare (*Vive le Roi*)
A. de Cabezòn 1510-1566	Prelude in the Dorian Mode
John Jenkins 1592-1678	Five-part Fantasy No. 1
William Lawes d. 1645	Fantasy and Air No. 1 (6-part)
J. S. Bach 1685-1750	*O Man, Now Weep for Thy Great Sin* (Choral Prelude) *See What His Love Can Do*
Bach-Dolmetsch	March (Brass Choir)

II. CLASSIC PERIOD

G. F. Handel 1685-1759

Music for the Royal Fireworks
3 Trumpets, 3 Horns, 24 Oboes, 12 Bassoons. (This version is not printed, and is practically unknown. The published version includes strings.)

March from *Scipio*
Originally written as slow parade march for the Grenadier Guards. Still played, or at least until recently, as *The Royal Guards March*. (Modern version published by Novello.)

Concerto in F
For double set of Wind Instruments and Strings. (Breitkopf & Härtel)

G. H. Stölzel 1690-1749

Concerto in 4 Choirs
2 Choirs of Trumpets and Tympani
1 Choir of Woodwinds
1 Choir of Strings, Divided

Frederick the Great 1712-1786

Military March
(Score: Berlin, Schlesinger)
(Frederick's Flute Concertos, etc., are well known.)

K. P. E. Bach 1714-1788

6 Small Sonatas (Hamburg, 1775)
2 Horns, 2 Flutes, 2 Clarinets, Bassoon

6 Small Pieces
2 Horns, 2 Oboes, 2 Clarinets, Bassoon

2 Small Pieces
2 Horns, 2 Oboes, Bassoon

2 Marches
2 Horns, 2 Oboes, Bassoon

	? Marches 3 Trumpets and Tympani
	6 Marches 2 Oboes, 2 Clarinets, 2 Horns, Bassoon
	4 Symphonies (Vienna)
	Duet 2 Clarinets
Leopold Mozart 1719-1787	*Marcia Villanesca*
Joseph Haydn 1732-1809	6 Feldpartien (1761) 2 Clarinets, 2 Oboes, 2 Horns, 3 Bassoons, 1 Serpent
	Serenade (1768) 2 Horns, 2 Flutes
	2 Marches 2 Clarinets, 2 Bassoons, 2 Horns, 1 Trumpet (Leipzig: Peters)
	Octet 2 Oboes, 2 Clarinets, 2 Horns, 2 Bassoons (Leipzig: Kahnt)
	Divertimento 2 Clarinets, 2 Horns (Copenhagen: Hansen) (AMP)
	Hungarian National March for Wind Instruments (1802)
	2 Nocturnes (F and G) for Wind Instruments
	Divertimento Flute, Oboe, Horn, Bassoon
	6 Divertimenti (Scherzandi) (1752) Flute, Oboe, Horn
	Concerto in E♭ for Trumpet (1796)
J. E. Altenburg 1734-1796	Concerto for 7 Trumpets and Tympani
	Miscellaneous Pieces for Trumpets
François Joseph Gossec 1734-1829	Three Symphonies for Wind Instruments
	Marche Lugubre (Modern versions published

by Buffet-Crampon and Affiliated Music Corp.)

Hymn to the Goddess of Reason

Hymn to the Supreme Being

Contredanse and Pieces (1769)
2 Clarinets, 2 Horns, 2 Bassoons

J. C. Bach 1735-1782

4 Marches
2 Oboes, 2 Bassoons, 2 Horns, 2 Clarinets

2 Marches
2 Clarinets, 2 Horns, 2 Bassoons

Michael Haydn 1737-1806

Turkish March for 12 Wind Instruments and Percussion

G. Paisiello 1741-1816

March of the First Consul
Composed for Napoleon, 1810 (Modern version, Buffet-Crampon)

Franz Anton Rossetti 1744-1792

Septet
Oboe, 2 English Horns, 2 Horns, 2 Bassoons

W. A. Mozart 1756-1791

Serenade (K. 361)
2 Oboes, 2 Clarinets, 2 Basset-horns, 4 Horns, 2 Bassoons, Contra bassoon

Serenade, E♭ (K. 375)
2 Oboes, 2 Clarinets, 2 Horns, 2 Bassoons

Serenade, C min. (K. 388)
2 Oboes, 2 Clarinets, 2 Horns, 2 Bassoons

Two Divertimenti (K. 166 & 186)
2 Oboes, 2 Clarinets, 2 English Horns, 2 Horns, 2 Bassoons

Two Divertimenti (K. 187 & 188)
2 Flutes, 5 Trumpets, 4 Tympani

Six Divertimenti (K. 213, 240, 252, 253, 270, 289)
2 Oboes, 2 Bassoons, 2 Horns
Five Divertimenti (K. Anh. 229)
2 Clarinets, Bassoon
2 Quartets (K. 285 & 298)
4 Flutes
1 Quartet (K. 370)
4 Oboes
Adagio (K. 411)
2 Clarinets, 3 Basset-horns
Adagio (K. 410)
2 Basset-horns, Bassoon
Quintet (K. 452)
Pianoforte, Oboe, Clarinet, Horn, Bassoon
Quartet Concertante (K. Anh. 1. 9)
Oboe, Clarinet, Horn, Bassoon and Strings

(*Mozart's works published in complete edition by Breitkopf & Härtel. Some in other editions.*)

Ignaz Joseph Pleyel 1757-1831	Serenade à 8-9 2 Oboes, 2 Clarinets, 2 Bassoons, 2 Horns and Double-bass ad lib. (Bonn: Simrock; or Costallat)
L. Cherubini 1760-1842 (Cherubini was at one time Bandmaster of the National Guard of Paris. He was decorated by Napoleon I for his services.)	*Marche du Préfet d'Eure-et-Loire* *Marche pour le Retour du Préfet* *Marche pour le Baron von Braun* 2 Military Marches March and Quickstep for the National Guard of Paris
Franz Danzi 1763-1826	Twelve Quintets (Op. 50, 56, 67, 68) Flute, Oboe, Clarinet, Horn, Bassoon (Berlin: Schlesinger)
A. Gyrowetz 1763-1850	Two Serenades, Op. 3 2 Clarinets, 2 Horns, Bassoon

	Serenade, Op. 32 Ditto (Offenbach a.M.: André)
Samuel Wesley 1763-1837	March Horns, Oboes, Bassoons, Serpent
L. van Beethoven 1770-1827	Two Marches in F for Band March in C for Band March in D for Band Polonaise in D for Band Ecossaise in D for Band March 2 Clarinets, 2 Horns, 2 Bassoons Sextet, Op. 71 2 Clarinets, 2 Horns, 2 Bassoons Trio, Op. 87 (orig. Op. 29) 2 Oboes, English Horn Octet, Op. 103 2 Oboes, 2 Clarinets, 2 Horns, 2 Bassoons Rondino Same Instruments as Op. 103 3 Duos for Clarinet and Bassoon 3 *Equali* for 4 Trombones Variations on *Reich Mir Die Hand* Flute, Clarinet, Bassoon Quintet, Op. 16 Pianoforte, Oboe, Clarinet, Horn, Bassoon

(*The above are published by Breitkopf & Härtel in the complete editions of B's works. Some in other editions.*)

Add (*unpublished*):

	Military March 2 Piccolos, 6 Clarinets, 10 Trumpets, Horns, Trombones, etc.

Anton Reicha 1770-1834	Two Quartets (Op. 12 and 27) 4 Flutes (Opus 12 reprinted by Cundy-Bettoney) Three Adagios (Op. 18) 4 Flutes Sonata (Op. 19) 4 Flutes Adagio English Horn, Flute, Clarinet, Horn, Bassoon Twenty-four Quintets (Op. 88, 91, 99, 100) Flute, Oboe, Clarinet, Horn, Bassoon (Op. 91, No. 5 and Op. 99, No. 1 reprinted. AMP.)
(Reicha was an eminent theorist and close friend of Beethoven.)	
J. N. A. Witassek 1771-1839	March and Allegro for Military Band (Leipzig: Hofmeister)
Ferdinand Paër 1771-1839	Four Grand Military Marches Composed for the wedding of Napoleon I and Marie-Louise of Austria, April 2, 1810. (Modern version published by Buffet-Crampon) Siz Waltzes for Military Band Fantasia for 2 Pianoforte, 2 Flutes, 2 Horns and Bassoon
(Paër, in addition to being one of the most celebrated opera-composers of his day, was maître-de-chapelle to Napoleon from 1807 to 1812.)	

NOTE: *In addition to the works listed above, there are hundreds of works by lesser composers such as Berr, Kleinheinz, Blasius, G. A. Schneider and others. Many of these men had a direct interest in military music and may be considered predecessors of Wieprecht. Those interested in Marches of the 17th and 18th Centuries should investigate the collections made by J. Kosleck (Breitkopf and Härtel) and L. Chomel (Buffet-Crampon). The concertos and sonatas for single wind instruments written by the composers of the period I have made no attempt to list, as such a catalogue would require almost another complete volume.*

R. F. G.

III. 1800-1937

A. Compositions for Large or Small Band

G. Spontini 1774-1851	Marches for the Prussian Guards
L. Spohr 1784-1859	Nocturne in C, Opus 34 For Wind Instruments and Turkish Band (Percussion)
C. M. von Weber 1786-1826	Waltz in E♭ March in C (Posthumous Works, No. 8) Flute, 2 Oboes, 2 Clarinets, 2 Bassoons, 2 Horns, 2 Trumpets, Bass Trombone (Leipzig: C. Peters)
G. Meyerbeer 1791-1864	Three Torch Dances (Re-arranged for modern use by Wieprecht and others. Available only in such arrangements.)
G. A. Rossini 1792-1868	3 Marches for the Marriage of The Duke of Orleans (Leipzig: Breitkopf & Härtel) March for the Sultan Abdul Medjid (Mainz: Schott)
G. Donizetti 1797-1848	*Luge Qui Legis* (Weep Who Reads) Funeral March Written for Military Band, 1842. (Milan: Ricordi)
Hector Berlioz 1803-1869	*Funeral and Triumphal Symphony* For Wind Band with Orchestra and Chorus ad lib. (Paris: Brandus; now Breitkopf & Härtel)
F. Mendelssohn 1809-1847	Overture in C, Opus 24 (Fischer and Breitkopf & Härtel; also Buffet-Crampon and others)
R. Wagner 1813-1883	*Huldigungsmarsch* Originally written for band, but not so published. Present band versions made from

		Raff's published version for orchestra. (Many editions)
		* *Trauersymphonie zur Besetzung C. M. von Webers.* (Weber Funeral Symphony) Written for an extremely large band, music adapted from themes of Weber's *Euryanthe.* (Breitkopf & Härtel)
A. Ponchielli	1834-1886	Two Funeral Marches (Ricordi)
		Fantasia Militare (Ricordi)
C. Saint-Saëns	1835-1921	March, *Orient and Occident* (1869)
		March, *Sur les Bords du Nil,* (On the Banks of the Nile) Op. 125
		Marche Interalliée, Op. 155 (1918)
		Quickstep, *Vers La Victoire* (Towards Victory) (1918)
		Hymne Franco-Espagnole (1900)

(*Saint-Saëns' works published by Durand, Paris.*)

P. I. Tchaikovsky	1840-1893	Military March (1892-93) Written by request of A. P. Tchaikovsky for the band of the 98th Infantry Regiment, of which the latter was Colonel. (Affiliated Music Corp.; Buffet-Crampon)
Edvard Grieg	1843-1907	Funeral March: *Zum Andenken an R. Nordraak* Originally written for Pianoforte in A minor. Arranged for band in G minor by Grieg himself. (Peters)
N. Rimsky-Korsakov	1844-1908	Concerto for Clarinet and Band (Affiliated Music Corp.)
		Variations on a Theme by Glinka for Oboe and Wind Band (Ms.)

Works marked * are described in this volume under the name of the composer.

	Concerto for Trombone and Band (In preparation — Affiliated Music Corp.)
Carl Busch 1862-	*Prelude (Schirmer)
	* *A Chant from the Great Plains* (Fischer)
	*Hymn and Processional (Fitzsimons)
Paul Gilson 1865-	*Valse Symphonique* (Breitkopf & Härtel)
	Norwegian Suite (Data unavailable on other works)
Max von Schillings 1868-1933	March, Opus 27
Albert Roussel 1869-1937	* *A Glorious Day* (Elkan-Vogel)
Florent Schmitt 1870-	*Dionysiaques* (Durand, Paris)
	Selamnik, Turkish Divertissement, Op. 48, No. 1 (Durand)
	March of the 163rd (Durand)
Henry Hadley 1871-1937	*Overture, *Youth Triumphant* (Fischer)
	*Festival March (Fitzsimons)
R. Vaughan Williams 1872-	* *Toccata Marziale* (Boosey & Hawkes)
	*English Folk-Song Suite (Boosey & Hawkes)
Gustav Holst 1874-1934	*First Suite for Band, in $E\flat$ (Boosey & Hawkes)
	*Second Suite for Band, in F (Boosey & Hawkes)
	Prelude and Scherzo, *Hammersmith* (Ms.)
Ottorino Respighi 1879-1936	* *Huntingtower Ballad* (Ricordi)
N. Miaskovsky 1881-	Solemn March (Affiliated Music Corp.)
Igor Stravinsky 1882-	Symphonies for Wind Instruments
	Volga Song for Wind Instruments (Schott)
Percy Grainger 1882-	*March, *The Lads of Wamphray* (F
	* *Molly on The Shore* (F

	**Shepherd's Hey* (F
	**Colonial Song* (F
	**Irish Tune from County Derry* (F
	*Children's March, *Over The Hills and Far Away* (F (Piano and Band)
	**Lincolnshire Posy* (A Suite)
	**Spoon River*
	**Blythe Bells*
	Harvest Hymn
Ernst Toch 1887-	*Spiel* for Wind Band (Schott) 1. Overture 2. Idyll 3. Buffo
Sergei Prokofiev 1891-	*Spartan March* (Affiliated)
Leo Sowerby 1895-	*An American Rhapsody* (Ms)
Paul Hindemith 1895-	*Concert Music for Wind Band* 1. Concertante Overture 2. Variations on *Prinz Eugen* 3. March (Schott)
Henry Cowell 1897-	*Celtic Set* 1. Reel 2. *Caoine* (An Irish Lament) 3. Hornpipe 4. Air
Ernst Křenek 1900-	*Three Joyous Marches for Wind Band* (Universal Edition, 1929)

B. Compositions for Brass Band

André Wormser 1851-1926	*Les Lupercales,* Symphonic Poem for Brass alone. (Buffet-Crampon)
Edward Elgar 1857-1934	*Severn Suite* Written for Brass Band and later re-arranged for orchestra. Published for Brass Band. (London: R. Smith, 1930)

Granville Bantock 1868-	*Oriental Rhapsody* (R. Smith, 1930)
	Symphonic Prelude, *Prometheus Unbound* (R. Smith, 1933)
Guillaume Lekeu 1870-1894	Introduction and Adagio (1891) (Not published)
Gustav Holst 1874-1934	*Moorside Suite* (R. Smith, 1928)
John Ireland 1879-	*Downland Suite* (R. Smith, 1932)
	Comedy Overture (R. Smith, 1934)
Herbert Howells 1892-	*Pageantry Suite* (R. Smith, 1934)

Other compositions by Percy Fletcher, Keighly, et al.

C. Compositions for Small Combinations of Wind Instruments (Without Piano or Strings)

C. M. von Weber 1786-1826	*Marcia Vivace* 10 Trumpets
G. A. Rossini 1792-1868	Quartet Flute or Oboe, Clarinet, Horn, Bassoon (Ricordi, 1929)
Franz Schubert 1797-1828	Menuet and Finale 2 Oboes, 2 Clarinets, 2 Horns, 2 Bassoons (Breitkopf & Härtel)
	Eine Kleine Trauermusik 2 Clarinets, 2 Bassoons, Contrabassoon, 2 Horns, 2 Trombones (Breitkopf & Härtel)
Franz Lachner 1803-1890	Octet, Opus 156 Flute, Oboe, 2 Clarinets, 2 Horns, 2 Bassoons (Leipzig: Kistner)
F. David 1810-1876	Two Nonets for Wind Instruments
Charles Gounod 1818-1893	*Petite Symphonie* (1885) Flute, 2 Oboes, 2 Clarinets, 2

	Horns, 2 Bassoons (Paris: Costallat)
Th. Gouvy 1819-1898	Octet, Opus 71 Flute, Oboe, 2 Clarinets, 2 Horns, 2 Bassoons (Leipzig: Kistner) *Petite Suite Gauloise*, Opus 90 Flute, 2 Oboes, 2 Clarinets, 2 Horns, 2 Bassoons (Universal Edition)
Joachim Raff 1822-1882	Sinfonietta, Opus 188 2 Flutes, 2 Oboes, 2 Clarinets, 2 Bassoons, 2 Horns (1876)
C. Reinecke 1824-1910	Octet, Opus 216 Flute, Oboe, 2 Clarinets, 2 Horns, 2 Bassoons (Leipzig: Kistner) Sextet, Opus 271 Flute, Oboe, Clarinet, 2 Horns, Bassoon (Leipzig: Zimmermann)
G. Lange 1830-?	Nonet Flute, 2 Oboes, 2 Clarinets, 2 Horns, 2 Bassoons (Dresden: Seeling, 1878)
S. Jadassohn 1831-1902	Serenade, Opus 104c (4 Mvts.) 2 Flutes, 2 Oboes, 2 Clarinets, 2 Horns, 2 Bassoons (A. P. Schmidt, 1890)
E. Flament 1836-1897	Fantasia con Fuga, Opus 28 Flute, Oboe, Eng. Horn, Clarinet, Horn, 2 Bassoons (Evette & Schaeffer, now Buffet-Crampon)
Th. Dubois 1837-1924 (D. won Grand Prix de Rome, 1861. Succeeded A. Thomas as Director of Conservatoire.)	First Suite 2 Flutes, Oboe, 2 Clarinets, Horn, 2 Bassoons (Heugel, 1898) Second Suite 2 Clarinets, 2 Flutes, Horn, 2 Bassoons (Paris: Leduc) *Au Jardin* (In the Garden) 2 Flutes, Oboe, 2 Clarinets,

	Horn, Bassoon (Heugel, 1908)
F. Codivilla 1841-?	Octet Flute, Oboe, Clarinet, Bassoon, Cornet, 2 Horns, Trombone (Bologna: Bongiovanni, 1918)
Henri Maréchal 1842-1924	*Air du Guet* (On an Old Provençal Theme) Flute, Oboe, Clarinet, Horn, Bassoon (Paris: Heugel)
Emile Pessard 1843-1917	*Aubade en Quintette* Flute, Oboe, Clarinet, Horn, Bassoon (Paris: Leduc)
Paul Taffanel 1844-1908 (T. was Founder of the Société des Instruments à Vent, Paris.)	Quintet Flute, Oboe, Clarinet, Horn, Bassoon (Paris: Leduc)
E. Bernard 1845-1902	Divertissement, Opus 36 2 Flutes, 2 Oboes, 2 Clarinets, 2 Horns, 2 Bassoons (Paris: Durand, 1927)
C. H. H. Parry 1848-1918	Nonet, Opus 71
Gustav Schreck 1849-1918	Nonet, Opus 40 2 Flutes, Oboe, 2 Clarinets, 2 Horns, 2 Bassoons (Breitkopf & Härtel, 1905)
L. Bonvin 1850-	Romance, Opus 19a Flute, 2 Oboes, 2 Clarinets, 2 Horns, 2 Bassoons (Breitkopf & Härtel) Melody, Opus 56b Same combination as above
A. J. Simon 1851-	Quartet, Opus 23 2 Cornets, Alto and Tenor Trombones Ensemble Pieces, Opus 26 Four Septets 3 Cornets, E♭ Altos, 2 Trombones Four Sextets 2 Cornets, 2 E♭ Altos, 2 Trombones

	Six Quintets 2 Cornets, 2 E♭ Altos, 1 Trombone Eight Quartets 2 Cornets, E♭ Alto, Trombone (Affiliated Music Corp.)
Vincent D'Indy 1851-1931	*Chanson et Danses*, Opus 50 Flute, Oboe, 2 Clarinets, Horn, 2 Bassoons (Paris: Durand, 1891)
Leoš Janáček 1854-1928	*Mládí* (*Youth*) Flute (Piccolo), Oboe, Clarinet, Horn, Bassoon, Bass Clarinet (Prague: Hudební Matiče, 1925)
L. De Wailly 1854- (Was a pupil of César Franck)	Octet Flute, Oboe, 2 Clarinets, Horn, 2 Bassoons, Trumpet (Paris: Rouart-Lerolle, 1905)
A. Mendelssohn 1855-1933	Suite for Wind and Percussion, Op. 6 (Leuckart, 1916)
J. Röntgen 1855-1932	Serenade in A, Opus 14 (Breitkopf and Härtel)
Edward Elgar 1857-1934	Quintet for Wind Instruments (Ms.)
A. Bruneau 1857-1934	Romance for 4 Clarinets (Ms.) (Opus 16)
S. Lazzari 1858- (L. was a pupil of César Franck)	Octuor Flute, Oboe, Eng. Horn, Clarinet, 2 Horns, 2 Bassoons (Paris: Evette & Schaeffer, 1920)
A. Périlhou d. 1936	Divertissement 2 Flutes, 2 Clarinets, 2 Oboes, 2 Bassoons, 4 Horns (Heugel)
M. Ippolitov-Ivanov 1859-1935	Two Kirghiz Songs Oboe, Clarinet, Bassoon, with Pianoforte ad lib. (Affiliated Music Corp., 1932)
Edward German 1862-1936	Serenade for Wind Instruments (Ms.)
Carl Busch 1862-	Septet, *An Ozark Reverie* Flute, Oboe, 2 Clarinets, 2 Horns, Bassoon (Fitzsimons)

Northland Suite (4 Mvts.)
Flute, Oboe, Clarinet, Bassoon (Fitzsimons)

Arioso and Fanfare
6 Cornets or Trumpets (Fitzsimons)

Impromptu
6 Cornets or Clarinets (Fitzsimons)

In Festive Mood
2 Trumpets, Horn, Trombone, Baritone, Tuba (Witmark)

Suite for 3 Trumpets (Witmark)

Four Miniatures
3 Cornets or Clarinets (Fischer)

Quietude, In Playful Mood, Evening Promenade
4 Cornets or Clarinets (Fischer)

Meditation
4 Trombones or Baritones (Fischer)

Gabriel Pierné 1863-1937

Preludio and Fughetta, Op. 40, No. 1
2 Flutes, Oboe, Clarinet, Horn, 2 Bassoons (Hamelle)

Pastorale, Opus 14, No. 1
Flute, Oboe, Clarinet, Horn, Bassoon (Paris: Leduc)

Pastorale Variée
Flute, Oboe, Clarinet, Horn, 2 Bassoons, Trumpet (Paris: Durand)

J. G. Ropartz 1864-

Two Pieces
Flute, Oboe, Clarinet, Horn, Bassoon (Paris: Durand, 1926)

Richard Strauss 1864-

Serenade in E♭, Opus 7
2 Flutes, 2 Oboes, 2 Clarinets, 4 Horns, 2 Bassoons, Tuba or Contra bassoon (Universal Edition, 1884)

Suite in B♭, Opus 4
13 Wind Instruments (Berlin: Fürstner, 1911)

Feierlicher Eintritt der Ritter des Johanniterordens (Solemn Entry of the Knights of the Order of Johannes)
12 Trumpets, 3 Solo Trumpets, 4 Horns, 4 Trombones, 2 Tubas, Tympani (Berlin: Schlesinger, 1909)

A. Glazounov 1865-1936 — *In Modo Religioso,* Opus 38
Trumpet, Horn, Tenor and Bass Trombone (Belaiev)

H. Scherrer 1865- — Old French Dances, Opus 11
Flute, Oboe, 2 Clarinets, Horn, Bassoon (Heilbronn: Schmitt, 1899)

Paul Gilson 1865- — Septet & Scherzo
2 Humoresques

O. E. Novaček, 1866-1900 — Sinfonietta
Flute, Oboe, 2 Clarinets, 2 Horns, 2 Bassoons (Breitkopf & Härtel, 1905)

Swan Hennessy 1866- — *Little Irish Suite*
Flute, Oboe, Clarinet, Horn, Bassoon

Trio, Opus 54
2 Clarinets and Bassoon (Paris: Eschig)

Jules Mouquet 1867-
(Prix de Rome, 1896.) — Suite
Flute, Oboe, Horn, 2 Clarinets, 2 Bassoons (Paris: Lemoine, 1910)

F. Casadesus 1870-
(C. was Founder and Director of the American Cons. at Fontainebleau, 1918-1922.) — *London Sketches*
2 Flutes, 2 Oboes, 2 Clarinets, 2 Horns, 2 Bassoons (Deisz, 1916)

Florent Schmitt 1870- — *Lied and Scherzo,* Opus 54
2 Flutes, 2 Oboes, 2 Clarinets, 2 Horns, 2 Bassoons (Durand)

G. Balay 1871-	Three Quintets Flute, Oboe, Clarinet, Horn, Bassoon (Buffet-Crampon)
August Reuss 1871-1935	Octet, Opus 37 2 Oboes, 2 Clarinets, 2 Horns, 2 Bassoons (Munich: Zierfuss, 1920)
Paul Juon 1872-	Quintet, Opus 84 Flute, Oboe, Clarinet, Horn, Bassoon (Berlin: Birnbach, 1930)
S. N. Vassilenko 1872-	Quartet on Turkmenish Themes, Op. 65 Flute, Oboe (Eng. Horn), Clarinet, Bassoon (Affiliated Music Corp.)
N. Tcherepnin 1873-	Six Quartets for Horns (Affiliated Music Corp.; one pub. by Cundy-Bettoney)
Max Reger 1873-1916	Romance Flute, Oboe, Clarinet, Horn, Bassoon and Contra bassoon (Simon)
D. G. Mason 1873-	Divertimento, Opus 26b 1. March 2. Fugue Flute, Oboe, Clarinet, Horn, Bassoon (Fischer; Witmark)
Henri Marteau 1874-1934	Serenade (4 Mvts.) 2 Flutes, 2 Oboes, 2 Clarinets, Bass Clarinet, 2 Bassoons (Steingräber, 1922)
Gustav Holst 1874-1934	Quintet Flute, Oboe, Clarinet, Horn, Bassoon (Ms.)
Arnold Schönberg 1874-	Quintet, Opus 26 Flute, Oboe, Clarinet, Horn, Bassoon (Schott)
Pierre Monteux 1875-	Two Little Pieces Flute, Oboe, Clarinet, Bassoon, Trumpet, Percussion (Paris: Mathot, 1922)

André Caplet 1878-1925	*Suite Persane* 10 Wind Instruments (Hurstel)
Josef Holbrooke 1878-	Miniature Characteristic Suite, Opus 33b (5 Mvts.) Flute, Oboe, Clarinet, Horn, Bassoon (Kent, England: Hull, 1910)
Franz Moser 1880-	Serenade, Opus 35 2 Flutes, 2 Oboes, Eng. Horn, 2 Clarinets, Bass Clarinets, 4 Horns, 2 Bassoons, Contra bassoon (Universal, 1922) Suite, Opus 37 17 Wind Instruments
Seth Bingham 1882-	Suite for Wind Instruments
Igor Stravinsky 1882-	*Octuor* Flute, Clarinet, 2 Bassoons, 2 Trumpets, 2 Trombones (Russian Musical Editions, 1924)
Percy Grainger 1882-	*A Walking Tune* Flute, Oboe, Clarinet, Horn, Bassoon (Schott) 2 *Hill-Songs* (see text)
E. Lendvai 1882-	Quintet, Opus 23 Flute, Oboe, Clarinet, Horn, Bassoon (Simrock, 1922)
Edgar Varèse 1885-	*Octandre* Flute, Oboe, Clarinet, Horn, Bassoon, Trumpet, Trombone, Bass (Curwen—rental only) *Hyperprism* Flute, Piccolo, Clarinet, 3 Horns, 2 Trumpets, 2 Trombones, 16 Percussion Instruments (Curwen—rental only)
Cesare Sodero 1886-	*Morning Prayer* *Valse Scherzo* Flute, Oboe, Clarinet, Horn, Bassoon (AMP)
Burnet Tuthill 1888-	*Hornpipe* Flute, Oboe, Clarinet, Horn, Bassoon (Fischer)

Hans Gal 1890-	Divertimento, Opus 22 Flute, Oboe, 2 Clarinets, 2 Horns, Bassoon, Trumpet (Leuckart, 1927)
Jacques Ibert 1890-	Three Short Pieces Flute, Oboe, Clarinet, Horn, Bassoon (Paris: Leduc, 1930) Two Movements 2 Flutes, Clarinet, Bassoon (Leduc, 1923)
H. Villa-Lobos 1890-	Quartet (Choros No. 4) 3 Horns, 1 Trombone Trio (Choros No. 2) Oboe, Clarinet, Bassoon Duet Flute and Clarinet (Paris: Eschig)
Sergei Prokofiev 1891-	Scherzo, Opus 12, No. 9 4 Bassoons (Affiliated)
Darius Milhaud 1892-	*Dixtuor* Piccolo, Flute, Oboe, Eng. Horn, Clarinet, Bass Clarinet, 2 Horns, 2 Bassoons (Universal)
Eugene Goossens 1893-	Fantasy, Opus 40 Flute, Oboe, 2 Clarinets, 2 Bassoons, 2 Horns, Trumpet (Curwen, 1926)
Paul Hindemith 1895-	Quintet, Opus 24, No. 2 Flute, Oboe, Clarinet, Horn, Bassoon (Schott) Sonatine 2 Flutes (Schott)
Leo Sowerby 1895-	Quintet Flute, Oboe, Clarinet, Horn, Bassoon (Society for The Publication of American Music, 1931) Quintet, *Pop Goes The Weasel* Flute, Oboe, Clarinet, Horn, Bassoon (Fitzsimons)

Francis Poulenc 1899- — Sonata
Horn, Trumpet and Trombone 1922 (London: Chester)
Sonata
Clarinet and Bassoon. 1922 (Chester)
Sonata
2 Clarinets. 1918 (Chester)
Fanfare
2 Clarinets, 2 Bassoons, Contra bassoon, 2 Horns, 2 Trumpets, 2 Trombones, Percussion (Chester)

P.-O. Ferroud 1900-1936 — Trio in E
Oboe, Clarinet, Bassoon (Paris: Durand)

Ernesto Halffter 1905- — *Suite Ancienne* for Wind Instruments

---

ADDENDA

Sobeck — Quintets, Op. 11 and 14 (Boosey & Hawkes)

A. Klughardt — Quintet, Opus 79 (Leipzig: Zimmermann, 1901)

D. Wind Ensembles With Pianoforte or Strings

(*This list is susceptible of great extension. It includes only a few representative works in which wind instruments are pre-dominant, and does not, of course, include sonatas for single wind instruments and pianoforte.*)

Louis Spohr 1784-1859 — Quintet, Opus 52
Pf., Flute, Clarinet, Horn, Bassoon

M. I. Glinka 1804-1857 — *Trio Pathétique*
Pf., Clarinet, Bassoon (Affiliated Music Corp.)

A. Rubinstein 1830-1894 — Quintet in F. Opus 55
Pf. and Wind Instruments (Schuberth)

A. Ponchielli	1834-1886	Quintet Pf., Flute, Oboe, E♭ Clarinet, B♭ Clarinet (Ricordi)
J. Rheinberger	1839-1901	Sextet, Opus 191b Pf., Flute, Oboe, Clarinet, Horn, Bassoon (Leuckart)
Antonin Dvořák	1841-1904	Serenade in D minor, Opus 44 2 Oboes, 2 Clarinets, 3 Horns, 2 Bassoons, 'Cello, Double Bass (Simrock)
N. Rimsky-Korsakov	1844-1908	Quintet Pf., Flute, Clarinet, Horn, Bassoon (Belaiev) (Affiliated Music Corp.)
Ch.-M. Widor	1845-1937	*Salvum Fac Populum Tuum,* Opus 84 3 Trumpets, 3 Trombones, Tympani, Organ (Heugel, 1916)
Vincent D'Indy	1851-1931	Sarabande and Minuet, Op. 24 bis Pf., Flute, Oboe, Clarinet, Horn, Bassoon (Hamelle)
A. Liadov	1855-1914	*Valse Badinage,* from Opus 32 Originally written for Pf. solo. Arranged by the composer for Piccolo, 2 Flutes, 3 Clarinets, Harp and Bells (Belaiev, 1897)
M. Ippolitov-Ivanov	1859-1935	*Evening in Georgia* Flute, Oboe, Clarinet, Bassoon, Harp or Pf. (Affiliated)
Paul Gilson	1865-	Trio Pf., Oboe, Clarinet (Brussels: Cranz)
Lucien Magnard	1865-1914	Quintet, Opus 8 Pf. and Wind Instruments (Paris: Rouart-Lerolle, 1904)
Albert Roussel	1869-1937	Divertissement, Opus 6 Pf. and Wind Instruments (Rouart-Lerolle)

Paul Juon 1872-	Divertimento, Opus 51 Pf. and Wind Instruments (Berlin: Schlesinger)
Gustav Holst 1874-1934	Quintet Pf. and Wind Instruments (Ms.)
Reynaldo Hahn 1874-	*Le Bal de Béatrice d'Este* Pf., 12 Wind Instruments, 2 Harps (Heugel)
André Caplet 1878-1925	Quintet Pf. and Wind Instruments
J. Holbrooke 1878-	Sextet, Opus 33 (Chester)
Burnet Tuthill 1888-	Variations on *When Johnny Comes Marching Home* Pf., Flute, Oboe, Clarinet, Horn, Bassoon (Galaxy, 1934)
Darius Milhaud 1892-	Sonata Pf. Flute, Oboe, Clarinet (Durand)
Paul Hindemith 1895-	Concert Music Pf., 2 Harps, 4 Horns, 3 Trumpets in C, 2 Trombones, Tuba (Schott, 1930)
A. Tansman 1897-	*La Danse de la Sorcière* Pf., Flute, Oboe, Clarinet, Horn, Bassoon (Paris: Eschig, 1924)
V. Rieti 1898-	Sonata Pf., Flute, Oboe, Bassoon (Universal)
Jeanne Leleu	Symphonic Suite (5 Mvts.) Pf., 2 Flutes, Oboe, Eng. Horn, Clarinet, Bassoon, Horn, 2 Trumpets, Trombone, Drums (Paris: Leduc, 1926)
M. Mirouze	Pièce en Septuor Pf., Flute, Oboe, Clarinet, Bassoon, Horn, Trumpet (Leduc, 1933)

E. Chorus or Voice and Wind Instruments

(Besides the innumerable compositions of the sixteenth and seventeenth centuries, in which voices and wind instruments may be used alternately or in conjunction, there are the following more modern works which are listed here for purposes of record.)

J. S. Bach 1685-1750	Cantata No. 118: *O Jesu Christ, Mein's Lebens Licht* (A Choral Motet) (Bach Gesellschaft XXIV 185) Score calls for: Lituus I and II Cornetto Trombone I, II and III No Strings
F. J. Gossec 1734-1829	Second *Te Deum* (1790) Chorus and Wind Band
L. van Beethoven 1770-1827	*Bundeslied* (Goethe), Opus 122 Soprano, Alto, 3-part Chorus, and Wind Instruments. Composed in 1822-23.
C. M. von Weber 1786-1826	Chorus from *Sappho* (1818) Chorus from *Carlo* (1820) *Hörst Du Der Klage Dumpfen Schall* For Mixed Chorus and Wind (1811) Dirge For Soprano, 2 Tenors, Bass, and Wind Instruments (1803)
G. Meyerbeer 1791-1864	*March of the Bavarian Archers* Cantata for 4 Voices and Male Chorus, with Brass Acc't.
G. A. Rossini 1792-1868	Cantata (?) (1819)
F. Mendelssohn 1809-1847	*An Die Künstler* (Schiller), Op. 68. Male Voices and Brass Instruments. Composed for the opening of the first German-Flemish vocal festival. Köln, 1846 (Simrock)

Franz Liszt 1811-1886 — *An Den Heiligen Franziskus*
Male Voices, Organ, Trumpets, Drums

Anton Bruckner 1824-1896 — *Germanenzug* (1863)
Male Chorus and Wind
Mass No. 2 in E minor (1866)
Mixed Choir, 8 Voices, Wind
Das Deutsche Lied (1892)
Male Chorus and Wind

Johannes Brahms 1833-1897 — Funeral Hymn, Opus 13
Mixed Chorus, Wind (2 Oboes, 2 Clarinets, 2 Horns, 2 Bassoons, 3 Trombones, Tuba, Tympani)

J. Rheinberger 1839-1901 — *The Roses of Hildesheim,* Op. 143. Male Chorus and Wind

---

Of modern works the following are of greatest interest:

Percy Grainger 1882- — *I'm Seventeen Come Sunday*
Mixed Chorus and Brass Band (Schott & Co.)
Marching Tune
Mixed Chorus and Brass Band (Schott & Co.)

There are very many interesting works by contemporaries for small combinations of wind instruments with a single voice or several voices. The following are representative:

Percy Grainger — *Died for Love*
Voice, Flute, Clarinet, Bassoon (Schott)

Igor Stravinsky 1882- — Pastorale
Soprano, Oboe, English Horn, Clarinet, Bassoon (Schott)
Pribaoutki (Pleasant Songs) (Chester)
Berceuses du Chat
Contralto and 3 Clarinets (Chester)

F. Fanfares

(*In addition to the few ancient Fanfares previously mentioned, the following modern Fanfares are of some interest. This list is by no means complete.*)

C. M. von Weber	1786-1826	Tusch (Fanfare) For 20 Trumpets
G. A. Rossini	1792-1868	*The Crown of Italy* (reprinted by Ricordi) *La Rendezvous de Chasse* (1828)
Richard Wagner	1813-1883	Fanfares for a Regiment at Bayreuth
A. Liadov and	1855-1914	Fanfares for the Rimsky-Korsakov Jubilee, 1904 (Belaiev)
A. Glazounov	1865-1936	
Claude Debussy	1862-1918	Fanfare from *The Martyrdom of St. Sebastian*
Paul Dukas	1865-1935	Fanfare from *Le Péri*
Florent Schmitt	1870-	*The Camp of Pompey,* from *Antony and Cleopatra* (Durand)

G. Curiosa

Charles Gounod	1818-1893	Method for Cornet-à-Pistons (1845)
Johannes Brahms	1833-1897	12 Etudes for Cornet or Trumpet (no opus no.)

POSTSCRIPT

For a long time only stringed instruments have had the privilege of commanding attention at musical gatherings. Ought not one to regret that the wind instruments, which by their nature are much closer to the human voice, are, so to speak, kept out?

The complaint levelled against the wind instruments is that there is no music written for them which is of sufficient interest to make anyone care to hear it performed.

The progress of instruments depends more on composers than on players. The masterpieces of Haydn and Mozart, which were so difficult to play once upon a time, have long since established the preponderance of stringed instruments. One must give credit to the amateurs for whom these works were written; they were not discouraged by the difficulties, and today we have reaped the benefit of their study and their courage.

It is by following the same path that we will arrive at the same end.

To study one's part carefully, to rehearse often, to perfect the ensemble in order to grasp the intentions of the composer —these are the essentials for the performance of these Quintets. In music which depends on the ensemble for its effect there are always some difficulties which appear great at first, but which are not hard to overcome. The fortes, mezzo-fortes, *etc., and above all the* pianos *should be strictly observed. The part which carries the melody must be allowed to dominate and must not be covered up. To arrive at perfection it is also necessary to be sure to observe the nuances which are indicated, for without them all music loses its interest.*

By carefully following the recommendations we have just made, one will succeed in playing these Quintets as they should be played. This is what we ourselves have endeavored to do. By following our example, teachers and players of wind instruments will encourage composers to enrich their repertory.

It is only by diligence and perseverance that they will arrive at such musicianship as to overcome the repugnance which many composers feel toward writing for wind instruments, and only in such a way will they establish a real rivalry with the stringed instruments, bringing to an end the priority of the latter, for which we have described the principal causes.

(*signed*) Messrs. VOGT, GUILLOU, DAUPRAT, BOUFFIL, HENRY
Members of the Royal School of Music and the Royal Theatre of Comic-Opera. Paris, 1817

This statement was printed on the first page of the original edition of Anton Reicha's *Six Quintets for Wind Instruments*, Opus 88, published by N. Simrock of Bonn in 1817. Time has hardly impaired its interest or its validity, and I preface it to the following remarks less as a historical curiosity than as a text for expansion.

The list of works for wind instruments which I have presented on previous pages, although it will perhaps surprise many people who have believed wind-instrument literature to be almost non-existent, will hardly serve to disprove or deprecate the priority of stringed instruments. In that respect circumstances have not greatly changed since 1817. If, however, today's plea for compositions for wind instruments is not something new, today's performers are nevertheless in a better position to act as well as plead.

There are today more good wind-instrument players than there have ever been before, and these players have the advantage of using much-improved instruments. There is an enormously greater number of bands. Paradoxically enough, one of the largest factors in the band's favor today is the heretofore heavy preponderance of stringed-instrument music. Orchestral writing over the last one hundred and fifty years has developed a tradition of such growing complexity that modern orchestral music is artistically inaccessible to all but the most complete and well-trained of orchestras. There are few orchestras, and not too many conductors, who can give a satisfactory performance of one of the more exacting of modern scores. There is the additional problem presented by the difficulty an orchestral composer experiences in obtaining a performance of his work. New works must compete with the huge repertory of standard music which is the orchestra's heritage.

The band should be more accessible to composers. It should be more eager to give the new composer a hearing, and it should likewise be less bound by a mass of tradition. This requires, of course, an interest on the part of bandmasters, and a willingness and ability to give good performances of new works, performances which will in every way meet the demands of the composer and realize his intentions.

The methods of accomplishing this end are already set forth in outline in the statement by Reicha's quintet players. Perhaps a number of bandmasters will ask why this is important. It is important for several reasons. It must be remembered that while the band has existed in a more or less satisfactory state on a diet of transcriptions, and that while theoretically there is no limit whatsoever to the production of new transcriptions, at the same time the musical audience is hearing (via radio, and via the extension of popular orchestral concerts) more and more of the standard orchestral repertory in its original form. That in itself is not a very weighty argument against transcriptions, but the fact remains that there are rather large numbers of people who prefer (or believe they prefer) to hear a composition in its original form, played by the instruments for which it was designed. Should this tendency continue (and there is no reason to suppose the contrary), the band will, unless it encourages new compositions, be reduced to echoing the orchestra on a lower plane, or to put it still more baldly, will exist simply as a means of producing loud noises for parades and picnics.

In preceding pages we have attempted to give the opposite side of the picture: the reasons why bands should continue to develop as a musical force, and the historical backgrounds which lead one to this conclusion. There remain a few considerations of practical interest touching on the subject.

Good performance means, among other things, attention to detail, sufficient rehearsal, and adequate instrumentation. The latter means not only the presence in the band of the indicated instruments, but their balance and distribution. A band in which there are more cornets than clarinets, for example, is under rather a handicap at the outset. A band in which there are no French horns or bassoons or oboes is likewise in difficulties. Often such situations are out of the control of the bandmaster; in that case he is wise to choose his repertory accordingly. What is even more important from a musical standpoint is the inflexibility of band instrumentation. This again is often a matter of circumstance, but in many cases it is due to the evidently popular conception that the more instruments used, the better the effect. To turn again to the orchestra for a parallel, we may remark that the orchestra of Richard Strauss is not the orchestra of Mozart. Would Mozart's music sound better played by Strauss' orchestra? When we answer that question and apply the answer to bands, we have one approach to the problem of instrumentation.

The orchestra's instrumentation is entirely the result of the scores written by composers, just as the tradition of the string quartet is the result of the works of Haydn and Mozart. The band, however, starts on the diametrically opposed principle. It says, in effect, "we have so many cornets, trombones, clarinets and saxophones, etc.—now you must write something for this combination." This is not an argument for the infinite extension of the band's instrumentation to include every possible instrument. Rather let it be construed as an argument for the utilization of the available instruments to best effect. Need every score for band include every instrument in the band? It seems somewhat odd that there are hardly any arrangements for an all-reed band, for example. The principle of choirs in the band has, as a general thing, been subordinated to the practice of writing for *soli* and *tutti*.

These ideas are presented in the most general way, in the hope that they may appear worthy of further consideration by individuals concerned. That the band can give as artistic a performance as the orchestra is a statement the truth of which most bandmasters take for granted. But that the assumption of its rightful place in musical life by the band depends upon its continued and ceaseless striving for artistic and esthetic perfection is something which should not be forgotten.

The following pages contain lists of standard works available for bands. It is impossible to deny that many of these works were never intended for performance by bands. At the same time it cannot be gainsaid that almost all of them can be made to sound well when properly performed by a good band. It will be found that certain works are better arranged than others. The bandmaster who has the artistic success of his band at heart will examine each arrangement carefully before he places it on a program for performance. It is more important for the success of the band that the arrangement be good than that the music be "classical" or "serious." A poor arrangement of a Beethoven symphony is, for example, of more doubtful value than a good arrangement of some intrinsically less impressive work. The best arrangement, let it be said, is not necessarily that which makes the band sound the loudest and strongest, but in general that which preserves a satisfactory tonal balance and provides contrast in dynamics and in timbres. A good arrangement is one which is in accord with the character of the music. Bandmasters must decide for themselves what music sounds best for band, and govern themselves accordingly. Band audiences, happily enough, are still for the most part in a receptive state. The bandmaster is in a position to experiment, and on the results of his experiments the future direction of band music will to a large extent depend.

It is not altogether outside the province of this book, and in fact may properly be considered one of its functions, to discuss briefly the question of building programs and choosing music. The purpose of this volume is to show what great quantities of material are available. In a field where there is so much to be done, it is regrettable that so little variety is obtained, that so little independence of choice exists. A bandmaster traveling through a certain state is likely to hear each band performing the same or nearly the same selections. While, for competitive purposes, it is often expedient to have a single number or group of numbers slated for intensive preparation, the advantages of this procedure on the cultural and artistic sides are neither obvious nor numerous. Standardization is possibly a provider of untold benefits in an industrial civilization, but it may profitably be borne in mind that the ultimate of standardization in musical taste means enjoyment by edict, and the eventual discouragement of all creative activity in the art. On the side of performance, it sets up the ideal of the player-piano. The attempt to "standardize" musical taste, insofar as it is being made, is more than likely to result in a complete stultification of the faculties for music appreciation.

In earlier paragraphs I have emphasized the close relation between the band and its audience. It is still impossible to have better band programs without better audiences, but the reverse is still also true, and that is where the responsibility of the bandmaster lies. The discharge of this responsibility will depend upon the ingenuity and resourcefulness of the bandmaster. One cannot make an audience like a given piece of music by hammering away at it constantly. If we assume that we are going, for example, to embark upon a campaign of feeding Bach to audiences, we shall not endear ourselves to the audiences by playing one Bach number over and over again. Out of six or seven Bach numbers, however, almost every one, in no matter what type of audience, will find some pleasure. If this pleasure is genuine (and it should be), the bandmaster will find his audience far more receptive to further experiment on his part. It is important for the bandmaster to create and foster this open-mindedness in his audience, but he must, of course, begin with himself. We must necessarily assume that bands exist for the purpose of making music. If this is true, it is clearly up to bandmasters to select more widely from the vast stores of music available, for music consists not only of a limited selection of overtures and tone poems (with marches for encores), but of all the notes put down on paper from the beginning of modern notation to the present day.

It is my belief, submitted in all due respect, that no bandmaster will, in attempting to act on the suggestions outlined below, find himself up against excessive resistance on the part of his audience. The problem, in any case, is to make the bandmaster as strong an influence upon his audience as his audience is upon him. In schematic form, and in order of what seem to me to be their importance, I present these considerations for program construction:

I. Freer exercise of choice in selection of music to be played, dependent on:
   a. Capacity of band (proficiency and instrumentation).
   b. Suitability of music chosen for band performance.

II. Performance of music written both before and after the nineteenth century; that is, a wider knowledge (and dissemination of knowledge) of the treasures of ancient and modern music.

III. Performance of works written directly for band, especially those which, by their successful idiomatic exploitation of the band's resources, will encourage living composers to write further for band.

IV. Performance of music by sections of the band; that is, the development of the possibilities inherent in the reed choir, the brass choir, the double-reed and saxophone choir, etc.

Action upon these suggestions will almost automatically provide that prime desideratum in a band program: *variety*. In a broad general sense, variety should be maintained not only musically, but technically. The exploitation of various sections of the band, of various instrumental combinations and colors, will do much to foster the development of a public which will listen to bands with renewed interest and greater comprehension.

Eventually there will be created a demand for wind-instrument chamber music, to parallel the position in musical life of the string quartet. For band players themselves, no better training and no deeper enjoyment can be imagined than the performance of music for small ensembles. Every band player of requisite proficiency should endeavor to find the opportunity of playing in a small group. The development of a good ensemble takes time and patience, but the results, in finer musicianship, in a feeling for the subtleties of line and tone, will do much to provide more elevated criteria for wind-instrument performances in general. It is obvious that wind-instrument chamber music will never have the appeal for the public that is the characteristic of music played by a full-bodied wind band, but a certain place it should, and will, indubitably have. And no other type of music should give as much of benefit or of joy to the really devoted amateur of wind instruments.

Key to Abbreviations of Publishers

ABC	American Book Company	88 Lexington Avenue, New York
Aff	Affiliated Music Corp. (representing State Music Publishers of Russia)	549 West 42nd Street, New York
AMP	Associated Music Publishers representing: Brietkopf & Härtel, Leipzig; Universal Edition, Vienna; Max Eschig, Paris; Schott & Co., London	25 West 45th Street, New York
Ba	C. L. Barnhouse	Oscaloosa, Iowa
Birch	C. C. Birchard Co.	Boston, Massachusetts
B&H	Boosey & Hawkes, Ltd.	295 Regent Street, London W1
	or Boosey-Hawkes-Belwin	43 West 23rd Street, New York
Brg	George F. Briegel	1674 Broadway, New York
C	Chappell	London, England
	Chappell-Harms, Inc.	1250 Sixth Avenue, New York
CB	Cundy-Bettoney Co.	Boston, Mass.
D	Oliver Ditson Co.	Boston, Mass.
EV	Elkan-Vogel Co. representing: Durand, Paris	1716 Sanson Street, Philadelphia, Pa.
F	Carl Fischer, Inc.	62 Cooper Square, New York
Fil	Henry Fillmore Music House	528 Elm Street, Cincinnati, O.
Fitz	H. T. Fitzsimons Co., Inc.	Chicago, Illinois

H	T. B. Harms, Inc.	1250 Sixth Avenue, New York
J	Walter Jacobs Co.	120 Boylston Street, Boston
K	Karl King Music House	Fort Dodge, Iowa
LF	Leo Feist, Inc.	1629 Broadway, New York
Lud	Ludwig Music Co.	414 W. Superior Avenue, Cleveland, Ohio
M	Edward B. Marks Music Corp.	1250 Sixth Avenue, New York
N	Novello	London, England
	c/o H. W. Gray Co.	159 East 48th Street, New York
P	Theodore Presser, Inc.	1712 Chestnut Street, Philadelphia, Pa.
R	Ricordi & Co.	12 West 45th Street, New York; London
Rem	Remick Music Corp.	1250 Sixth Avenue, New York
Rob	Robbins Music Corp.	799 Seventh Avenue, New York
Ru	Rubank, Inc.	736 S. Campbell Street, Chicago
S	G. Schirmer, Inc.	3 East 43rd Street, New York
SF	Sam Fox Music Co.	1250 Sixth Avenue, New York
W	M. Witmark & Sons	1250 Sixth Avenue, New York
Wil	Ernest Williams School of Music	153 Ocean Avenue, Brooklyn, N. Y.

Bibliographical Note

In a work of this nature a complete bibliography becomes an impediment rather than an aid to the reader or student. Hundreds of volumes have figured, by the contribution of perhaps but a single fact each, in the compilation of this book. The principal task of the conscientious list-compiler and note-writer is to rummage through as many books, periodicals and catalogues as he can obtain, in order to trace or to verify facts. To list all of these would be to send the student off, in most cases, on false scents. However, certain essential works dealing with various phases of this book may be indicated.

The reader anxious to pursue further study in the field of ancient wind-instrument music should refer to the following:

Denkmäler deutsche Tonkunst (Leipzig: Breitkopf & Härtel, 65 vols. 1892-1931)

Denkmäler der deutsche Tonkunst in Oesterreich (Vienna, 82 vols. 1892-1937)

Denkmäler der Tonkunst in Bayern (Leipzig: Breitkopf & Härtel)

Arnold Schering: Geschichte der Musik in Beispielen (Leipzig: Breitkopf & Härtel, 1931)

J. A. Kappey: Short History of Military Music (Boosey & Co., 1894—out of print)

Georges Kastner: Manuel Général de Musique Militaire (Paris, 1848—out of print)

H. G. Farmer: The Rise and Development of Military Music (London: W. Reeves, 1912)

E. Neukomm: Histoire de la Musique Militaire (Paris: L. Baudouin, 1889)

For documentation of works by given composers, especially with regard to publication or preservation of Ms., the following books are indispensable (in addition to the preceding):

R. Eitner: Quellen-Lexikon (Leipzig: Breitkopf & Härtel, 1901-04)

A. M. Hofmeister: Handbuch der Musikalischen Literature (Leipzig: C. F. Whistling)

F. Hofmeister: Verzeichnis (Leipzig: Hofmeister)

W. Altmann: Kammermusik-Literature (Leipzig: C. Merseburger, 1918)

For general reference:

Oxford History of Music (Oxford Univ. Press. 2nd Edition, 1929-34)

Burney's History of Music (New Edition: Harcourt, Brace & Co., 1937)

Grove's Dictionary of Music and Musicians (Macmillan, 3rd Edition, 1935)

Riemann's Musik Lexikon (11th Edition, Berlin: M. Hesse, 1929)

On bands in general:

Edwin Franko Goldman: Band Betterment (Carl Fischer)

On brass bands:

J. F. Russell and J. H. Elliot: The Brass Band Movement (London: J. M. Dent, 1936)

For almost each composer represented in this volume at least one good biography (and in many cases an autobiography) is available and should be consulted for further reference. Most of these have been done into English and are available to the American or British reader.

For documentation of works by given composers especially with regard to publication or preservation of Ms. the following books are indispensable (in addition to the [illegible]):

R. Eitner: Quellen-Lexikon (Leipzig: Breitkopf & Härtel, 1900-04)
A. W. Hofmeister: Handbuch der Musikalischen Literatur (Leipzig: C. F. Whistling)
F. Hofmeister: Verzeichnis (Leipzig: Hofmeister)
W. Altmann: Kammermusik-Literatur (Leipzig: C. Merseburger, 1918)

For general reference:

Oxford History of Music (Oxford Univ. Press, 2nd edition, 1929-34)
Burney's History of Music (New Edition, Harcourt, Brace & Co., 1935)
Grove's Dictionary of Music and Musicians (Macmillan, 3rd Edition, 1935)
Riemann's Musik Lexikon (11th Edition, Berlin: M. Hesse, 1929)

On Bands in general:

Edwin Franko Goldman: Band Betterment (Carl Fischer)

On brass bands:

J. F. Russell and J. H. Elliot: The Brass Band Movement (London: J. M. Dent, 1936)

For almost each composer represented in this volume at least one good biography (and in many cases an outstanding one) is available and should be consulted for further reference. Most of these have been done into English and are available to the American or British reader.

PART TWO
PROGRAM MATERIAL

Adolphe Charles Adam

BORN Paris, July 24, 1803
DIED Paris, May 3, 1856

WORKS ARRANGED FOR BAND:

Overtures: IF I WERE KING (F; B&H; AMP
QUEEN FOR A DAY (F; B&H
LE POSTILLON DE LONGJUMEAU (C
LE TORÉADOR (B&H
GIRALDA (CB; B&H

ADOLPHE CHARLES ADAM ranks with the most successful of his time in the composition of comic opera. He was a pupil of Boieldieu (q. v.), by whose advice he greatly benefited. Encouraged by his early successes, Adam composed somewhat too rapidly to do justice to himself, but he nevertheless maintained his position as a leading composer. In 1847 he attempted to found a national theatre especially to produce the works of young and aspiring comic-opera composers. This enterprise was upset by the Revolution of 1848, and shortly thereafter Adam accepted the Professorship of Composition at the Conservatory, succeeding his father.

Although few of his theatrical works are still performed, the overtures of several hold their places in the band repertory. These overtures, such as *If I Were King* and *Queen for a Day*, are distinguished by the elegance rather than the originality of their style, and by the effective simplicity of their content. His best-rounded work for the stage is probably *Le Postillon de Longjumeau*, which was written in 1836.

Don Isaac Albeniz

BORN Camprodon, Catalonia, May 29, 1860
DIED Cambo les Bains, Pyrenees, June 16, 1909

WORKS ARRANGED FOR BAND:

TANGO IN D (W
MIDSUMMER NIGHT'S SERENADE (S

ALBENIZ, although identified almost exclusively with Spanish "national" music, received most of his training as composer and pianist in other European countries. After his earliest successes as a child prodigy in Barcelona, he pursued his studies under Marmontel and Liszt. His tours as pianist, including one to America, were enormously successful.

The latter part of his life was devoted almost entirely to composition. His operas have not held the stage, but his piano compositions have earned a permanent place in the repertory. His most important piano works, such as the *Iberia Suite,* were written after he had come under the influence of Debussy. Albeniz sought to suggest the character of Spanish regional music rather than to transcribe it literally.

Noteworthy in Albeniz' more ambitious works are the modal cadences, the contrasting rhythms, and the guitar-like character of the harmonies.

Tango in D: The *Tango in D* is probably the best-known composition of Albeniz, although it is far more conventional in every way than many of his other works.

Daniel François Esprit Auber

BORN Caen, France, January 29, 1782
DIED Paris, May 14, 1871

WORKS ARRANGED FOR BAND:

Overtures: MASANIELLO (D; B&H; F
FRA DIAVOLO (B&H; F; AMP
THE BLACK DOMINO (F; CB
THE BRONZE HORSE (B&H; F; CB;
THE CROWN DIAMONDS (B&H; F
ZANETTA (F
and many others (various editions)

Selections from: FRA DIAVOLO (B&H; CB
THE CROWN DIAMONDS (CB
and others (various editions)

AUBER belongs to that distinguished group of nineteenth-century French comic-opera composers which included Boieldieu, Hérold and Adam. In many ways he may be considered the last of the line, summing up in his music the qualities which made his predecessors and contemporaries famous. Spontaneity of melody, grace of line and elegance of style are the greatest merits of his compositions; these are qualities characteristic of the entire French school.

Auber's reputation during his lifetime was very great. Of his more than forty operas, however, few are performed today. He was made Director of the Paris Conservatory by Louis Philippe in 1842, succeeding Cherubini, and became court composer to Napoleon III in 1857.

The overtures of Auber, with the exception of *Masaniello*, are not to be taken as dramatic prologues or illustrations. They were conceived as "curtain-raisers" for comedies. They are slight, but transparent in structure and full of subtle refinements. They owe their appeal to a verve and freshness of feeling, an occasional piquancy of rhythm, and a simplicity of melodic line which derives from the tradition of French folk-song.

✓ ✓ ✓

Overture, Masaniello: Masaniello, the one serious opera composed by Auber, has very little in common with his other works. It is set apart not only by the nature of its subject, but also by the character of the music. The libretto was written by Eugene Scribe (1791-1861), a man whose name is inseparably bound up with the history of nineteenth-century French opera. The story concerns Thomas Aniello (better known as Masaniello), a fisherman who was the leader of a revolt in Naples in 1647, and who was assassinated by his enemies. The opera was produced in Paris on February 29, 1828, only two years before the revolt of 1830, and was evidently not devoid of political significance. It is said to have been almost as widely sung as was the Marseillaise in the French Revolution. In Brussels, where the opera was presented in 1830, riots broke out following the performance; these riots were the first signals for the revolt which freed Belgium from the Netherlands.

The opera is also known as *The Mute of Portici,* due to an odd accident which occurred at the first performance. The singer who was to have taken the part of Fenella, sister of Masaniello, was at the last moment unable to appear, and the role was given to a pantomimist. The effect was so unusual and so successful that it has been perpetuated in all subsequent productions.

The overture to the opera is very dramatic in character. Except for the short andante section which forms part of the introduction, all the themes are from the opera. It is recorded that Wagner was greatly impressed by *Masaniello,* which he heard during his youth. He particularly admired the bold harmony and instrumentation and the original use of the chorus.

Johann Sebastian Bach

BORN Eisenach, Germany, March 21, 1685
DIED Leipzig, Germany, July 28, 1750

WORKS ARRANGED FOR BAND:

FUGUE (*orig. A Minor*) (S
FUGUE IN G MINOR ("The Little") (EV
FUGUE À LA GIGUE (B&H
CHORALE & FUGUE, *G Minor* (Bach-Abert) (S
PRELUDE & FUGUE, *B♭ Minor* (F
TOCCATA & FUGUE, *C Major* (B&H
Choral Preludes:
WE ALL BELIEVE IN ONE GOD (W
SLEEPERS WAKE (F
FERVENT IS MY LONGING (EV
JESU, JOY OF MAN'S DESIRING (F
Choral Melody: COME SWEET DEATH (F
SICILIENNE (F
BOURRÉE (S
BRANDENBURG CONCERTO #1 (*Two Mvts*) (B&H

THERE is no greater name in the history of music than that of Bach. The Bach family, from about 1560 to 1800, presented the world with no less than seven generations of musicians. Its genius reached its highest development in the fourth generation, with the works of Johann Sebastian, the dominant musician of his era, and one of the artistic giants of history.

J. S. Bach's position midway in his family's musical evolution is in a way symbolic of his position in the annals of music. Summarizing much of the old, he was at the same time able to foreshadow subsequent developments to such an extent as to earn the popular designation of "father of music." But let no one forget the predecessors of Bach! The contrapuntal idiom, which was the natural means of expression for Bach, was the result of centuries of growth and development. Bach used this idiom with a variety, a richness and a grandeur equalled by few before him and none after him; he gave it a new plasticity, and by emphasizing an ordered system of tonality, pointed the way to the further development of harmonic music. In all, Bach was a transitional artist; like many such (Giotto, Leonardo, Beethoven, etc.) he represented a pinnacle of artistic achievement.

Bach's music was primarily of the church; in it is found the culmination of the ecclesiastical styles evolved in Germany and the Netherlands. To this style, in which he worked with such wonderful creative fluency and resourcefulness, Bach brought his own intellectual force and emotional depth. His exploitation of the forms of the fugue, the choral prelude and the cantata was so complete that his successors (his sons, for example) were literally forced into another style of composition, a style which J. S. Bach had touched upon but had not explored.

Bach's music remained in comparative obscurity for many years after his death. A difference in the external conditions of music, a changing world and a changing audience, made simpler music more greatly relished. Occasional musicians "re-discovered" Bach (Mendelssohn and Franz, for example); but even until recently it was considered a sort of intellectual snobbery to prefer Bach to the composers of the tuneful eighteenth century or the soulful nineteenth. The major part of Bach's work was popularly supposed (as is the work of such as Josquin today) to be historically interesting, ingenious, but dry. With the beginnings of the healthy reaction against the extreme phases of romanticism, the music of Bach is once again taken for what it is: pure, lofty, logical and magnificent design in sound, owing nothing to any art but music, and capable of stirring its hearers as no music written since.

Fugue (A Minor): The *A Minor Fugue* is one of the most celebrated of Bach's compositions in that form. Originally written for organ, it has been transcribed many times; Liszt's pianoforte arrangement is particularly well known. In the band version, the key has been altered from A minor to C minor, and the prelude, which forms a part of the original work, has been omitted. No words can convey any impression of the work; if it is said that it is one of Bach's grandest, then enough has been said. The vigor of the subject, the variety of the episodes and the power of the climax make the fugue an incomparable musical experience for any listener.

Fugue in G Minor ("The Little Fugue"): Bach's two fugues in G minor, written for organ, are usually referred to, for purposes of identification, as the "Great Fugue" and the "Little Fugue."

Fugue à la Gigue: This fugue, taken from a work of Bach written for the harpsichord, was arranged for band by Gustav Holst, the famous English composer (1874-1934). There is no evidence to show that Bach ever called the work by this title, but the rhythm of the composition supports the title's aptness. The fugue is written in 6/8 time, and proceeds at the lively tempo characteristic of the Gigue. It thus provides an example of the manner in which Bach exploited the infinite possibilities of variation within the set form of the fugue.

Chorale and Fugue in G Minor (Bach-Abert): This chorale and fugue is taken from a combination of works by Bach arranged for orchestra by Johann Joseph Abert (1832-1915), and known as the *Prelude, Chorale and Fugue.* Abert was a well-known German composer and conductor. The prelude used in this work is the fourth of Bach's *Well-Tempered*

Clavichord, while the fugue is no other than the "Great Fugue" in G minor, originally composed for the organ. Between these two, Abert placed a chorale of his own composition. This chorale, played by the brass alone, is later worked into the fugue.

Prelude and Fugue in B♭ Minor: The *Prelude and Fugue in B♭ Minor* forms one of the most celebrated portions of *The Well-Tempered Clavichord.* The measured gravity, intensity of expression and richness of texture which characterize both of these inseparable pieces, set them on the level of the great preludes and fugues for organ, and leave no doubt that here are no mere student pieces or occasional compositions, but creations of a great master.

Toccata and Fugue, C Major: The toccata was a form frequently used during the sixteenth and seventeenth centuries, and, like so many others, broadened and deepened by Bach. There are few definable characteristics of the form; originally the name signified that the composition was intended to show off the "touch" of a performer on a keyed instrument; the music was thus of a running and rapid pattern, and often assumed the character of improvisation. This *Toccata and Fugue* of Bach was written originally for the organ.

Choral Prelude: We All Believe In One God: This chorale prelude is also known as "The Giant Fugue," deriving the name from the unusual passages in the bass which include skips of such large intervals as to suggest the strides of a giant. The choral prelude is based on a hymn by Martin Luther, set to a melody from the Plainsong of the Credo (1524). As was Bach's custom in his choral preludes, the original simple melody was used as the basis of a free and sometimes elaborate composition, using the contrapuntal devices which were the very essence of his music.

Choral Prelude: Fervent Is My Longing: The original melody on which Bach based this moving composition was a secular tune by Hans Leo Hassler (1564-1612), one of the most renowned German composers of his day. Bach's genius transformed this simple tune into a composition of great eloquence and pathos.

Choral Prelude: Sleepers Wake: Of Bach's two hundred and ninety-seven church cantatas (one hundred and ninety survive), none is more justly popular than *Sleepers Wake,* the one hundred and fortieth of the series. It is founded on a hymn by Philipp Nicolai (1556-1608) published at Frankfort in 1599, and bearing the full title, *Wachet Auf, Ruft Uns Die Stimme.* The present choral prelude is Bach's setting of the second verse of this hymn. Bach wrote this cantata for the Sunday next before Advent, either in 1731 or 1742. The original score calls for soprano, tenor and bass soli, chorus and orchestra, the latter consisting of strings, two oboes, alto oboe, bassoon, horn and organ.

Choral Prelude; Jesu, Joy of Man's Desiring: Bach's one hundred and forty-seventh church cantata bears the title, *Be Thou Cheerful, O My Spirit.** The cantata is divided, as are all of Bach's like works, into several sections, in the style of a short oratorio. The chorale, *Jesu, Joy of Man's Desiring,** which occurs at the close, is based on a melody of Johann Schop (ca. 1590-1664), and is one of the best known

* The Chorales "Werde Munter, Mein Gemüte" and "Jesu, Meiner Seelen Wonne" are based on the identical melody. *Vide* Nos. 233 and 365 of Bach's four-part chorales (Peters Ed.).

of Bach's settings. It is especially popular in numerous piano transcriptions.

Choral Melody: Come Sweet Death: This grave and moving melody is taken from a set of *Geistliche Lieder* (*Sacred Songs*) composed by Bach in 1736. It is not, as sometimes said, an excerpt from a choral prelude or cantata. In its simplicity and eloquence, this melody is an admirable counterpart of Handel's celebrated *Largo*.

Sicilienne (*Siciliano*): The Sicilienne is a dance-form, allied to the Pastorale and the Canzonetta; the rhythm is 6/8 or 12/8 and the tempo is moderate; the mode is usually minor. As the name implies, the form derives from Sicily. Siciliennes are frequently found in suites of the eighteenth century, both as instrumental and vocal numbers. The present *Sicilienne* is taken from Bach's second sonata for harpsichord and flute.

Bourrée: This well-known composition is taken from a sonata for violin (unaccompanied) by Bach. An arrangement of the work by Saint-Saëns, for pianoforte, first gave it extreme popularity. It is from this arrangement that most subsequent adaptations have been made. The Bourrée is a dance of ancient origin, found in one form or another in many countries of Europe. It is strongly marked, in 2/4 or alla breve rhythm, and is usually in regular two part form. It occurs in many eighteenth-century suites. Tradition has it that the Bourrée was first introduced to Paris at the end of the sixteenth century, and that Lully was the first to transform it from a folk dance into a form suitable for concert suites.

Michael William Balfe

BORN Dublin, May 15, 1808
DIED Dublin, October 20, 1870

WORKS ARRANGED FOR BAND:

Overtures: THE BOHEMIAN GIRL (F; D
THE SIEGE OF ROCHELLE (F; D
THE WELL OF LOVE (F; B&H
THE CASTLE OF AYMON (Brg

Selections: THE BOHEMIAN GIRL (F; B&H; D; CB; Ba; Fil
THE CASTLE OF AYMON (B&H
THE PURITAN'S DAUGHTER (B&H

BALFE's life was that of a traveling virtuoso who went from triumph to triumph. In this he closely resembled his compatriot and contemporary, Wallace (q. v.). Although Balfe commenced his career as a violinist, he soon became attracted to the theatre where he made a considerable reputation as an opera singer. At the same time he began to compose for the Italian stage, and produced a number of successful ballets and operas.

His first English opera was *The Siege of Rochelle*, performed at the Drury Lane Theatre in 1835 with brilliant success. Not content, however, Balfe went to Paris, where he composed two of his best known works: *The Well of Love* and *The Castle of Aymon*. These were produced at the Opéra Comique in 1843 and 1844, respectively. He returned to England in 1843, bringing with him *The Bohemian Girl*, the most successful and the most enduring of his works. It was acclaimed enthusiastically and during Balfe's lifetime was translated into several languages and sung throughout Europe. It still holds a place in the repertories of many opera companies. Many of the airs are familiar today, especially *Then You'll Remember Me* and *A Heart Bowed Down*.

Antonio Bazzini

BORN Brescia, Italy, March 11, 1818
DIED Milan, Italy, February 10, 1897

ARRANGED FOR BAND:

Overture, SAUL (F; B&H

BAZZINI was one of the great violin virtuosi of the last century. He gave concerts throughout Europe from 1836 to 1864, when he returned to his native city in order to devote himself to composition. In 1882 he became Director of the Milan Conservatory.

He wrote many symphonic works and several string quartets, but oddly enough for an Italian composer, only one opera, which was unsuccessful. His studies of Bach and Beethoven helped him to achieve a solidity of structure and a richness of harmony in his works, while his native gift for melody remained unspoiled. He is best remembered outside of Italy for the overture he composed for *Saul,* a drama by Vittorio Alfieri (1749-1803), one of the greatest of Italy's tragic poets.

Ludwig Van Beethoven

BORN Bonn, Germany, December 16, 1770
DIED Vienna, March 26, 1827

WORKS ARRANGED FOR BAND:

Overtures: FIDELIO (B&H; C
LEONORE NO. 3 (F; C
EGMONT (F; B&H; D
CORIOLANUS (F; B&H
KING STEPHAN (B&H

SYMPHONY NO. 1 IN C, complete (B&H
SYMPHONY NO. 5 IN C MINOR (complete) (C
Andante from SYMPHONY NO. 1 (CB
Larghetto from SYMPHONY NO. 2 (F; D
Andante from SYMPHONY NO. 5 (F
Allegretto from SYMPHONY NO. 8 (F
"MOONLIGHT" SONATA, complete (B&H
"MOONLIGHT" SONATA, *First Movement* (F
SONATA IN A♭, OPUS 26: *Funeral March* (F
ECOSSAISES (F
GERMAN DANCES (F
Turkish March from THE RUINS OF ATHENS (B&H; F; J
Selections from FIDELIO (F; B&H
"THE PRAISE OF GOD IN NATURE" (F; Ba;
MENUET IN G (F; J

ORIGINAL WORKS FOR BAND:

MARCH IN D (AMP
TWO MARCHES IN F (AMP
POLONAISE IN D (AMP
MARCH IN C (AMP
ECOSSAISE IN D (AMP

THE FIGURE OF BEETHOVEN dominates the music of his period as perhaps that of no other musician in any age has ever done. Even Bach in his time is not an exception. Beethoven was more than a great composer: he was a historical necessity. It was logical that following Mozart the classic sonata be broadened and expanded, for Mozart had brought it to formal perfection, and it was inevitable that music begin to reflect the new attitude toward art that was expressed in Goethe, Chateaubriand, Coleridge and others at the turn of the century. It was Beethoven's greatness to fulfill more than adequately the mission that was obviously his. In general terms the conventional summary of Beethoven's work is just: he summed up the classic school and announced the beginning of the romantic period.

It is customary to divide Beethoven's creative life into three periods. The works of his first period, until approximately 1803, include those in which he more or less followed the models of Haydn and Mozart. These include the first two symphonies, and most of the compositions up to Opus 18. The second period, commonly dated from about 1803 to about 1813, is that in which Beethoven began to express in his music something purely personal and subjective, something on a scale at once grander and warmer than anything in music before his time. In this period are classified the greater number of the often-played and most familiar works: the Symphonies from No. 3 to No. 8, *Fidelio,* the overtures to *Egmont, Coriolanus* and *Prometheus,* the Violin Concerto, the Piano Sonatas from Opus 13 to Opus 90, many quartets and other compositions. Here, for the first time since Bach (but on a different basis from that of Bach), we have music whose aim is to elevate the soul as well as to fascinate the ear, to be at one time the expression of emotion and the means of creating emotion. This concentration on expressiveness is carried still further in Beethoven's third period. This later music is marked by a greater withdrawal of the composer into himself, a more intense exploration and exploitation of the elements of "pathos" in music. But in Beethoven's case (and this is not invariably true of his successors in the romantic period) the expression was always strictly delimited within formal patterns; despair or joy never became in his work a formless or onomatopoetic mass of sound.

Beethoven was far from unrecognized or unsuccessful in his lifetime. His musical education began in his fourth year, and indications of his gifts were soon evident. Interest in the progress of his career was shown by musicians and patrons alike, and it was through the influence of the latter that Beethoven settled in Vienna in 1792. He continued his studies with Haydn and Albrechtsberger, composed steadily and acquired a huge reputation as a pianist and extemporizer. His deafness, which began soon after 1800, caused him to withdraw from society to a certain extent, but he continued to give concerts and to enjoy the acclaim which greeted most of his works. Toward the latter part of his life, as his suffering increased, he became less and less agreeable in company, more nervous and depressed, and at times even imagined that he was in financial want. Such was not the case, however. The esteem in which he was held by musicians and public alike was comparable to that enjoyed by Haydn. Beethoven's funeral was attended by more than twenty thousand people, gathered to pay homage to a composer whom they recognized as the greatest of their time.

Overtures, Fidelio and Leonore No. 3: Beethoven wrote four overtures in all for his single opera, *Fidelio,* which when originally produced in Vienna in 1805, was known as *Leonore.* At the first performance the overture used was that now known as *Leonore No. 2.* Shortly afterwards Beethoven composed a new overture for a revised production; this was the *Leonore No. 3.* In 1806 the opera was still further revised and was scheduled for production under its present title. Beethoven composed still another overture for this production, which, however, did not take place. The third overture is now known as *Leonore No. 1.* Finally, in 1814, the opera was produced in approximately its present form, with the overture known as *Fidelio*. All of these overtures bear the opus number 72, with the exception of *Leonore No. 1,* which is listed as Opus 138.

The *Leonore No. 3* is the most famous and the most magnificent of the four. It is a model of musical structure and dramatic power. The introduction is elaborate, opening with scale passages in the full band and continuing with Florestan's air from the opera itself. The principal section of the overture follows closely the dramatic outline of the opera, but achieves a fusion of musical and dramatic quality such as few composers besides Beethoven have been able to effect. Notable in the overture are the trumpet calls which occur during the development and which foreshadow the triumphant character of the concluding section.

The *Fidelio* overture was the last of those composed by Beethoven for his opera, and dates from 1814. It is quite different in structure from the other overtures and makes use of different thematic material. The introduction is extremely elaborate, opening *allegro,* shifting to *adagio,* returning to the *allegro* and then back to the *adagio*. Four themes are introduced in this section, the first theme of the *allegro* being suggestive of the principal theme of the overture itself. The main section opens and continues *allegro,* following the usual pattern, but concluding with a reminiscence of the *adagio* of the introduction followed by an energetic coda, *presto*. The first performance of the *Fidelio* overture took place in Vienna on May 23, 1814.

Overture, Egmont: Early in 1810 Beethoven was occupied with the composition of incidental music for Goethe's *Egmont,* a historical drama based on the Spanish occupation of the Netherlands in the sixteenth century. The play, with an overture and nine other numbers by Beethoven, was privately produced in Vienna on May 24, 1810. The music ranks with Beethoven's best in its dramatic force and direct expressiveness. The overture opens with the usual introduction, based principally on a heavy and sombre theme sounded in full chords with a marked rhythm. This theme is closely related to the second theme of the overture proper. The *allegro,* or principal section, opens with a sweeping theme, followed by the theme derived from the introduction. Both are elaborately developed. The concluding section of the overture introduces new material and is marked by triumphant fanfares in the brasses. The overture has been interpreted by some as a condensed version of the drama itself, with the sombre opening reflecting the oppression of the Dutch people and the conclusion indicating their ultimate triumph under the inspiration of the heroic Egmont.

Overture, Coriolanus: Beethoven's overture *Coriolanus* was composed not for Shakespeare's tragedy, but for a play on the same subject by one Heinrich von Collin. It was first performed in Vienna in December, 1807. The overture is somewhat unusual in that it opens without any introductory section. The first theme is heroic in character and is succeeded by a lyric second theme. These are briefly worked up before the appearance of the third theme, a fugato subject. The customary development section is telescoped, and the overture proceeds to a recapitulation of the three chief themes with little variation. The coda is unusually expressive and is generally taken to represent the death of Coriolanus. The overture concludes *pianissimo,* on a note of tragedy.

Overture, King Stephan: For the opening of the New Theatre in Pesth (Buda-Pesth) in 1812, the poet Kotzebue was commissioned to write a trilogy on Hungarian subjects, and Beethoven was commissioned to compose the incidental music.

The music for *The Ruins of Athens* and that for *King Stephan* were the results of this commission. The music for *King Stephan* consisted of an overture and nine other numbers, of which only the overture is frequently played today. It is a work in heroic style, befitting the nature of the subject, Hungary's great national hero and benefactor. The overture opens with trumpet calls, succeeded by a march-like theme which is interrupted by the trumpet calls again and then proceeds. The principal section begins with a noble theme which is developed and which then gives way to a theme reminiscent of that of the choral finale of the Ninth Symphony. The middle section of the overture is built on these two themes, brilliantly worked out. The overture ends with a dashing coda.

Symphony No. 5, in C minor:

I. Allegro con brio
II. Andante con moto
III. Allegro (Scherzo)
IV. Allegro, Presto

The Fifth Symphony is probably the best-known of Beethoven's nine, and is generally considered to be the most comprehensive single expression of his genius. It was completed almost at the same time as the Sixth, and first performed in Vienna on December 22, 1808.

Almost every critic, and many musicians, have written about the Fifth Symphony in more or less rhapsodical terms, many of them reducing the music to nothing more than an illustration of some pseudo-poetic idea and apparently feeling that the symphony is the better for it. The most familiar story is of course that concerning Beethoven's characterization of the opening theme in the words, "So Fate knocks at the door." From that admirably succinct statement the interpretations spread like sermons on a Biblical text.

The opening movement is dominated by the "Fate" motive, a rhythmic rather than a melodic figure which recurs almost incessantly. The second theme, in E♭ major, is gentle and smooth, offering a strong contrast. In form the movement is fairly conventional, differing from pre-Beethoven types more by elaboration than by structural innovation. The movement is marked by the constant interchange of thematic material between the choirs of the ensemble; it ends on an agitated passage derived from the second theme.

The *Andante* opens with a graceful and placid melody of exquisite contour. This alternates with a bolder and more stirring theme which asserts itself powerfully. An echo of the "Fate" theme of the first movement is heard towards the end of the movement.

The *Scherzo* opens softly but soon leads into a section based on the rhythmic pattern of the "Fate" motive, now in a distinct melodic form. The trio continues with the same vigor. The *Scherzo* leads without a break into the *Finale* by means of a "bridge" section in which the tympani continue to emphasize the dominant rhythmic figure. The *Finale* proper opens with a swinging, joyous theme of irresistible sweep. The movement becomes more and more animated, until it is interrupted by a passage reminiscent of the *Scherzo*. After this episode the movement continues to gather speed and energy until the rousing *presto* climax.

Symphony No. 1, in C Major: The first performance of Beethoven's First Symphony took place in Vienna on April 2, 1800. Beethoven had worked at it for some years previous, but with that painstaking method characteristic of him had not hurried its completion. In general style the First Symphony is not a far cry from its Mozartean models, although isolated passages contain suggestions of the later Beethoven.

In its simplicity and melodic purity it stands almost alone among Beethoven's larger works.

The second movement is marked *Andante cantabile con moto.* It opens with a simple and graceful theme in F major, which is answered canonically. The use of the tympani and the dynamic contrast in the movement foreshadow the effects Beethoven was later to attain with these means.

Symphony No. 2, in D Major: The distance, musically, between the Second and Third Symphonies of Beethoven is immense. The Second contains almost none of the drama and pathos which mark the work composed only a year or so later. It is nearer to the First Symphony in its straightforward character, its delicacy and its grace. The work was completed in 1802 and received its first performance in Vienna on April 5, 1803.

The *Larghetto,* which is the only movement published for band, is one of the most familiar symphonic excerpts in the concert repertory. There is little to single out for analysis or description in the movement, which is an almost unbroken *cantilena* from start to finish.

Symphony No. 8, in F Major: The Eighth Symphony is one of the gayest and most appealing works Beethoven ever penned. It was written at Linz in 1812, the same year which saw the composition of the magnificent Seventh. Beethoven himself spoke of the Eighth as "the little symphony in F" the "little" being, presumably, more of an expression of endearment than a measure of size.

Only the *Allegretto* (second movement) has been arranged for band. This movement takes the place of the usual *adagio* or *andante,* and is a measure of the general brightness of the whole symphony.

The principal theme is staccato and light; except for a

brief interlude of a more flowing nature it continues throughout the movement. Much of the effect of the music is dependent on the instrumentation, which, in Beethoven's orchestral score, is of immense ingenuity and charm.

First Movement from the *"Moonlight" Sonata* (*Opus 27, No. 2*): The title of "Moonlight Sonata," which has become attached to Beethoven's fourteenth piano sonata, is due more to the romanticism of Beethoven's critics than to that of the composer himself, for he left no indication either explicit or implied that any such title was in order. The sonata no doubt has romantic associations, suggested by its dedication to the Countess Giulietta Guicciardi, a lady whose relations with the composer have been the subject of considerable idle speculation, but the music itself is a *tabula rasa* for anyone's interpretation. Beethoven entitled the work *Sonata quasi una Fantasia,* and it was so published in 1802. The first movement, which is played almost to the exclusion of the others, is too well known to require description; its most notable features are the placidity of the melodies and the tranquil regularity of the accompaniment in triple figure. The originality of the movement from the formal standpoint consists largely in the fact that it replaces the *Allegro* generally found as first movement of a sonata. The original key of the *"Moonlight" Sonata* is C# minor.

Funeral March from *Pianoforte Sonata in A♭, Opus 26:* The movement which replaces the usual *adagio* in Beethoven's twelfth sonata for the pianoforte has as its full title *Marcia Funebre sulla Morte d'un Eroe* (*Funeral March for a Hero's Death*). Grove relates that its composition was inspired by a similar march in an opera of Ferdinand Paër; Beethoven, if the story is not apocryphal, desired merely to show that he could write a better one. The march is solemn and dignified, well suited to its given subject, and an excellent example of the richness of Beethoven's harmonies. The sonata was composed in 1801, and published in the following year with a dedication to Prince Carl Lichnowsky, patron of the composer.

Ecossaises: Early in the last century a considerable vogue for Scotch and Irish music seems to have swept the European continent. *Ecossaises* (*Scotch Pieces*) and Irish songs were produced in great numbers by German, Polish, French and Viennese composers. Beethoven *Ecossaises* for piano are probably the best known of these, although Chopin's and Schubert's are occasionally heard. The *Ecossaise* is not very precisely defined as a musical form; it is derived from a Scotch dance-form generally in 2/4 time with marked rhythm. Beethoven's effort in this form is a delightful bagatelle frequently heard on concert programs.

German Dances: (*Contredanses*): Beethoven wrote a number of German Dances and Contredanses for orchestra as well as several for pianoforte. Many of these are in the form of the *Ländler,* a folk dance popular in some sections of Austria and Bohemia. The *Ländler* is best described as a slow and rustic waltz; it generally consists of two sections of eight bars each, with repeats.

Turkish March from *The Ruins of Athens:* Beethoven composed the incidental music to two plays of Kotzebue for the opening of the New Theatre in Pesth in 1811. *The Ruins of Athens* was the second of these. Beethoven wrote an overture and eight further numbers for the occasion. Of these, the *Turkish March* is the best known and most frequently heard.

Selections from *Fidelio: Fidelio,* Beethoven's only opera, was first produced in 1809. It was revised several times, but it was not produced in its final form until 1814. While certainly not ranking with the most popular or the most excellent operas in the world, it is still occasionally performed. The action of the opera takes places near Seville and concerns the unjust imprisonment of a Spanish nobleman and his salvation through the devotion and cleverness of his wife. The *Prisoner's Song* and the *Aria of Florestan* (heard in the *Leonore* overtures) are perhaps the most famous numbers in the score.

The Worship of God in Nature: This well-known and frequently arranged composition of Beethoven was originally written as a song for soprano voice, one of a set of six to words of Gellert, published as Opus 48. It is probably the most universally popular of Beethoven's vocal compositions.

Vincenzo Bellini

BORN Catania, Sicily, November 1, 1801
DIED Puteaux, France, September 24, 1835

WORKS ARRANGED FOR BAND:

Overtures: NORMA (F
I PURITANI (B&H
Selections: NORMA (F
I PURITANI (D
LA SONNAMBULA (F

BELLINI was the son of an organist and received his first musical training at home. His instruction, however, both there and at the Naples Conservatory, was neither thorough nor regular, and he profited most by his private study of the works of Haydn, Mozart, and his great idol, Pergolesi. His first opera was performed in 1825; its success was great and encouraged the composer to devote his musical abilities to the stage. He wrote rapidly, and achieved a tremendous reputation which reached its peak with the production in 1831 of both *Norma* and *La Sonnambula.*

After the emergence of Meyerbeer and later of Wagner, the operas of Bellini were all but forgotten. Their prettiness and ingenuousness could not hold the stage against the dramatic thunder and musical elaborateness of the new style. Yet Bellini is nevertheless remembered today, and his operas have been occasionally revived. The grace and fluidity of Bellini's melodies, and above all their idiomatic vocal qualities, have made them great favorites with singers. None of the composer's works possesses great dramatic feeling, but all have a pleasant lyricism.

❧ ❧ ❧

Norma: The opera *Norma* is based on a French melodrama dealing with the Druids in the time of the Roman conquest. The libretto is neither accurate historically nor convincing dramatically, but the score is full of brilliant melodies of a type calculated to exhibit a singer's virtuosity to the utmost. Particularly famous are the arias *Casta Diva* (*Chaste Goddess*) and *Mira, O Norma* (*Hear Me, Norma*), familiar to all music-lovers.

Norma was first produced in Milan on December 26, 1831; the first American performance took place in New York ten years later.

La Sonnambula (*The Sleep-Walker*): *La Sonnambula* was produced at Milan on March 6, 1831, not quite ten months before *Norma.* The year was thus a great one indeed for Bellini, since both operas were triumphant successes. They differ greatly in character, *Norma* being based on melodrama and *La Sonnambula* on an idyllic ballet, the work of the famous Scribe.

The plot of *La Sonnambula* concerns the misadventures of Amina, the heroine, who walks in her sleep and strays into the room of a Count. This gentleman, fortunately, is gallant enough to leave the chamber, but misunderstandings naturally arise. They are straightened out, and the curtain falls on a scene of happiness. The music throughout is of a graceful and gentle character, and has much charm. The role of Amina was a favorite of both Malibran and Patti.

I Puritani (*The Puritans*): *I Puritani* was Bellini's last great success. It was commissioned in 1834 by the Italian Theatre in Paris, and produced there on January 25, 1835. The first American performance took place in New York in 1844. The story concerns the struggles between the "Royalists and the Puritans" in the reign of Charles I. The heroine, daughter of a lord, loves a Puritan; parted from him by the war, she becomes demented, but all ends well with the reunion of the lovers and the restoration of reason. The music is by turns brilliant and tender, very representative of Bellini's graceful style and virtuoso treatment of the voice. The most famous air is that sung by the heroine during her madness.

Arthur Bergh

BORN St. Paul, Minnesota, 1882

ARRANGED FOR BAND:

Festival March: HONOR AND GLORY (Rem

HONOR AND GLORY is a fine example of the festival march in broad and impressive style. A spirited first section is followed by a bold and flowing melody in which, as the composer suggests, traces of his Norwegian ancestry will be found. The march was originally written for pianoforte and later arranged for band.

The composer is known for the melodramas, *The Raven* and *The Pied Piper of Hamelin,* which he wrote for David Bispham. He has written numerous works for piano, violin and male chorus, as well as many songs. He was formerly a violinist with the New York Symphony and the Metropolitan Opera House, and was for many years in charge of all recording activities of the Columbia Phonograph Company.

Hector Louis Berlioz

BORN near Grenoble, France, December 11, 1803
DIED Paris, March 8, 1869

WORKS ARRANGED FOR BAND:

Overtures: BENVENUTO CELLINI (S; B&H
ROMAN CARNIVAL (F
BEATRICE AND BENEDICT (F
JUDGES OF THE SECRET COURT (B&H
Excerpts from FANTASTIC SYMPHONY (B&H
March to the Scaffold from THE FANTASTIC SYMPHONY (F
RAKOCZY MARCH (F
DANCE OF THE SYLPHS (F
TROJAN MARCH (F
Selections from THE DAMNATION OF FAUST (B&H

IT IS possible to say that never in the history of music has there been a composer more violently original than Berlioz. Beginning his career at the time that "romanticism" was a new gospel in art, Berlioz threw himself whole-heartedly into the new movement, and carried it to the point of extremity. The romantic school believed in "self-expression" and in effecting a fusion of literature and music. Berlioz followed both precepts on the grand scale. His baroque imagination and his literary bias colored every score he composed. Program music has known no more ardent defender or more robust practitioner.

His technical skill, especially in orchestration, was immense. He was capable of writing pure and beautiful melody, yet he often sacrificed continuity and form for effect. His extravagant romanticism, depending more on theatricality than on structural solidity, was the complete antithesis of the classical tradition.

Berlioz, we are told, was an impatient student, determined to follow his own ideas. He won the Prix de Rome in 1830 only after considerable opposition from Cherubini and others, who had evidently been more startled than pleased by the young composer's early efforts. Berlioz was a storm center throughout his lifetime. The polemics written about his works would, if collected, fill volumes; many of the most readable of these were written by the composer himself, who was no less distinguished as a critic and pamphleteer than as a musician. His tours through Europe were in general more successful than his appearances in his own country; he was never able to realize his desire to become a professor at the Paris Conservatory, although near the end of his life he was made a member of the Academy and received the Legion of Honor.

His treatise on Instrumentation was long the definitive work on the subject. He wrote, in addition to that, numbers of essays, the libretti to two of his operas, and a fascinating volume of Memoirs.

✓ ✓ ✓

Overture, Benvenuto Cellini: The opera *Benvenuto Cellini* was composed in the years 1835-1837. It was Berlioz' first attempt at writing for the stage, and although the overture was warmly applauded, the opera itself was greeted with derision. The disciples of the new "romantic" school, however, especially those gathered around Liszt at Weimar, were enthusiastic about the work. The libretto was based on episodes from the Italian sculptor's autobiography, but made use of much fictitious material as well.

The overture was the last part of the opera that Berlioz composed. Almost all of the material in it is taken from the opera itself. There is a long introduction, with several changes of tempo, before the principal section begins. This latter, marked *Allegro deciso con impeto,* is in fairly strict form, and contains many passages of great dramatic power.

✓

Overture, Beatrice and Benedict: Beatrice and Benedict, a comic opera in two acts, was brought out at Baden-Baden in 1862 and was very well received. The libretto, written by the composer, is founded on Shakespeare's *Much Ado About Nothing.* The opera is hardly ever played today, but the overture, which is a delightful and sparkling composition, remains a favorite.

Berlioz writes thus about the opera in his memoirs: "To return to the opera of *Beatrice.* I had taken the book from *Much Ado About Nothing,* and added the songs and episodes of the musician. . . . Critics, come expressly from Paris, praised the music warmly, especially the songs and the duet. Some thought there was a great deal of rubbish in the rest of the score and that the spoken dialogue was stupid. It is copied almost word for word from Shakespeare.

"The work is difficult of performance, especially the men's parts, but I think it is one of the most spirited and original I ever wrote."

Overture, Judges of the Secret Court (Les Francs Juges): This remarkable overture was written in 1828, in the composer's twenty-fifth year. Berlioz had written the greater part of an opera dealing with the Vehmic Judges, and the overture was to form part of it. The opera, however, was never performed; Berlioz used much of the music in other works and published the overture separately. The composition depicts the terror and indignation aroused by the proceedings of the Holy Vehme, a secret tribunal which flourished in Germany in the fifteenth century. This extra-legal body, the counterparts of which are unfortunately not unknown today, met in secret and meted out sentences of death to its victims, carrying them out without mercy.

The overture is ominous and sombre in character, picturing in music both the dread power of the Court and the rage and despair of the victim. The middle section contains a remarkable chorale for wind instruments (in the original version); the climax develops out of a fugal episode of great power.

Overture, The Roman Carnival: This brilliant overture was first performed in Paris on February 3, 1844, under the direction of the composer. The thematic material of the work is drawn from Berlioz' opera *Benvenuto Cellini,* which had been unsuccessfully presented in 1838; the overture itself had been intended as an introduction to the second act of that opera. The principal theme is a Saltarello (a very fast Italian dance) which appears in the opera's first act. This alternates with an andante melody derived from an aria sung by Cellini. The prevailing spirit of the overture is that of the Saltarello, with its gay suggestion of Carnival scenes and merriment.

Fantastic Symphony: The *Fantastic Symphony,* subtitled *Episodes in the Life of an Artist,* is one of the major works of Berlioz, and the one which perhaps most completely illustrates the rare quality of his imagination. It was written in 1828-29. Each movement of this strange composition has its own legend, given in great detail. The work as a whole is intended to depict the reflection of a love-affair in the mind of a young artist who can only be described as over-sensitive. A recurrent theme, described by Berlioz as the *idée fixe* (fixed, or set, idea), represents the artist's beloved or his idea of love.

The *idée fixe* dominates the first movement, which sets out to illustrate the quality of the young artist's spiritual troubles. In the second movement, the scenes of a gala ball are depicted in an ingenious waltz through which the strains of the principal theme are heard. The third movement shows the unhappy youth in the fields, where amidst pastoral scenes and sounds, he cannot forget his beloved. A storm, inevitably rising, adds further to his despondency, and the movement ends gloomily.

In the fourth movement the composer portrays the further misery to which the young artist's extravagant passion leads him. Certain that his love is not returned, the hero takes poison which, alas, does not end his suffering but merely casts him into a stupor. He dreams that he has murdered his beloved and is awaiting execution. The march to the scaffold begins; bells chime, drums roll, the *Dies Irae* is heard. Above it all, the theme of the beloved continues to sound, until the fatal stroke of the executioner's axe.

The fifth movement continues where the fourth leaves off. Witches and devils gather around for the artist's interment. A frenzied orgy takes the place of the funeral he has forfeited by his crime.

Trojan March (*Marche Troyenne*): This stirring march is taken from Berlioz' grand opera, *The Trojans,* his last great work. It was intended to be his masterpiece, and its failure was a bitter blow to the composer. The opera was written in two parts: *The Capture of Troy* and *The Trojans at Carthage.* The second part was performed in Paris during the lifetime of Berlioz, in 1863, but the first complete performance did not take place until 1897, when it was produced at Karlsruhe under Felix Mottl. Berlioz wrote his own libretto for the gigantic work, which although unequal in quality, contains some of the most magnificent music he ever wrote.

The Damnation of Faust (*Selections*): *The Damnation of Faust,* "a dramatic legend," was completed in 1846 and had its first performance the same year. It is in many ways the most complete expression of Berlioz' remarkable genius. It is divided into four tableaux, embracing eighteen scenes, during the course of which Faust undertakes many wanderings and undergoes many experiences, both physical and spiritual, which were unknown to Goethe. There is a great deal of extraordinary music in the score, much of it among the best Berlioz composed. It is interesting to compare the treatment of the Faust legend by Berlioz with that by Gounod. Berlioz' version is much more supernatural and unrestrained, exuberant in energy and original in conception.

The Rakoczy March: This march occurs in the elaborate opera *The Damnation of Faust* which Berlioz composed in 1845-46. The *Rakoczy March* is the national air of Hungary, and takes its name from that of Prince Franz Rakoczy, one of whose court musicians, named Michael Barna, composed the tune. Berlioz, showman that he was, decided to interpolate the march in his opera on the occasion of its performance in Budapest. To do this, he had to make Faust visit Hungary, but this was no great feat for anyone with the composer's ingenuity. The success of this gesture was, according to Berlioz' Memoirs, overwhelming.

Dance of the Sylphs: This sprightly number occurs in the second tableau of *The Damnation of Faust,* that amazing work into which Berlioz poured so much energy. Faust has been conducted by Mephistopheles to a beautiful meadow, where he falls into deep sleep. His vision of a chorus of sylphs is presented as a ballet on the stage. Like so many of Berlioz' other works, this dance is brilliant and original and full of novel orchestral effects.

(Sir) Henry R. Bishop

BORN London, November 18, 1786
DIED London, April 30, 1855

ARRANGED FOR BAND:
Overture, GUY MANNERING (F

BISHOP was a prolific composer whose success in the realm of ballad-opera was marked. He composed over eighty works for the stage in addition to a number of oratorios and cantatas. He was knighted in 1842 and received the degree of Doctor of Music from Oxford in 1853.

Guy Mannering, founded on the novel of Sir Walter Scott, was one of the six operas he composed during the year 1816. A number of traditional Scottish melodies are used in the music.

Georges Bizet
(Alexandre César Léopold Bizet)

BORN Paris, October 25, 1838
DIED Bougival, France, June 3, 1875

WORKS ARRANGED FOR BAND:

Suites: L'ARLÉSIENNE #1 (F; B&H
L'ARLÉSIENNE #2 (F; B&H
Prelude from L'ARLÉSIENNE #1 (Ru
CHILDREN'S GAMES (B&H
Selections from: CARMEN (F; D; C; Fil
THE PEARL-FISHERS (F
Overture, PATRIE (F
SÉRÉNADE ESPAGNOLE (F

BIZET is now properly recognized as one of the greatest geniuses of nineteenth-century French music: a composer of genuine originality and distinction whose works are of considerably greater significance than those of his more successful contemporaries. Bizet's reputation in his own day was not great; not until three years before his death did he attain anything like success. Yet his career started brilliantly. He studied at the Paris Conservatory under Halévy (whose daughter he married), and in 1857, at the age of nineteen, won a prize offered by Offenbach for a comic opera. In the same year he won the Prix de Rome. He composed two comic operas while in Rome, as well as a concert overture and two movements of a symphony. Returning to Paris, however, his fortunes changed. His first grand opera, *The Pearl-Fishers* (1863) was unsuccessful, as were his succeeding works, *La Jolie Fille de Perth* (1867), and *Djamileh* (1872).

With the incidental music to *L'Arlésienne* Bizet acquired a measure of recognition. His masterpiece, *Carmen,* might have started him again on a glorious career, but he died three months after its production, wearied and disappointed after his long struggle.

What Bizet might have accomplished had he lived longer is a matter for speculation. All that was best in the French tradition is apparent in his music: its finish, refinement and directness. To that Bizet brought much that was strong and original. His harmonies have a subtlety, his melodies a vigor and his instrumentation a boldness which set them apart. His taste for the exotic, which unquestionably lent color to many of his works, was always kept within bounds; he never abandoned musical honesty for specious "local color." Above all, his music was never insipid or trite; almost everything he wrote is characterized by its conciseness and by its individuality.

Suite No. 1, L'Arlésienne (The Woman of Arles):
I. Prelude
II. Minuetto
III. Adagietto
IV. Carillon

Suite No. 2, L'Arlésienne:
I. Pastorale
II. Intermezzo
III. Menuet
IV. Farandole

L'Arlésienne is the title of a play written by Alphonse Daudet (1840-1897). It was first produced in Paris on October 1, 1872, with incidental music written by Bizet. Although the play was not very successful, Bizet's music was well received. It was the first work of the composer to gain popular favor. Bizet later arranged the music in two concert suites, both of which gained and have held places in the standard repertory. The numbers offer striking contrasts; all, however, are markedly original and colorful, exhibiting the freshness of the composer's inspiration. The *Prelude* of the first suite is based on a Provençal March (*March of the Kings*), which is sometimes erroneously ascribed to Jean-Baptiste Lully. The melody of this march occurs again in the *Farandole* in the second suite. The farandole is a popular dance of Provence.

Overture, Patrie: Bizet, Massenet and Guiraud were commissioned by Jules Pasdeloup in 1873 to compose new works for the Pasdeloup Orchestra. Massenet wrote his famous *Phèdre* overture for the occasion, while Bizet, taking as his subject a drama by Sardou, composed the above work. It was performed at a Pasdeloup concert early in 1874 and was enthusiastically received. The choice of a patriotic subject was a happy one, in view of the feelings of the French public so soon after the disasters of 1870. The work is written with Bizet's usual brilliance, and has maintained greater favor than any of Bizet's orchestral works with the exception of the *Arlésienne* suites.

Carmen (*Selections*): *Carmen* has made the name of its composer immortal, yet when this opera was first performed in 1875 it scored but a mild success. Bizet's death three months later was undoubtedly hastened by disappointment.

Carmen is founded on a story by Prosper Mérimée (1803-1870), one of the most distinguished authors of the period. Both story and opera are notable for swiftness and intensity of action. For movement, color and conviction, the opera *Carmen* has few if any equals. It may seem strange now that Bizet was accused of "Wagnerism" by his contemporaries. Certainly the perennial freshness of the music of *Carmen*, its brilliant vividness and directness, seem to refute such an accusation almost automatically.

The first American production of the work took place in New York on October 23, 1879, with Minnie Hauk, Campanini and Del Puente. Since then it has been performed constantly. It has had thousands of productions throughout the world, but it grows steadily, rather than declines in popularity. Eames, Calvé, Farrar, and many other famous stars have appeared in the title role.

The Pearl-Fishers (Selections): *The Pearl-Fishers* was the first grand opera Bizet composed. It received its first performance at the Théâtre Lyrique in Paris on September 29, 1863. The American première took place in Philadelphia in 1893. The opera was not a great success when first played, but steadily gained in popular favor. The principal role was a favorite of Caruso.

The action of the opera takes place in the Orient. The story deals with the rivalry of two humble pearl-fishers for the love of a priestess, and the magnanimity of the unsuccessful suitor. The music is rich in color and of considerable dramatic force. Some critics maintain that the score of *The Pearl-Fishers* is more striking and beautiful than that of *Carmen.*

Suite, Children's Games (Jeux d'Enfants):

I. March (Trumpet and Drum)
II. Berceuse (The Doll)
III. Impromptu (The Top)
IV. Duo (Little Husband, Little Wife)
V. Galop (The Ball)

This charming work was performed at the initial concert of the Colonne Orchestra in Paris, March 2, 1873. Originally written for pianoforte, four hands, it was later arranged for orchestra by the composer. The pieces need no explanations beyond their titles, for their illustrative qualities are self-evident. The delightful humor of the imagery and the freshness of the music have endeared the suite to all audiences, whether children or "grown-ups."

François Adrien Boieldieu

BORN Rouen, France, December 16, 1775
DIED Jarcy, France, October 8, 1834

WORKS ARRANGED FOR BAND:

Overtures: THE CALIPH OF BAGDAD (F; SF
LA DAME BLANCHE (F; B&H
JEAN DE PARIS (F

ONE of the greatest names associated with the development of comic opera in France is that of Boieldieu. Although in many ways he but carried on the tradition of Grétry (1741-1813), in other respects he introduced a new technique which was developed by Hérold, Adam and Auber. Boieldieu's first opera was produced when he was eighteen; his first real success, *The Caliph of Bagdad,* when he was twenty-five. Up to that time, Boieldieu's study had been desultory and irregular; berated by Cherubini for his "undeserved success," the young composer proceeded to equip himself more thoroughly, and as a result, his later operas proved to be much more substantial.

Boieldieu spent many years in Russia, from 1803 to 1811, with a contract to turn out three operas per year, and a number of marches. The atmosphere was uncongenial, however, and none of the works of this period ranks with the composer's best. His return to Paris was a triumph in many ways. His reputation grew constantly. In 1817 he was appointed Méhul's successor as Professor of Composition at the Conservatory; in 1821 he received the Legion of Honor. He collaborated in a number of works with Cherubini, Méhul, Hérold and Auber. Among his pupils were Adam and Fétis.

It is interesting to note the enormous vogue which the works of Boieldieu and co-workers had in France. The musical taste of the period assured a living to any composer who

could turn his hand to the comic opera. Those who d
viously, occupied the position of popular composer
temptation to work rapidly and to turn out as much a
sible was therefore very strong. Much of the music of
Boieldieu reveals a too great facility; the best of it, however, is marked by a high degree of finish and a melodic charm closely related to that of the French folk-song.

✓ ✓ ✓

Overture, The Caliph of Bagdad: The Caliph of Bagdad was produced in 1800, with great success. The music is simple, engaging and elegant. The overture, which has survived the opera as a whole by some hundred years, is highly characteristic of the period, being not un-reminiscent of Mozart or Rossini. The short introduction is of great charm; the main section of the overture is brilliant and sparkling, with just enough contrast to keep it interesting throughout.

✓

Overture, Jean de Paris: Jean de Paris was the third opera Boieldieu produced after his return from Russia in 1811. Its performance in 1812 occasioned tremendous enthusiasm; it was the greatest success Boieldieu had enjoyed thus far in his career. The overture is simple in character, extremely tuneful, and exhibits the polish characteristic of Boieldieu's best work.

✓

Overture, La Dame Blanche: From 1818 to 1825 Boieldieu remained inactive due to ill-health. He returned to the operatic stage in the latter year with his masterpiece, *La Dame Blanche* (*The White Lady*), and scored an unparalleled success. This opera is still the best-remembered of all that Boieldieu composed. The libretto was founded on a fusion of two novels by Sir Walter Scott, *The Monastery* and

Guy Mannering. Scottish airs are used in the music; they are somewhat Gallicized, but they lend a special quality to the score. The overture, which includes a number of these tunes, is sometimes mistakenly referred to as *Pique Dame*.

Arrigo Boito

BORN Padua, Italy, February 24, 1842
DIED Milan, June 10, 1918

ARRANGED FOR BAND:

Selections from MEFISTOFELE (B&H

BOITO was a man of unusual talent and was as much a poet as a musician. He was closely associated with Verdi, having written the librettos for *Falstaff* and *Othello*. *Mefistofele* was first performed in 1868, at Milan. The libretto is made up of episodes from the whole of Goethe's *Faust*, and the music is of a dramatic, indeed often sensational, character.

Alexander Porphyrievitch Borodin

BORN St. Petersburg, November 12, 1834
DIED St. Petersburg, February 28, 1887

WORKS ARRANGED FOR BAND:

Symphonic Sketch, IN THE STEPPES OF CENTRAL ASIA (B&H

From PRINCE IGOR: *Overture* (B&H
Polovtsian Dances (B&H; C
Polovtsian March (B&H

BORODIN was one of a group of amateurs who gathered around the composer Balakirev and formed the neo-Russian school. By profession Borodin was a physician, but his gift for music was unquestionably of the first order. Like the other composers who followed Balakirev, Borodin felt that he was a Russian rather than an internationalist in music; his compositions show the distinct formative influence of Russian legend and folk-melody.

Overture, Prince Igor: Borodin's opera, *Prince Igor,* is at once the most deeply Russian and the most popular of his works. The libretto, fashioned by the composer and Vladimir Stassov, is based on a medieval epic from the Kiev cycle, dating from the Tartar epoch. The legend recounts the campaign of Prince Igor and his son Vladimir against the Polovtsi, a semi-barbaric tribe of Central Asia. Borodin's music is notable for its abundant use of native material, both rhythmic and melodic. The dances are sweeping in their color and vigor, while the arias are remarkable for their breadth and richness.

The opera was unfinished at Borodin's death. Completed by Rimsky-Korsakov and produced at Kiev in 1891, it met with instantaneous success. The overture was never written down by the composer, but Glazounov, who had heard him play it over on the piano, wrote it out from memory and orchestrated it. It is based on melodies which occur during the opera itself, the broad melody serving as second theme of the overture is that of Prince Igor's Song.

Polovtsian Dances from *Prince Igor:*
I. Introduction: Andantino—Allegro vivo
II. Allegro
III. Presto—Moderato—Presto—Allegro con Spirito

The famous *Polovtsian Dances* occur at the end of the second act of Borodin's opera. Prince Igor and his son Vladimir are prisoners in the camp of Konchak, the Polovtsian chief. This courteous warrior promises to free Igor if he will promise never to fight again. He then orders the tribal dances performed in honor of the prisoners.

In the opera the dances follow one another without interruption. The same thematic material is used throughout, brilliantly orchestrated and skillfully varied. As performed by the ballet the various movements include dances by the young boys and maidens of the tribe, by the warriors, and by the entire tribal assemblage.

Polovtsian March from *Prince Igor:* The March of the Polovtsi is heard in the third act of *Prince Igor,* during the celebration of the Polovtsian victory over Prince Igor's army. Although bearing the title of "March," the number has more of the character of a ballet selection. It is full of color and makes use of the type of material heard in the famous Polovtsian Dances.

Symphonic Sketch, In the Steppes of Central Asia: Borodin composed this colorful work in 1880, for the twenty-fifth anniversary of the accession of Tsar Alexander II. On that occasion a series of *tableaux vivants,* or animated pictures, was given by the ballet as part of the entertainment. *In the Steppes of Central Asia* was one of these. Like the music of *Prince Igor,* this symphonic sketch reflects the composer's interest in the music of the Asiatic provinces of Russia. A note to the score gives the following as the composer's program: "Over the uniform sandy Steppes of Central Asia come the unwonted sounds of a peaceful Russian song. From the distance are heard the stamping of horses and camels and the peculiar sound of an Oriental melody. A native caravan draws near. It pursues its way, safe and free from care, through the boundless desert under the protection of Russian arms. It moves farther and farther off. The song of the Russians and the melody of the Asiatics combine to form a common harmony, the echo of which is gradually lost in the air of the Steppe."

Johannes Brahms

BORN Hamburg, Germany, May 7, 1833
DIED Vienna, April 3, 1897

WORKS ARRANGED FOR BAND:

ACADEMIC FESTIVAL OVERTURE (F
HUNGARIAN DANCES (One or several pub. by F; B&H; CB; ABC; J
WALTZES (One or several by B&H; F
CRADLE SONG (F; Brg
TRAGIC OVERTURE (AMP

BRAHMS is generally considered the inheritor of the musical tradition of Beethoven and the last of the great German symphonists. His life was extremely uneventful, and almost entirely devoted to composition. Robert Schumann was among the first to recognize the genius of Brahms. Indeed his championing the cause of the young composer was a turning point in Brahms' career.

Of Brahms' music, much can be said. It is generally felt that Brahms is one of the greatest composers of all time. Critics have pointed out that he enlarged and enriched the classical forms, making them the vehicles for the expression of noble and profound ideas. In any case Brahms stands as the greatest German exponent in the nineteenth century of "absolute" music as opposed to "program" music or opera. In this he was the complete antithesis of Wagner. Critics of the period staged a war by proxy between the two composers, even though many of the faults of Wagner are not unnoticeable in Brahms. Today it seems more than likely that the reputation of Brahms will continue to grow.

Few of Brahms' major works have been arranged for band. He is known to band audiences primarily by a number of shorter pieces which reflect him in his lightest mood.

The Academic Festival Overture: In 1879 the University of Breslau offered to Brahms the degree of Doctor of Philosophy. In 1880 Brahms composed the *Academic Festival Overture* as a token of his appreciation. It was first performed at Breslau early in the year 1881, Brahms himself conducting the orchestra. The overture is really a fantasia on German student songs, of which Brahms was very fond, and in the singing of which he loved to join.

Hungarian Dances: Brahms originally published in Hungarian dances in four volumes as piano duets. Because of the wide popularity they immediately attained, they were soon published in almost every conceivable form. Brahms' fondness for the characteristics of Magyar music is apparent in many of his original works. These dances are said to be transcriptions of performances by Gypsy bands.

Waltzes: The sixteen waltzes for piano are possibly the best known of all Brahms' compositions. They have been arranged for many combinations of instruments.

Cradle Song: Many of the songs of Brahms bear the legend "Volkslied" or folk song. In some cases this indicates that the words are traditional, while in others it indicates merely that the style of writing is closely akin to the popular song. Such a work is the well-known *Wiegenlied* (*Cradle-Song*), which, like many of Brahms' shorter compositions, has been arranged in many forms.

Max Bruch

BORN Cologne, Germany, January 6, 1838
DIED Friedenau, Germany, October 2, 1920

WORKS ARRANGED FOR BAND:

KOL NIDRE (F

ALTHOUGH during his lifetime Bruch was famous for his choral works, his reputation today rests upon two compositions: the *Violin Concerto in G Minor,* and the *Kol Nidre.* This latter was originally arranged by Bruch as a set of variations for 'cello and orchestra, the melody being the traditional Hebrew one used on the Day of Atonement. Bruch wrote music in every form, but his work is remarkable more for its polish than for its originality.

Dudley Buck

BORN Hartford, Connecticut, March 10, 1839
DIED Orange, New Jersey, October 6, 1909

ARRANGED FOR BAND:

TRIUMPHAL MARCH (S

AS ORGANIST, composer and educator, Dudley Buck exercised profound influence on the American musical life of his time. He received his musical training abroad, returning to the United States in 1862. From that time on he held positions as church organist in many cities and became an influential factor in the growth and development of choral music in America. In 1875 he became assistant conductor to Theodore Thomas, and in 1877 assumed the conductorship of the Apollo Club of New York. This position he held until his retirement.

Buck composed in almost all forms, but the greater part of his work was written for chorus. Several of his cantatas enjoyed wide popularity. Among these the best known are *The Golden Legend* (1880) and *The Light of Asia* (1885). His *Triumphal March* was published as Opus 26, and is a straightforward example of the Grand March.

Carl Busch

BORN Bjerre, Denmark, March 29, 1862

WORKS WRITTEN FOR BAND:

A CHANT FROM THE GREAT PLAINS (F
PRELUDE (S
Hymn and *Processional* from the LIBERTY MEMORIAL ODE (Fitz
Also many marches and music for small ensembles (see introduction)

CARL BUSCH, one of the best-known figures in American musical life today, came to this country in 1887, settling in Kansas City, where he has since remained. To him more than to any other person is due the increase of musical activity in that city. He organized and conducted numerous orchestras and other musical organizations, and from 1912 directed the Kansas City Symphony.

His compositions have brought him world-wide recognition, and have been performed by leading orchestras here and abroad. He has won more prizes than can be enumerated here, and has been knighted by the Danish Government in recognition of his services to Scandinavian music. Most numerous among Dr. Busch's compositions are his cantatas and other choral works. Dr. Busch's interest in bands is, however, of long standing. In addition to the works he has composed for full band, he has written a number of pieces for small brass ensembles. Dr. Busch is a noted collector of old wind instruments, and is known as an authority on the subject.

Symphonic Episode, A Chant from the Great Plains: This composition won a prize of $250.00 offered by Edwin Franko Goldman in 1919 for the best original work for band.

The judges were Percy Grainger and Victor Herbert. The program of the composition is as follows: Indian scene from an outdoor pageant illustrating early life in the West. A quiet summer day in the village with the children engaged in games and the old men looking on. In the distance is heard the chanting of the victorious braves returning from war, and bringing with them their dead and wounded. As they approach the village, they form in solemn procession and pass on to the burial ground. The pastoral life, which ceased during the procession, is once more taken up. The principal motive is an idealization of a theme from Alice C. Fletcher's *A Study of Omaha Indian Music.*

Prelude: This composition was written by Dr. Busch in appreciation of his election to honorary membership in the American Bandmasters' Association. He has submitted the following notes concerning it: "The title 'Prelude' has been affixed to this composition in lieu of a better one. Since this term has never been associated with any particular form in music, it has given me an opportunity to proceed freely as my imagination prompted. With the different choirs appearing separately and in various combinations, I trust it may serve as a study in band scoring, and thus justify me in presenting it at this concert."

Hymn and Procession from *Liberty Memorial Ode:* The *Liberty Memorial Ode* is a choral work written by Dr. Busch for the dedication of the Liberty Memorial in Kansas City, Mo., on November 11, 1926. Since this work was performed in the open air under the composer's direction, the accompaniment was written directly for band. In their present form, therefore, these excerpts are not transcriptions.

Peter Buys

BORN Amsterdam, Holland, 1881

ORIGINAL WORKS FOR BAND:

Fantasies: CHILDHOOD DAYS (Ba
THE ANGELUS (Ba
SAUCY SUSAN (Ba
Paraphrase: CHRISTMAS GREETING (Ba
Numerous marches, waltzes and smaller pieces

PETER BUYS began the study of the violin at the age of six, and soon afterwards undertook comprehensive studies of theoretical subjects as well as of other instruments. His early training was thus well-rounded and thorough.

He came to the United States in 1902, and accepted a position at the United States Military Academy, where he was soon put in sole charge of band and orchestra arranging. Returning to New York City, he joined Sousa's Band and was entrusted by Mr. Sousa with arranging for his organization. Later, Mr. Buys became bandmaster at Juniata College in Pennsylvania, holding that position until the city of Hagerstown, Maryland, offered him a larger field as Director of its Municipal Band. In Hagerstown, Mr. Buys also founded his well-known School of Music. Mr. Buys was one of the first members of the American Bandmasters' Association, and has been chairman of its committee on instrumentation for several years.

As composer and transcriber for band, Mr. Buys holds a distinguished place in American musical life. Sousa, on different occasions, presented programs made up almost exclusively of Buys' compositions. Mr. Buys has made frequent appearances as guest conductor, while his own concerts in Hagerstown have an impressively large following.

Fantasy, Childhood Days: This fantasy tells the story of a day of play in the life of a child, using as its material childhood songs which are sung the world over. Beginning with *Lazy Mary Will You Get Up,* and concluding with *Rockabye Baby,* the music shows the child singing, playing and dancing by turns. Well-known tunes which are heard include *The Farmer In The Dell, London Bridge Is Falling Down, Jingle Bells, Pop Goes The Weasel,* and many others.

Sacred Fantasy, The Angelus: Many of the most beautiful of the old hymns are included in this fantasy. A skillful blending of the tunes and a dignity of presentation have made this fantasy a popular favorite.

Descriptive Fantasy, Saucy Susan: The basis of this fantasy is the famous frontier song, *O Susanna.* The composer has taken the tune and demonstrated what can be done with a simple melody when developed in various styles. The variations include many characteristic manners, ranging from the religious to the humorous.

Paraphrase, Christmas Greeting: This number is an elaboration of the celebrated Christmas song, *Silent Night, Holy Night.* It is worked out in symphonic style and is full of dignity.

Alexis Emmanuel Chabrier

BORN Ambert, France, January 18, 1841
DIED Paris, September 3, 1894

WORKS ARRANGED FOR BAND:

Rhapsody, ESPAÑA (F
WALTZ SUITE (C

BY REASON of his spontaneity, brilliance and ingenuity in harmonic and orchestral coloring, Chabrier may be said to be one of the forerunners of the modern French school. He first took up music as an amateur while studying law, but soon afterwards devoted himself entirely to composition. He composed several operas and operettas, of which the best-known is *Gwendolyn,* first performed at Brussels in 1886.

In 1882 he visited Spain, where he became enthusiastic about Spanish dancing. Several of his compositions were inspired by this visit, none more notably than the rhapsody *España.* The Spanish themes used in the work are entirely original, however, although they are based on characteristic Spanish dance forms such as the Jota and the Malagueña. It is said that when the players in the orchestra first saw the parts, they were bewildered by the novel rhythms! Today, by comparison to the Spanish music of De Falla, Chabrier's rhapsody no longer seems so daring, but its vigor and tunefulness contribute to keeping it constantly popular.

Cécile Chaminade

BORN Paris, France, August 8, 1861

WORKS ARRANGED FOR BAND:

SCARF DANCE (F; B&H; J; CB
LA LISONJERA ("The Flatterer") (F; B&H; CB
Ballet Airs:
PIERRETTE (F; CB
SERENADE (F; B&H
PAS DES AMPHORES ("Vase Dance") (F; J
PAS DES CYMBALES (B&H
MEDITATION (B&H

CÉCILE CHAMINADE was a gifted composer of salon pieces and ballet music. Many of her works, which are characterized by graceful outline and agreeable lyricism, still enjoy wide popularity. Of her Ambroise Thomas wrote: "This is not a woman who composes, but a composer who happens to be a woman." Mme. Chaminade was a pupil of Benjamin Godard.

The popular *Scarf Dance* is part of Mme. Chaminade's "ballet-symphony" *Callirhoë*, successfully produced in Marseilles in 1888.

Luigi Cherubini
(Maria Luigi Carlo Zenobio Salvatore Cherubini)

BORN Florence, Italy, September 14, 1760
DIED Paris, March 15, 1842

WORKS ARRANGED FOR BAND:

Overtures: LODOÏSKA (B&H
ANACREON (W

CHERUBINI was one of the dominant figures of early nineteenth-century music. Living and working in Paris, London and Vienna, as well as in his native Italy, Cherubini was truly an international influence. The greater part of his life was passed in Paris, where he became one of the first inspectors of the Conservatory. He became professor of composition at the institution in 1816, and from 1821 to 1841 was its director.

Cherubini was a great contrapuntist, but in his operas he showed neither the dramatic sense of Mozart nor the seriousness of Gluck. His works nevertheless had considerable influence on such composers as Grétry, Méhul, and even Rossini. The overtures, which remain in the standard repertory, are extremely pleasing and show an exceptional finish of form. Aside from these works, Cherubini is best remembered by his famous *Requiem in C Minor*, a work characteristically eighteenth century in its melodic content, but remarkable for its contrapuntal richness.

⸗ ⸗ ⸗

Overture, Lodoïska: In 1789, one Léonard, the hairdresser of Queen Marie-Antoinette, obtained permission to establish a theatre for Italian Opera in Paris. Cherubini became conductor there, and held the position until 1792. During that period, he brought out the works of his contemporaries and completed the score of one of his own most successful operas. This was *Lodoïska,* first performed in 1791. While not competing with Gluck (q. v.) on his own ground, Cherubini effected in this work a certain enlargement of the conventional opera of the period, giving the whole a generally greater dramatic content and more breadth in the treatment of the orchestra and ensemble.

Overture, Anacreon: Orchestra audiences today know Cherubini best by the overture to *Anacreon,* a one-act ballet-opera written and produced in 1803. The work is thoroughly representative of Cherubini's style, exhibiting a pleasing sense of melody, a wealth of scholarly detail, a structural clarity and a great restraint in the employment of musical devices. The overture is in straightforward classical style. The opening *largo* of twenty-seven bars forms an introduction to the main *allegro* of the overture. The working out of the themes forms the principal interest of the work. Although *Anacreon* was written before Cherubini made the acquaintance of Beethoven, the work shows clearly a certain affinity of feeling between the two contemporaries.

Frederic François Chopin

BORN near Warsaw, February 22, 1810
DIED Paris, October 17, 1849

WORKS ARRANGED FOR BAND:

FUNERAL MARCH (F; B&H
WALTZES (Various selections and editions)
NOCTURNES (Various selections and editions)
MAZURKAS (Various selections and editions)
POLONAISES (Various selections and editions)
PRELUDES (Various selections and editions)

CHOPIN, as is well known, composed almost exclusively for the pianoforte, and was one of the greatest virtuosi on that instrument in the history of music. His works did more to enrich the pianist's repertory than those of any other composer. They created an entirely new idiom, both technically and artistically. In spite of their essentially pianistic character, many of Chopin's works may be played with good effect by bands.

Robert Schumann called Chopin "the boldest and proudest poetic spirit of the times." It is true that Chopin's music is of a poetic or lyric character, but it must also be pointed out that Chopin never descended to the commonplaces of so-called poetic composition. He titled his compositions after the forms in which they were cast: waltz, mazurka, scherzo, etc., and also used such ambiguous classifications as prelude, etude, impromptu and nocturne, relying for effect on the content of the music itself rather than on the suggestions which might be embodied in banal titles. All of his music is notable for a simplicity and perfection of form as well as for an extraordinary rhythmic variety and a wealth of melodic invention.

Funeral March: Chopin's famous *Funeral March* was written as the second movement of his *Sonata in B♭ Minor* for piano. It has been transcribed for almost all combinations of instruments and its use has become a tradition.

Nocturnes: The nocturne has no prescribed form, but represents a type of composition made famous by Chopin. The use of the word nocturne as a title, however, was not original with him; it was popularized by the composer John Field (1782-1837) whose style influenced Chopin to a considerable extent. Chopin's nocturnes are characterized by floating melodies and graceful embellishments; the general effect is one of tranquillity.

Preludes: Chopin's twenty-four preludes cover almost every possible variety of writing for the pianoforte, as well as a wide range of musical expression.

Mazurkas: The mazurka is a Polish national dance in three-quarter or three-eighth time, and of slower tempo than the waltz. It is usually characterized by a strong accent on the third beat of the bar. Chopin wrote fifty-two mazurkas in all, greatly enlarging and refining the original simple form.

Waltzes: Chopin's waltzes have a distinctive character which sets them far apart from the simple dance or salon piece. Most of them are so well known and are so frequently heard as to require no comment.

Polonaises: The polonaise, like the mazurka, is a dance of Polish origin. In the hands of Chopin it was altered from a simple dance into a glowing expression of his love for his native land. The *Polonaise Militaire*, with its fiery spirit and strong rhythm, may be considered as an expression of Chopin's faith in the destiny of his country.

Francesco Cilea

BORN Calabria, Italy, July 29, 1866

WORK ARRANGED FOR BAND:

Selections from ADRIANA LECOUVREUR (B&H

CILEA's music is little-known in America, but many of his operas have been and still are performed with great success in Europe, particularly in Italy. His most famous work is the opera, *Adriana Lecouvreur,* which established his international reputation. The libretto is founded on a drama by Scribe. The music shows the influence of the later Verdi rather than that of Cilea's successful contemporaries Mascagni and Giordano. The opera was first produced in Milan in 1902.

Domenico Cimarosa

BORN Aversa, Italy, December 17, 1749
DIED Venice, Italy, January 11, 1801

ARRANGED FOR BAND:

Overture: THE SECRET MARRIAGE (B&H; S

CIMAROSA was one of the leading Italian composers of the eighteenth century. Like his compatriots, he devoted the greater part of his energy to the composition of works for the stage. He achieved his first success at the age of twenty-three with a comic-opera in the prevailing style. This initial effort was followed by others equally successful. All of these early works were remarkable for their gaiety and humor. So marked was Cimarosa's success in Naples, and later in Florence, that Empress Catherine II of Russia persuaded him to go to St. Petersburg in 1788. He remained there four years, during which time he composed an almost incredibly large number of works.

Later Cimarosa accepted the appointment of Chapel-Master to Emperor Leopold of Austria, and it was while he was in Vienna, in 1792, that he composed his finest comic opera, *The Secret Marriage.* The opera was so well received that the Emperor had the performance repeated as an encore on the very evening of its first presentation. The work maintained its popularity for many years, and is revived occasionally even today.

The overture is characteristically eighteenth century in style, full of vivacity and grace, and reminds the listener somewhat of Mozart in its elegance and clarity of structure.

Samuel Coleridge-Taylor

BORN London, August 15, 1875
DIED Croydon, England, September 1, 1912

WORKS ARRANGED FOR BAND:

Rhapsodic Dance, THE BAMBOULA (B&H
Suite from the Ballet, HIAWATHA (B&H
SUITE DE CONCERT (B&H
Incidental music to FAUST (B&H
Incidental music to OTHELLO (B&H
THREE DREAM DANCES (B&H
Waltz Suite, THREE FOURS (B&H
CHRISTMAS OVERTURE (B&H
ST. AGNES EVE (B&H
FOUR CHARACTERISTIC WALTZES (N
HIAWATHA'S WEDDING-FEAST (N

SAMUEL COLERIDGE-TAYLOR, one of the foremost composers of his race, was the son of an English mother and African father, who was a physician in his native Sierra Leone. His education was acquired in England. In composition he was a student of Sir Charles Villiers Stanford; he also played the violin. His early works aroused much favorable criticism, and it was not long before he enjoyed world-wide fame. Much of his best work was commissioned for various festivals in England and America, and for theatres in London. He visited America thrice, in 1904, 1906 and 1910.

His music discloses a fine sense of form and has a very rich melodic quality. His orchestration is very colorful. In some of his music, vigorous and almost barbaric rhythms predominate.

⸙ ⸙ ⸙

Rhapsodic Dance, The Bamboula: Coleridge-Taylor was commissioned by an American publishing house to make a collection of African melodies. Among them was this festival dance-tune, which like the others was originally published for violin and pianoforte. In 1910 the composer enlarged this piece to its present form. It received its first performance at the festival in Norfolk, Conn., in 1911.

Suite from the Ballet, Hiawatha:

I. The Wooing
II. The Marriage Feast
III. (a) Bird Scene
(b) Conjurer's Dance
IV. Departure
V. Reunion

The best-known of Coleridge-Taylor's works is probably the Hiawatha trilogy, consisting of *Hiawatha's Wedding Feast, The Death of Minnehaha* and *Hiawatha's Departure*. This work, based on Longfellow's poem, was written in the form of a cantata for chorus and orchestra. The three parts were brought out in 1898, 1899 and 1900, respectively. Much later the composer arranged these five numbers from the work in the form of a ballet suite. The music is very colorful and original and shows the indubitably great talent of the composer.

Petite Suite de Concert:

I. La Caprice de Nanette (Nanette's Caprice)
II. Demande et Réponse (Question and Answer)
III. Un Sonnet d'Amour (Love Sonnet)
IV. La Tarantelle Frétillante

This little suite, Opus 77, was written during the last years of Coleridge-Taylor's life. It was originally scored for orchestra, and has achieved considerable popularity both in that form and in its band arrangement.

Christmas Overture: Shortly before his death, Coleridge-Taylor began the composition of the incidental music to *The Forest of Wild Thyme*, by Alfred Noyes. The entire work was not completed, but portions of it were published as Opus 74. The *Christmas Overture* is the best known of these. It received its first performance on Christmas day, 1924, by the Symphony Orchestra of the British Broadcasting Company, under the baton of Hiawatha Coleridge-Taylor, the composer's son.

The overture, which is charmingly written and brilliantly scored, incorporates a number of famous English Christmas carols and concludes with a quotation of *Hark! The Herald Angels Sing.*

Three Dream Dances: The *Three Dream Dances* are part of the incidental music which Coleridge-Taylor wrote for *The Forest of Wild Thyme*, by Alfred Noyes.

Incidental music to Faust: Coleridge-Taylor wrote the incidental music to a number of romantic plays produced at His Majesty's Theatre, London, around 1910. The *Faust* for which this music was written was the work of Stephen Phillips. The production of the play took place in 1908. The three numbers written by Coleridge-Taylor are said to have greatly enhanced the effect of the production. The numbers are:

1. The Dance of the Witches (Brocken Scene)
2. The Four Visions (Helen, Cleopatra, Messalina and Margaret)
3. Devil's Kitchen Scene

Suite, Othello:

1. Dance
2. Children's Intermezzo
3. Funeral March

4. The Willow Song
5. Military March

This suite is taken from Coleridge-Taylor's incidental music to the play of Shakespeare, as given at His Majesty's Theatre, London, in 1911.

Peter Cornelius

BORN Mainz, Germany, December 24, 1824
DIED there, October 26, 1874

ARRANGED FOR BAND:

Overture: THE BARBER OF BAGDAD (F

CORNELIUS, after failing to achieve great success as an actor, began the serious study of music in Berlin. He eventually found his way to Weimar, where Liszt was performing prodigies as musical director. Cornelius attached himself to Liszt's devoted following, became an early admirer of Wagner, and set about the composition of *The Barber of Bagdad.* Liszt produced this opera in 1858; its failure—due largely to non-musical reasons—so angered Liszt that he left Weimar. Cornelius then followed Wagner to Vienna and Munich, at which latter place he became reader to King Ludwig II of Bavaria. His operatic masterpiece was produced with great success after his death. Aside from this work, Cornelius is best known for his songs.

✓ ✓ ✓

The Barber of Bagdad is based on a story from "The Arabian Nights," the composer himself writing the libretto. The overture is based entirely on themes from the opera. It opens with an *allegretto* in which the theme of the barber is heard in the brasses, while the woodwinds take up the barber's patter song. An *andante* section follows, leading into the main section of the overture, a very brisk and spirited *allegro.*

There are several versions of this overture, but the one generally used is that orchestrated by Liszt from the piano sketches of Cornelius. The masterly counterpoint and wealth of melody of the overture were greatly admired by Liszt.

Bainbridge Crist

BORN Lawrenceburg, Indiana, February 13, 1883

WORKS WRITTEN FOR BAND:

CHINESE PROCESSION (W
VIENNA—1913 (W
JAPANESE NOCTURNE (W
BEDOUIN DANCE

WORKS ARRANGED FOR BAND:

ARABIAN DANCE (F
CHINESE DANCE (F

BAINBRIDGE CRIST received his education in Washington, D. C., graduating from law school there in 1906. He practiced law in Boston for six years after that, but the urge to pursue a career in music, which he had studied since the age of five, finally prevailed. He abandoned his law practice and went to London, Paris and Berlin where he studied singing and composition. Paul Juon, the eminent composer, was one of his teachers. Returning to Boston, he devoted his time to composition and the teaching of singing.

Mr. Crist has been recognized as one of the most gifted of present-day American composers. His songs are widely known and his orchestral works have received many performances here and abroad. His music is characterized by exquisite craftsmanship and by an original and imaginative sense of color. The composer's interest in bands was stimulated by correspondence with Edwin Franko Goldman, who first drew his attention to the field. Mr. Crist has given careful thought to the problems of writing music for the concert band. The following statement from Mr. Crist will therefore be of considerable interest:

"First of all—when I had been asked to write something

directly for symphonic band—I saw clearly that the reason why much band music does not come off is because it was not conceived for band. I perceived that to gain effects with a band that were as telling as those obtained through the medium of an orchestra, one must conceive everything for band while actually creating. In other words, that one must hear a band playing one's thoughts; not an orchestra. I saw that if one merely transcribed Violin I for Clarinet I, 'Cello to Baritone, and so on, one could never achieve interesting and original effects. I am convinced that if composers will only be sensible enough to put an orchestra out of their minds when they wish to write for band, we shall have band music of great beauty and importance...."

✓ ✓ ✓

Chinese Procession: Chinese Procession, Mr. Crist's first work written directly for symphonic band, reflects the composer's interest in exotic subjects and imaginative themes. In many of his other compositions Mr. Crist has made use of colors and rhythms suggested by his studies of the Orient. *Chinese Procession* is an excellent illustration of the tonal color possibilities of the modern band.

✓

Vienna—1913: In this work, the composer has endeavored to catch the subtle atmosphere of the Austrian capital in the days before the war. Waltz strains ingeniously used suggest the Viennese beauty and gaiety. The composition was written directly for band.

✓

Two Oriental Dances (Arabian and Chinese): These two characteristic dances were originally composed for grand orchestra. They reflect the composer's fondness for exotic colors and rhythms and show his remarkable ability to suggest them in his music.

Claude Achille Debussy

BORN Saint-Germain-en-Laye, France, August 22, 1862
DIED Paris, March 26, 1918

WORKS ARRANGED FOR BAND:

PETITE SUITE (B&H
CHILDREN'S CORNER:
Serenade for the Doll (B&H
The Little Shepherd (B&H
Golliwog's Cakewalk (EV; B&H
CLAIR DE LUNE (EV
THE GIRL WITH THE FLAXEN HAIR (EV

NO COMPOSER of his generation was more influential than Claude Debussy, and few composers of any time have created so individual a style. Yet Debussy's music may be said to belong to the end of the nineteenth century rather than to the beginning of the twentieth, for it is in many ways the tonal equivalent of the decadent poems of Verlaine and Mallarmé. Like these, Debussy's music is exquisite and suggestive, restrained and yet over-refined, subtle in shading but limited in range. The best of it has a quality entirely unique, intangible and evocative.

Debussy's musical education was received at the Conservatory of Paris, where his originality occasionally disturbed his teachers. Nevertheless, he won the Prix de Rome in 1884 with his cantata, *L'Enfant Prodigue*. His earliest published works are more or less in the traditional French manner. It was not until the last decade of the century that his personal style appeared fully evolved with such works as *The Afternoon of a Faun*. Debussy's largest work, the opera *Pélléas and Mélisande,* is the fullest expression of his musical genius. It is a milestone in the development of the opera, being perhaps the only opera in which restraint rather than exaggeration is the guiding principle, and in which perfectly balanced declamation takes the place of set airs and pieces.

Debussy experimented freely with modal and whole-tone scales, breaking away from the major-and-minor system and the forms with which it is associated. He explored the effects of the upper overtones and used them for novel harmonic effects. Much of his music, although it is most easily recognizable by its harmonic color, is constructed on a linear basis; the adaptation of medieval diaphony is often quite apparent.

Petite Suite:

I. En Bateau (Boating)
II. Cortège
III. Menuet
IV. Ballet

Debussy's *Little Suite* was written in 1888, for piano duet. In its orchestral form it has long been one of the most popular examples of the composer's earlier style. The music is simple and contains few suggestions of Debussy's subsequent "impressionism."

The Children's Corner:

Serenade for the Doll
The Little Shepherd
Golliwog's Cakewalk

These numbers are taken from *The Children's Corner,* a set of six pieces for piano which Debussy wrote for his daughter. They were published in 1908. Although they are essentially humorous in conception and slight in substance, they are fairly representative of the composer's mature style, having the freedom of expression and individuality of idiom found in his more substantial works. *The Little Shepherd,* with its expressive melody, is often played as a flute solo;

few pastoral pieces are more effectively suggestive of shepherds' piping. The *Golliwog's Cakewalk,* perhaps the most popular of the set, was a conscious imitation of the American ragtime of the period; it testifies not only to Debussy's ability to work in novel rhythms but also to his lively sense of humor.

Claire de Lune (*Moonlight*): The beautiful *Claire de Lune* is taken from the *Suite Bergamasque,* an early work of Debussy, yet one which plainly shows the originality and genius of the composer. None of Debussy's piano compositions is played more often than this one, either in recital or in the home.

The Girl with the Flaxen Hair: The two books of preludes for piano are perhaps the best-known works of Debussy, and *The Girl with the Flaxen Hair* is probably the best-known of these preludes. It is the tenth prelude of the first book. Like Chopin's twenty-four preludes, Debussy's cover a wide range of pianistic effects, but unlike the former, they bear fanciful and occasionally cryptic titles. Debussy's piano music is extremely idiomatic and makes great use of the harmonics of the keyboard, yet many of his piano compositions are very effective for band or orchestra.

Clément Philibert Léo Délibes

BORN St. Germain du Val, France
DIED Paris, January 16, 1891

WORKS ARRANGED FOR BAND:

Ballet Suites: SYLVIA (F; B&H
COPPELIA (C; D; F; B&H
LA SOURCE (F; B&H
Pas des Fleurs from NAÏLA (F; B&H
March and *Procession of Bacchus* from SYLVIA (S
Selections from LAKMÉ (F; CB

LÉO DÉLIBES, like many other French composers of the last century, began his career as a composer of comic opera. He might have been extremely successful in this field alone had not his unusual talent for the ballet been revealed almost by chance. In 1866 he received a commission to collaborate with another composer on the music for the ballet *La Source.* Délibes' part of this work was so far superior to that of his collaborator that his reputation was immediately established. Many more commissions followed. Délibes produced a number of successful ballets, many charming songs, and one opera, *Lakmé,* which is still performed throughout the world. The composer received the Legion of Honor in 1871 and succeeded Réber as Professor of Composition at the Paris Conservatory in 1881.

Coppelia, Ballet Suite:

I. Fanfare et Marche de la Cloche (March of the Bell)
II. Valse des Heures (Waltz of the Hours)
III. Musique des Automats (Dance of the Automatons)
IV. Noce Villageoise (Village Wedding)
V. Intro. et Valse de la Poupée (Introduction and Waltz of the Doll)

VI. Marche des Guerrières (March of the Warriors)
VII. Czardas (Hungarian Dance)

Coppelia or *The Girl with Enamel Eyes* is considered by many critics to be the most pleasing of Délibes' ballets. It was first produced at the Grand Opera in Paris in 1870 and scored a triumphant success. The *Czardas* from this suite is often performed separately, and holds its popularity.

Sylvia, Ballet Suite:

I. a. Prelude
b. Les Chasseresses (The Huntresses)
II. a. Intermezzo
b. Valse Lente
III. Pizzicato Polka
IV. Marche et Cortège de Bacchus

Sylvia or *The Nymph of Diana,* was first presented at the Paris Opera in 1876. The scenario by Barbier uses a mythological setting, but is unrelated to any of the classical Greco-Roman myths. The action, which is of a light and pastoral character, is presented in five tableaux. The suite used for concert purposes is made up of numbers from the various tableaux arranged for their purely musical effectiveness. *Sylvia* was Délibes' most successful work in this form and put the crowning touch on his reputation as a ballet composer.

La Source, Ballet Suite:

I. Pas des Voiles (Dance of the Veils)
II. Andante
III. Variation
IV. Danse Circassienne (Circassian Dance)

La Source (*The Spring*) is the work which set Délibes on the road to recognition and fame. It was commissioned by the Paris Opera in 1866, to be composed jointly by Délibes and another musician already well-known for his ballets. The work revealed Délibes' genuine talent for writing vivacious and original dance music. It was later produced in Vienna under the title of *Naïla,* with several additional numbers. (See below.)

Pas des Fleurs from *Naïla:* For the production of his ballet, *La Source,* in Vienna, Délibes added this charming number, which has become the most popular of the entire suite. The name of the ballet was altered to *Naïla* for the Vienna production.

Selections from *Lakmé: Lakmé,* an opera in three acts, was first produced in Paris April 14, 1883. It was the most successful of Délibes' several operas and the only one that has survived. The libretto was taken from the romantic novel, *Le Mariage de Loti,* by Pierre Loti (1850-1923). Although Délibes was not possessed of great dramatic gifts, this opera has maintained its place in the repertory by reason of its wealth of melody and color. It contains one of the most famous coloratura airs ever written, the well-known *Bell Song.* The first American performance of the work took place in the same year as the original production.

Camillo De Nardis

WORKS ARRANGED FOR BAND:

Tone Poem, THE UNIVERSAL JUDGMENT (F
Suite, ABRUZZIAN SCENES (R; Italian Edition

THERE is little information available about Camillo De Nardis, whose reputation in America has been established almost exclusively by the popularity of his tone-poem, *The Universal Judgment.* De Nardis was for many years Director of the Royal Conservatory of Music in Naples. Many of his orchestral compositions are popular in Italy, and a number of them have been arranged for Italian band combinations.

The Universal Judgment won first prize in a competition for orchestral compositions at Naples in 1878. It is admirably adapted to band uses by reason both of the character of the melodic and harmonic structure and of the generous use of woodwind and brass in the original. Undoubtedly the various groups of brass instruments which, according to the original score, should be placed on the right, the left and the center of the stage, are intended to represent the choirs of heavenly trumpets heralding the Judgment Day.

Gaetano Donizetti

BORN Bergamo, Italy, November 29, 1797
DIED There, April 8, 1848

WORKS ARRANGED FOR BAND:

Selections from: LUCIA DI LAMMERMOOR (B&H; F
LA FAVORITA (F; B&H; D; CB
DAUGHTER OF THE REGIMENT (D; B&H
LUCREZIA BORGIA (F
L'ELISIR D'AMORE (F
LINDA DI CHAMOUNIX (CB

Overture: THE DAUGHTER OF THE REGIMENT (D

DONIZETTI was a composer of unusual facility and a representative of an important period in the development of Italian opera. He lived in the age of great vocal virtuosi and composed many of his most celebrated arias especially for them. His career was an almost unbroken string of successes, at least a part of which were due to the eminence and virtuosity of the singers who performed his works. Donizetti's operas, even in their time, were not noted for their dramatic qualities; they were brilliant, if superficial, vehicles for vocal fireworks. For that reason many of them have been forgotten. The best of them, however, are still performed, and are full of sparkling melodies.

Donizetti stands midway between Rossini and Verdi in the operatic tradition. He achieved no great renown until Rossini had ceased composing, and when Verdi began his series of much solider works, the art of Donizetti suffered a severe eclipse. But the mention of operas such as *Lucia di Lammermoor, L'Elisir d'Amore, The Daughter of the Regiment* and *Lucrezia Borgia* serves to remind one that Donizetti's best work may still be heard in the opera houses of the world.

ʼ ʼ ʼ

Lucia di Lammermoor (*Selection*): Donizetti's opera *Lucia* is founded on Sir Walter Scott's novel *The Bride of Lammermoor,* and is undoubtedly the most popular of all the composer's works. Donizetti himself wrote the libretto for the last act. *Lucia* was first performed in Naples in 1835 and was a tremendous success. As a result of this, Donizetti was appointed Professor of Counterpoint at the Royal College of Music at Naples.

Many of the melodies from *Lucia* are familiar, but none more so than the *Sextet,* which occurs at the beginning of the second act.

L'Elisir d'Amore (*Selection*): The melodious opera *L'Elisir d'Amore* (*The Elixir of Love*) stands about midway in the list of the composer's sixty-three operas. It was first produced in Milan in 1852, and is a delightful specimen of genuine opera buffa. The story deals with the commotion produced in a small Italian village by the arrival of a quack doctor, promoting the sale of a love potion.

The Daughter of the Regiment (*Selection*): Donizetti moved to Paris in 1839 after some trouble with the censors in Naples. He composed several of his best-known works while there. Among these is *The Daughter of the Regiment,* the fifty-third of Donizetti's operas, first performed in 1840. It was not a tremendous success in Paris and indeed it was not until Donizetti himself had translated the libretto into Italian that the opera became a favorite with such singers as Patti, Albani and Jenny Lind.

Lucrezia Borgia (*Selection*): The opera, *Lucrezia Borgia,* was first produced in Milan in 1833. The libretto, which is singularly melodramatic, was founded on Victor Hugo's novel. When the opera was produced in Paris in 1840, Hugo indignantly forbade further performances. The opera is seldom performed today but much of the music, especially the famous *Brindisi,* or drinking song, is still popular.

Linda di Chamounix (Selection): Linda di Chamounix, one of Donizetti's last operas, was written and produced while the composer was in Vienna in 1842. The action takes place in the French Alps during the reign of Louis XV. The opera is famous for several arias of a brilliant nature which are standard items in the repertory of coloratura sopranos.

La Favorita (Selection): La Favorita contains some of the most dramatic music Donizetti ever wrote. The last act in particular is notable in this respect. An indication of the composer's amazing facility is the fact that this entire act was written in less than four hours. The opera is based on a French melodrama and was first produced in Paris in 1840.

Paul Dukas

BORN Paris, October 1, 1865
DIED Paris, May 18, 1935

ARRANGED FOR BAND:

Scherzo: THE SORCERER'S APPRENTICE (B&H

DUKAS has long been considered in France one of the leading composers of his time. Outside of France he is famous for three or four compositions, but the main body of his work, which embraces an enormous variety of forms, is not extremely familiar. The music of Dukas exhibits a characteristically French perfection of craftsmanship, and a polish in the writing which does not, however, exclude considerable depth of content.

Dukas' opera, *Ariane and Bluebeard,* has been performed in America, and achieved considerable success throughout the world. Dukas' orchestration is exceptionally brilliant.

Scherzo, The Sorcerer's Apprentice: This popular descriptive composition is founded on Goethe's ballad of the same name. It concerns the apprentice of a magician who, when his master leaves the house, proceeds to experiment with the latter's magic formulae. He begins by commanding a broom to fetch water to put in the pitchers. The broom obeys, and the unfortunate apprentice then discovers that he cannot stop it. Soon the room begins to fill with water; finally, in desperation, the apprentice decides on heroic measures. As the broom enters with more water, he takes a hatchet and splits the broom in halves. This puts the finishing touches to the calamity, for both parts of the broom then commence to carry water. The sorcerer, however, arrives at that moment, takes in the situation, commands the broom to stop, and properly rebukes the experimenter.

The Sorcerer's Apprentice was first performed in Paris in 1897. It was first played in America, under the direction of Theodore Thomas, at a concert in Chicago, in 1899.

Antonin Dvořák

BORN Mulhausen, Bohemia, September 8, 1841
DIED Prague, May 1, 1904

WORKS ARRANGED FOR BAND:

"NEW WORLD" SYMPHONY: *Largo* (B&H; F
Scherzo (B&H
Finale (F
SLAVONIC DANCES Nos. 1, 2, 3, 4, 6, 7, 10, 11 (B&H
SLAVONIC DANCES Nos. 1, 3, 7, 8 (F) No. 4 (D
SLAVONIC DANCES Nos. 1-8, 10, 16 (AMP
BOHEMIA OVERTURE (F
HUMORESQUE, Opus 101, No. 7 (F; CB; EV; D; B&H; AMP; J
SONGS MY MOTHER TAUGHT ME (F
INDIAN LAMENT (F
LEGENDS (Opus 59) (AMP

DVOŘÁK, together with Smetana, represents both the foundation and the culmination of the Bohemian (Czech) school of music. Like Grieg and the composers of the neo-Russian school, Dvořák grounded himself firmly in the folk-music of his native land. To this background, Dvořák brought exceptional gifts; he has been compared to Schubert for the spontaneity and warmth of his many compositions. In regard to the form of his compositions he modeled himself on the classical masters, and particularly admired Brahms, who was his staunch friend and adviser.

Dvořák was exceptionally successful during his lifetime. His early works were well received, and with the appearance of the *Slavonic Dances* in 1878, he became a world figure. He was twice invited to England as conductor, and received the honorary degree of Doctor of Music at Cambridge in 1891. He also made successful tours in Germany and Russia. He received many honors from his own country as well as others.

In 1892, Dvořák came to America to accept the directorship of the National Conservatory of Music in New York. He remained three years in America, spending part of the time at the Czech colony at Spillville, Iowa. Some of his most famous compositions date from this period.

On his return to Prague, Dvořák resumed his duties as Professor of Composition at the Conservatory. He was appointed Director of the Conservatory in 1901, and spent the last years of his life composing a series of operas and symphonic poems on national subjects.

✓ ✓ ✓

Symphony No. 5 in E Minor ("From the New World"): This work, one of the most famous and popular of all symphonies, was written while the composer was in New York. It received its first performance at a concert of the New York Philharmonic Society, under the direction of Anton Seidl, in 1893. Contrary to a wide-spread belief, the work is entirely original in conception, although some of the themes resemble Negro spirituals and Indian folk songs. Dvořák was greatly attracted to the music of the Negro people, but all the music he wrote bears the stamp of his own personality.

The *Largo* contains one of Dvořák's most familiar melodies in the shape of the English horn solo with which the movement opens. The very song-like character of the theme has caused it to be arranged in many forms. It is said that Dvořák had in mind the story of Hiawatha and Minnehaha when composing this movement.

The *Scherzo,* like all other movements of the symphony, begins with a few bars of introduction. The tempo of the movement is *molto vivace.* The main section of the *Scherzo* has two themes, both presented in the wood-winds. The principal theme of the first movement makes itself heard fragmentarily. The trio offers a momentary contrast, after which the *Scherzo* returns, with the theme from the first movement again heard in the coda.

The *finale* recapitulates the material of all the other movements. The principal theme is announced in the brasses after a few measures of introduction. A lively bridge passage leads to the second theme, which is much quieter and more song-like in character. During the development echoes of the themes of preceding movements are heard: notably the English horn melody of the slow movement and the main theme of the first movement. These are worked in with the material from the *Finale* itself. The recapitulation is rather short and is followed by a coda based on the principal themes of the first movement and the *Finale,* but also including material from the remaining movements of the symphony.

Slavonic Dances: The *Slavonic Dances* justly established Dvořák's fame. They were originally written for pianoforte (four hands), but are best-known in orchestral form. In these brilliant and typical dances, Dvořák utilized not only Czech melodies but also those of other Slavonic nations such as the Jugoslavs and Poles. The forms include the Furiant, Polka, Reel and slow Waltz.

Legends (*Opus No. 59*): Dvořák composed ten *Legends* for piano duet which he arranged for orchestra in 1881. Like many of his works these legends were inspired by episodes from Bohemian history, and represent an idealization of Bohemian national music.

Humoresque: There is little left to say about this famous composition, which is as well-known as any piece of music ever written. It was originally composed for pianoforte, and is the seventh of a set, Opus 101, published in 1894. This composition, which has come to be known as *The* Humoresque, has so completely overshadowed the other Humoresques of the set, that almost none of the latter is known.

Indian Lament: The *Indian Lament* is taken from Dvořák's *Sonatina for Violin and Piano,* Opus 100. A product of Dvořák's sojourn in America, it reflects the interest taken by the composer in the indigenous music of the American natives.

Waltz: Among Dvořák's numerous shorter compositions for pianoforte are many waltzes, a good number of them based on Bohemian tunes. Several of the more popular ones were arranged for orchestra and later adapted for band, in which form they are extremely pleasing and effective.

Songs My Mother Taught Me: This popular composition is one of a set of Gypsy songs written by Dvořák. The songs are melancholy in character, having been written "to commemorate the sorrows of a wandering race." This song has the nostalgic quality of Gypsy music. "And when I sing these songs to my own children," the verse concludes, "the tears run down my brown cheeks also."

Overture, "Bohemia": Those wishing to compare this band arrangement with an orchestral original will not succeed in finding an overture by Dvořák entitled "Bohemia." This title was given by the arranger to Dvořák's orchestral overture, Opus 62, which bears the title *Kde Domuv Muj,* literally translatable as *Where Is My Home?* and usually given as simply *My Home.* In many catalogues the German equivalent, *Mein Heim,* is given.

The overture, by whatever name it may be called, is one

of the many which Dvořák wrote in a purely nationalistic vein. It is founded on a Czech hymn, and was in fact written as part of the incidental music for a Czech play, *J. K. Tyl*, produced in 1882.

(Sir) Edward Elgar

BORN Broadheath, England, June 2, 1857
DIED London, February 23, 1934

WORKS ARRANGED FOR BAND:

Marches: POMP AND CIRCUMSTANCE (B&H
Triumphal March, THE CROWN OF INDIA (B&H
Suites: "THE CROWN OF INDIA" (B&H
THREE BAVARIAN DANCES (B&H
THE WAND OF YOUTH (N
Overture: COCKAIGNE
CORONATION ODE (B&H
SURSUM CORDA (B&H
SALUT D'AMOUR (B&H; F; J
EMPIRE MARCH (B&H
Numerous Salon Pieces and Miscellaneous (N; B&H

ALTHOUGH SIR EDWARD ELGAR is known to band audiences primarily as the composer of the *Pomp and Circumstance* Marches, he was the outstanding English composer of his day, and perhaps the best-known figure in English music since Purcell. He composed in almost all of the large forms, many of his major works now occupying a regular place in the choral and orchestral repertory. These works include the magnificent oratorio, *The Dream of Gerontius,* which first revealed Elgar's great talent to the world, the *Enigma Variations,* two symphonies and numerous other compositions of various types. Elgar's position during his lifetime was practically unique in that he was regarded almost as the "official" national composer, or composer-laureate. He was knighted in 1904, received the Order of Merit in 1911, and was made "Master of the King's Musick" in 1924.

Marches: Pomp and Circumstance, Opus 39. The *Pomp and Circumstance* marches for orchestra, five in number, appeared between 1904 and 1907, during the most productive period of Elgar's career. The first of them is the most famous; its trio, arranged by the composer as part of an Ode for the coronation of Edward VII, is known to all as *Land of Hope and Glory*. All of these marches have a great breadth and irresistible swing, together with a brilliant sense of pageantry.

Three Bavarian Dances:
I. Sonnenbichl (The Dance)
II. In Hammersbach (Lullaby)
III. Bei Murnau (The Marksmen)

These three dances are orchestral adaptations of the first, third and sixth numbers of Elgar's choral suite, *From the Bavarian Highlands,* Opus 27, written after a sojourn in the Bavarian Alps. The titles of the pieces are the names of communities, and it is to be supposed that the composer wished to sketch their characters in notes. The dances are of a pleasing and graceful nature, patterned somewhat after the German country dances.

Suite: The Crown of India:
I. Dance of the Nautch Girls
II. Menuetto
III. Warrior's Dance
IV. Interlude
V. March of the Mogul Emperors

This suite was arranged from a Royal Masque composed by Elgar for the Delhi Durbar of 1912, when King George V, in accordance with British custom, was proclaimed Emperor of India. Several numbers which originally formed part of the Masque are not included in this suite. The music is full of color and, like much of the composer's work, is marked by intense national feeling. The marches in particular are splendid examples of Elgar's mastery of the "symphonic march," a medium which he may be said to have created and carried to its height in the famous *Pomp and Circumstance* series.

Triumphal March, The Crown of India: (see above.)

The Triumphal March, *The Crown of India,* was a part of the music Elgar composed for the Royal Masque given at the Delhi Durbar in 1912. It was not, however, included in the concert suite which the composer later extracted from the Masque, but was published separately.

Suite No. 2: The Wand of Youth:

I. March
II. The Little Bells
III. Moths and Butterflies
IV. The Fountain Dance
V. The Tame Bear
VI. The Wild Bears

Elgar composed two suites under the title *The Wand of Youth.* They bear the opus numbers 1a and 1b. Both suites are arrangements of music the composer wrote for a children's play when he was about twelve years of age. From these early sketches Elgar developed the two suites as they now stand, changing little but the instrumentation. The music has a great deal of youthful charm and shows a highly developed poetic imagination. The first concert performance of the second suite took place at the Worcester (England) Music Festival in 1908.

Overture, Cockaigne (In London Town): Were it not for the fact that Elgar's *Cockaigne* overture more or less adheres to the traditional form, it could more properly be called a tone-poem or orchestral picture of London. In the composer's words, it is intended to describe "the sights a pair of lovers encounter during an afternoon's stroll in that city." It is not a mystical picture of the city, like Delius' *Paris,* but a simple series of street scenes, full of animation, and what might be called "every-day-ness." The lovers enjoy their romance, are interrupted by children, watch a marching military band, go into a church and encounter such things as may quite reasonably be expected. The themes for each of these are easily recognizable and are interwoven with great skill in the score. The overture was first performed at a concert of the London Philharmonic Society in 1901.

Coronation Ode: This majestic composition was written for the coronation of George V in 1911. It is in several movements, the most familiar of which is that based on the trio of the first *Pomp and Circumstance* march. In the *Coronation Ode* this broad and inspiring melody is used with the words, *Land of Hope and Glory.*

Sursum Corda (*Lift Up Your Hearts!*) Op. 11: *Sursum Corda* was originally written for brass, strings and organ. In its brief length it is extremely expressive, conveying a sentiment of elevated religiousness and noble strength. The serene and broad quality of Elgar's best music pervades the composition, which is one of the composer's most popular shorter works.

Salut d'Amour (*Love's Greeting*), Opus 12: This popular salon piece was originally written for violin and piano, but has since been arranged for any other combinations. It represents the composer of *The Dream of Gerontius* in a light and pleasing vein.

Carl Engel

BORN Paris, July 21, 1883

WRITTEN FOR BAND:

ACADEMIC PROCESSIONAL MARCH (S

DR. CARL ENGEL is one of the leading musical scholars of the present day. He received his musical education in Europe. Upon coming to the United States, Dr. Engel became editor and adviser for a Boston music publisher, and in 1921 was called upon to succeed O. G. Sonneck as chief of the Music Division of the Library of Congress, remaining in this post for many years until he once again returned to editorial and administrative work in the publishing field. Dr. Engel is known for his many penetrating and scholarly contributions to *The Musical Quarterly* and other periodicals; he has been editor of *The Musical Quarterly* for the past several years.

In addition to his other pursuits, Dr. Engel has composed a number of works for piano, voice and violin. The *Academic Processional March* was written for band in 1938. It was "written for and dedicated to Oberlin College" in recognition of the bestowal of an honorary degree upon the composer by that institution.

Paul Fauchet

BORN France, 1858

WRITTEN FOR BAND:

SYMPHONY IN B♭ FOR BAND (Overture & Finale) (W

LITTLE is known about the composer of what is possibly the first symphony ever written for band. Fauchet was *chef-de-chant* (chorus-master) at the Opéra Comique of Paris, and also composed a number of light operas. His symphony was first performed by the Garde Républicaine band in 1926, and received its first American performance in 1933 at a concert of the Carleton Symphonic Band under James R. Gillette.

The symphony is really more like a concert suite than a true symphony. Its four movements are entitled *Overture, Nocturne, Scherzo* and *Finale*. The *Overture* and *Finale* are both in elaborated two-part form rather than in sonata and rondo form. The score calls for a large band.

Friedrich von Flotow

BORN Mecklenburg, Germany, April 27, 1812
DIED Darmstadt, Germany, January 24, 1883

WORKS ARRANGED FOR BAND:

Overture: MARTHA (F; B&H
Selections: MARTHA (CB; F; Ba; Ru; Fil
Overture: STRADELLA (C; CB; F
Selections: STRADELLA (F

FLOTOW was the son of a landed nobleman, and was educated with a view to the diplomatic service. A stay in Paris, however, where he came into contact with the artistic life of the period, awakened in him the desire to compose. A number of his operas attained some success during his lifetime, but today only *Stradella* and *Martha* are remembered.

✓ ✓ ✓

Martha was first written as a ballet, and as such was produced in 1844. Later Flotow enlarged and remodelled it. In its final form it was produced in Vienna, Nov. 25, 1847, where it was enthusiastically received. The opera is full of well-known airs, including *The Last Rose of Summer*.

✓

Stradella was first brought out as a short lyric sketch in 1837. Rewritten as an opera, and produced in Hamburg in 1844, it had an extraordinary success. This libretto is founded on the life of a famous Italian composer of the seventeenth century, whose talents for intrigue were on a par with his gifts for music.

César Auguste Franck

BORN Liège, Belgium, December 10, 1822
DIED Paris, November 8, 1890

WORKS ARRANGED FOR BAND:

Symphonic Piece from THE REDEMPTION (F; C
SYMPHONY IN D MINOR (Finale) (W

CÉSAR FRANCK brought to nineteenth-century French music a dignity and earnestness which to a great extent it lacked. Although born in Belgium, he passed most of his life in Paris, was influenced by the artistic life of France, and in turn influenced an entire school of French composers who followed him.

His life was the peaceful one of a church organist; his name is always associated with that of the church of Ste. Clotilde to which he was appointed in 1858. He was almost completely unappreciated as a composer during his lifetime, except by a devoted group of disciples. Gounod greeted the first performance of his great symphony with a disdainful sneer, and most of his other works were complete failures with the public. A small group gathered about him and championed his work, but it was not until a year before his death that Franck could be said to have known success.

Franck was appointed Professor of Organ at the Conservatory in 1872, and it is from this date that his best work begins. In 1887 he was belatedly recognized by the government and awarded the Legion of Honor. Even then, he was recognized not as a composer but as a teacher of organ.

It was not unnatural that the tranquil richness of Franck's music should suffer in competition with Gounod's shallow theatricality. Franck's musical expression was largely determined by his practice as organist; it was hence contrapuntal in texture and undramatic in substance.

Since his death his single symphony, in D minor, has taken its place in the great symphonic tradition, and has become one of the most beloved of all symphonies among concert audiences. His organ works rank with the greatest for that instrument.

Symphonic Piece from *The Redemption:* Franck originally wrote *The Redemption* as a setting of a poem by Edouard Blau, calling the work a "poem-symphony." The best-known portion of the work is this instrumental interlude, which is often played in concert. It is representative of Franck's sober beauty of musical expression and religious feeling. The work falls into three sections, followed by a coda. As is often the case in Franck's music, themes from the first section are worked in contrapuntally with the themes of the finale, giving unusual unity of structure. *The Redemption* was composed in 1872, from earlier sketches, and thus stands at the beginning of the composer's mature period.

Symphony in D Minor (*Finale*): César Franck's only symphony had its first performance at the Paris Conservatory on February 17, 1889. Whether envy or stupidity lay behind its cold reception, the fact remains that the composer was above being troubled by the lack of applause, and remarked only that "it sounded well." According to Vincent D'Indy, it was considered absolutely criminal of the composer to have given a solo passage to the English horn; such a thing was quite unheard of by the professors at the Conservatory. Gounod, too, expressed the sentiment that the symphony was "the affirmation of incompetence pushed to dogmatic lengths." It is reported that the composer of *Faust* swept from the hall surrounded by his numerous hangers-on, pontificating mightily.

The *D Minor Symphony* is in many ways the fullest expression of Franck's genius. Its development and structure depend altogether on the quality of the ideas; they are purely personal, original, completely integrated. With Franck the material in hand dictated the necessary formal plan. His symphonic structure certainly differs from that of Beethoven, yet the logical sequence is easily enough ascertainable.

The symphony is in three movements, of which only the *Finale* has been published for band. Marked *allegro non troppo,* in 2/2 time, the *Finale* opens with a sweeping theme (originally in the 'cellos) which is extensively developed. The brasses introduce the second theme, after which a sombre third theme is sounded in the basses. The development brings back the beautiful English horn solo of the second movement, sonorously restated by the full band. This section is in 3/4 time. For the coda, the time goes back to 2/2. Reminiscences of the themes of the first two movements are heard, but the work closes with a triumphant restatement of the principal theme of the *Finale.*

(Sir) Edward German

BORN Shropshire, England, February 17, 1862
DIED London, November 11, 1936

WORKS ARRANGED FOR BAND:

WELSH RHAPSODY (N
Three Dances from HENRY VIII (F; N
Dances from NELL GWYN (C
Three Dances from TOM JONES (C
Three Dances from AS YOU LIKE IT (N
Fantasie: MERRIE ENGLAND (C; B&H
Suite: THE TEMPTER (C
BOURRÉE AND GIGUE (N
CORONATION MARCH and HYMN (N
Overture to RICHARD III (N

THE real name of this popular English composer was Edward German Jones. To him belongs the distinction of being the most successful composer who followed in the footsteps of Sir Arthur Sullivan. His comic operas, however, have not kept place alongside those of the immortal Savoyard, and he is best known today for his incidental music to various plays. He was knighted in 1928.

In 1888 German was engaged as conductor at the Globe Theatre in London, then under the direction of Richard Mansfield. He thus was given the opportunity for writing the incidental music to many Shakespearean productions. Much of this music, arranged as concert suites and extracts, has attained universal popularity.

ʼ ʼ ʼ

Three Dances from *Henry VIII:* (1. Morris Dance; 2. Shepherd's Dance; 3. Torch Dance). These dances are taken from the incidental music to Shakespeare's *Henry VIII*, as given by Sir Henry Irving in London in 1892. The music was hailed by theatre-goers as something much better than what was expected from such incidental music, and did much to establish German's reputation. The first of these pieces is a fine example of a modern adaptation of the ancient English Morris Dance. All three have become extremely popular.

Dances from *Nell Gwyn:* (1. Country Dance 2. Pastoral Dance 3. Merrymakers' Dance). These three beautiful dances form part of the incidental music to an historical play presented at the Prince of Wales Theatre in 1900. They are rather similar in character to the more famous dances from *Henry VIII,* having a distinctly English character due to the use of traditional English folk-dance rhythms.

Three Dances from *Tom Jones:* German's comic operas compare quite favorably with those of Sir Arthur Sullivan, whose tradition he carried on. *Tom Jones,* produced in 1907, contains some of the composer's finest writing. It was produced in New York after achieving a great success in London.

Bourrée and Gigue: These two delightful numbers are taken from the incidental music written by German for the production of Shakespeare's *Much Ado About Nothing* at the St. James Theatre, London, in 1898. They show German's admirable and original handling of dance-forms, and have attained wide popularity.

Coronation March and *Hymn:* The *Coronation March* and *Hymn* were written for the coronation of George V in 1911, and were performed at Westminster Abbey. The music is stately in character and shows German's talents for writing serious music. Indeed, aside from the dances which are associated with his name, German composed two symphonies, several symphonic poems, and other works in large forms.

George Gershwin

BORN Brooklyn, New York, September 28, 1898
DIED Hollywood, California, July 11, 1937

ARRANGED FOR BAND:

RHAPSODY IN BLUE (H

GEORGE GERSHWIN started his professional career at the age of seventeen as a "piano-plugger" for a popular music house. Not long afterwards he began to compose popular tunes and to contribute musical numbers to musical comedies. His success in this field was prodigious, and he rapidly achieved the reputation of being one of the most gifted of the popular composers. Gershwin, however, had the desire to do bigger and more serious things, and continued his studies of theory and composition in New York under Rubin Goldmark. The first and most celebrated of his larger compositions was written during this period. This was the *Rhapsody in Blue,* first performed by Paul Whiteman and his orchestra in 1923. From that time on, Gershwin was known as the leading "jazz" composer of the day and the leader of the group interested in "symphonic jazz."

Gershwin's other large works, although less known, are equally worthy of attention. These include a *Concerto* for Piano and Orchestra, a *Cuban Overture,* a *Second Rhapsody,* and *An American in Paris.* In addition Gershwin composed two operas, *Porgy and Bess* and *135th Street.* His numerous musical comedy scores include *Of Thee I Sing* (Pulitzer Prize, 1931), *Strike up the Band, Lady, Be Good,* etc.

James Robert Gillette

BORN Roseboom, N. Y., May 30, 1886

WORKS WRITTEN FOR BAND:

CABINS (W
VISTAS (W
FUGAL FANTASY (W
MUSING (D
COTTON BLOSSOMS (D
CROSSROADS (Kjos

JAMES R. GILLETTE is well known as organist and composer. He was formerly conductor of the Carleton Symphony Band of Carleton College, Northfield, Minnesota, and was also professor of organ at that institution. Under his direction the Carleton Band became known as one of the best college bands in America. Mr. Gillette has written many works for organ and symphony orchestra, and in addition to his original compositions has made a number of symphonic transcriptions for band.

Mr. Gillette has composed a *Symphony* and a *Sinfonietta* for band in addition to the compositions enumerated above.

Cabins: This number is in the form of a rhapsody. The material is Southern in idiom and pictures a plantation on a warm summer evening.

Vistas: This composition is of a meditative and tranquil character, the music evoking the idea of distances and broad expanses.

Fugal Fantasy: This number is a free fantasy on the fugal subject which serves as its main theme.

Musing: The composer states that the reflective mood of this piece is perhaps suggestive of a pleasant dream.

Cotton Blossoms: This composition, like the composer's *Cabins,* is Southern in idiom and treatment.

Crossroads: In this number the composer has attempted to picture rural life as lived at a crossing of the country highways.

Alexander Constantinovitch Glazounov

BORN St. Petersburg, Russia, August 10, 1865
DIED Paris, March 21, 1936

WORKS ARRANGED FOR BAND:

Ballet, THE SEASONS (C
Bacchanale from THE SEASONS (F
Overture, CARNIVAL (C
CONCERT WALTZ (B&H
NOVELETTE (F
MEDITATION (F

ALTHOUGH GLAZOUNOV was a member of Balakirev's group, he was less purely Russian in his music than most of the famous Russian composers. Influences of Brahms, in particular, may be discerned in Glazounov's art. Glazounov's symphonies show his fondness for the classical forms. These works, together with a violin concerto and a number of smaller compositions, have securely established Glazounov's fame.

⁄ ⁄ ⁄

Suite from the Ballet, The Seasons:

I. Barcarolle
  a. Andante
  b. Variation
  c. Coda
II. Waltz of the Cornflowers and Poppies
III. Petit Adagio
IV. Bacchanale

Glazounov has written a number of effective ballets in addition to his more imposing symphonies and concertos. *The Seasons* is the best known of these. The ballet is divided into four tableaux, corresponding to the seasons. The suite consists of selected numbers from the entire ballet, and has no connection with its choreographic divisions. The first number, the *Barcarolle,* is interesting for the clarinet solo which occurs during its middle part. The *Bacchanale* is vividly compelling in its movement. Not as unrestrained as the title indicates, it nevertheless presents a tableau of lively action and high color.

Overture, Carnival: This overture was written in 1893 and originally scored for orchestra and organ. It is brilliant and energetic in character, as the title would suggest. The themes are developed in a highly interesting manner, with a number of strongly contrasting episodes. The form is rather free, but derived from the classical outlines of the sonata. The closing section is worked out in brilliant contrapuntal fashion.

Concert Waltz: This band arrangement has been made from Glazounov's *First Concert Waltz* for orchestra, Opus 47. It is a light and pleasing number in quasi-ballet style.

Novelette: This is the second of two piano pieces written by Glazounov as Opus 22.

Meditation: This pleasing melody is taken from a composition for violin and pianoforte, bearing the opus number 32.

Reinhold Moritzovitch Gliere

BORN Kiev, Russia, December 30, 1874

WORK ARRANGED FOR BAND:

Russian Sailors' Dance ("Yablochko")
from THE RED POPPY (F

GLIERE studied at the Moscow Conservatory under such famed composers as Taneiev and Ippolitov-Ivanov. His works include several symphonies and other orchestral compositions as well as a number of songs and some chamber music. He is at present Professor of Composition at the Moscow Conservatory.

The Ballet, *The Red Poppy,* was written and produced in 1927. It deals with an uprising on board a Chinese ship and the successful intervention of Russian sailors. The *Dance of the Russian Sailors* is the best known excerpt from the ballet, and is founded on the Russian folk tune, *Yablochko* (*Little Apple*). The dance takes the form of a series of variations on this striking tune.

(*Yablochko* itself has an interesting history. One of the most popular tunes of Russia, it has been used in turn as a revolutionary and as a counter-revolutionary song. Words are fitted to it to suit the occasion. The leader of a peasant movement in the Crimea, one "Batka" Makhno, made it peculiarly his own during the years of the Revolution and Civil War.)

Michael Ivanovich Glinka

BORN Novospasskoi, Russia, June 2, 1803
DIED Berlin, February 15, 1857

WORKS ARRANGED FOR BAND:

Overtures: RUSSLAN AND LUDMILLA (F; B&H
A LIFE FOR THE TSAR (F; AMP
Finale from A LIFE FOR THE TSAR (F
Fantasia, KAMARINSKAIA (B&H
RUSSIAN DANCE (D
Polonaise from A LIFE FOR THE TSAR (N; B&H
Selections from A LIFE FOR THE TSAR (B&H
VALSE FANTASIE (Birch

GLINKA was brought up in an intensely musical atmosphere, but his formal studies in music were rather desultory. Like many of the greatest Russian composers, his attitude toward his art was that of the amateur. He had no intention of devoting himself to composition until after his return from a trip to Italy, where he had become friendly with Donizetti and Bellini. He was then entering his thirtieth year; only at that time did he begin to feel truly drawn to the work of composing. His great ambition was to compose a Russian national opera. In this he was warmly encouraged by the section of the Russian intelligentsia which was struggling toward a revival of native traditions, as opposed to those who favored the Westernization of Russian culture.

His success in his efforts was complete with the productions of *A Life for the Tsar* and *Russlan and Ludmilla.* (See notes below.) He intended to add a third opera to these, but never realized the intention. As his fame grew, he traveled more and more. Journeys to Italy, France and Spain occupied his time; his visit to Spain inspired several of his later works. Toward the end of his life he returned to St. Petersburg, where he completed his *Autobiography*, an interesting commentary on the musical life of Russia in that period.

⸙ ⸙ ⸙

A Life for the Tsar: The production of *A Life for the Tsar* in 1836, actually marked the birth of a genuinely Russian school of music. Glinka's enthusiasm for the work was so great that during its composition he was continually ahead of his librettists. The music is brilliant and sparkling, and makes excellent use of Russian folk material with its characteristic five-beat and seven-beat measures. Nor is the music alone national; the libretto is founded on a famous episode in Russian history: the delivery of Russia from the Poles through the heroism of Ivan Soussanine, who gave his life for the Tsar Michael Feodorovitch, founder of the Romanoff dynasty (1613-1645). Glinka emphasized the central theme of the opera by making use of Polish tunes as well as Russian in his score.

The first performance of the work, at the Imperial Theatre in St. Petersburg on December 9, 1836, caused wild enthusiasm. The impetus given by Glinka's work to the art of musical composition in Russia can hardly be overestimated.

The overture to *A Life for the Tsar* is constructed along classical lines. A slow introduction leads to the main section, which is very rapid in tempo and light in movement. The development is rather briefer, and the coda rather longer than is usual.

The finale is an elaborate scene featuring two choruses and two stage bands. It depicts the Tsar's triumphant entry into Moscow, and is brilliant in its movement and orchestral coloration.

⸙

Overture, Russlan and Ludmilla: After the completion of *A Life for the Tsar*, Glinka immediately began work on an opera based on Pushkin's famous opera, *Russlan and Ludmilla.* The composition of his second opera, however, occupied Glinka several years, during which time he had considerable trouble with his librettists. The first performance of the work was not given until 1842. It did not have the immediate success which was accorded to the first opera, although today it is a favorite. There is some similarity of musical treatment in Glinka's two operas. In *A Life for the Tsar,* the composer contrasted Russian and Polish melodies; in *Russlan and Ludmilla,* the contrast is between Russian and Tartar airs. These are not used in the overture, which is thematically independent of the opera, and in classic form. The overture is further remarkable in that it remains in one tempo from beginning to end. It is a brilliant orchestral tour-de-force, full of the liveliest animation and exuberance.

Kamarinskaia: The fantasia, *Kamarinskaia,* sometimes called *A Slavonic Wedding,* was composed in the fall of 1848. Glinka had been examining a collection of Russian folk-tunes and had found among them a number of "wedding-songs," several of which aroused his enthusiasm. (Russian folk-music is particularly rich in these "wedding-songs"; almost the whole of the third volume of Rimsky-Korsakov's collection is given over to them.) The composer selected two: *Over the High Hills,* and the dance-song, *Kamarinskaia,* intending to write a piece for pianoforte based on them. He soon developed the work into an orchestral fantasia, entitled *Wedding Song and Dance.* According to his autobiography, he had no programmatic intentions whatsoever in connection with the composition, and was both surprised and amused when critics commented on his realistic representation of peasant scenes.

After a few bars of introduction the melody of *Over the*

High Hills appears. The dance-song *Kamarinskaia,* occurs as second theme. The music becomes more and more rapid as the themes are worked out, and at the conclusion the dance assumes the form of the Hopak. The score is marked by passages of the utmost brilliance and ingenuity, and throughout has an irresistible swing.

Christoph Willibald Gluck

BORN Weidenwang, Germany, July 2, 1714
DIED Vienna, November 15, 1787

WORKS ARRANGED FOR BAND:

Overture, IPHIGENIA IN AULIS (F; B&H
Hymn from ALCESTIS (F
Selections from IPHIGENIA IN TAURIS (B&H
Selections from ORPHEUS (B&H

TO GLUCK belongs the distinction of having inaugurated a series of profound reforms in the domain of Grand Opera. At the time Gluck began composing, Grand Opera in France had reached a very low level. For the most part, the operas of the time consisted of series of superficial airs strung together with little regard for dramatic effect. Gluck was a serious thinker as well as a great musician, and his revolt against the prevailing type of operatic composition caused the same kind of critical storm which later greeted Wagner.

Gluck's early operas were performed in Vienna and London with no great success. It was not until the production of *Iphigenia in Aulis* at the Paris Opera in 1774 that the genius of the composer was fully appreciated. The bitter disputes between the partisans of Gluck and those of Piccinni ultimately resulted in the triumph of the former.

Although Gluck composed in forms other than that of the opera, his fame rests entirely upon his dramatic compositions. He banished superficiality from his work, introduced dramatic declamation, enlarged the orchestra and increased its importance, and in short restored opera to a dignified and elevated plane. Toward the end of his life his art was universally appreciated and he died in the enjoyment of fame and fortune.

Overture, Iphigenia in Aulis: Iphigenia in Aulis was the first of Gluck's greater operas. It follows closely Racine's classic tragedy, just as the latter followed that of Euripides. Gluck's music is lofty in conception and succeeds in creating an epic atmosphere. The dramatic effects are extremely skillful and the whole composition is rich in invention.

The overture was a favorite of Richard Wagner who made the concert version now generally used. Speaking of the overture, Wagner said that "it prepares us for a drama the highest meaning of which it reveals to us at the outset, and so leads us to understand the action which immediately follows."

Hymn from *Alcestis: Alcestis* was one of the first operas to reveal the full power of Gluck as a dramatic composer. The work is founded on the tragedy of Euripides, and in the music Gluck gave a most intense musical expression to the idea of noble self-sacrifice. The orchestral parts of this opera are of the greatest interest and worth, while the choruses are often overpowering in effect. The *Hymn* is one of the finest numbers in the entire range of eighteenth-century opera.

Alcestis was first produced in Vienna in 1767. Gluck later re-arranged it for the Paris Opera, where its production in 1776 was a brilliant success.

Selections from *Iphigenia in Tauris: Iphigenia in Tauris* is generally accepted as the greatest of Gluck's operas. It is based on the tragedy of Euripides; both in content and in style it is an admirable sequel to *Iphigenia in Aulis,* written and produced some five years earlier. The later opera was first given in Paris on May 18, 1779, at the height of the furious controversy between the Gluckists and the Piccinnists. Gluck's opera was greeted with deserved success; Piccinni immediately began work on an opera using the same theme. The latter's work, however, only resulted in his own discomfiture, for his music seemed insipidly pretty compared to the grandeur and intensity of his rival's score.

Selections from *Orpheus: Orpheus and Eurydice,* produced at Vienna in 1762, was the first opera in which Gluck attempted to carry out some of his fundamental ideas of opera reform. Although its success was unmistakable, it was not followed immediately by other works of the same quality, for Gluck had much difficulty in obtaining support. It was not until the success of *Iphigenia in Aulis* in 1774 that Gluck was sufficiently encouraged to rewrite *Orpheus* for the Paris Opera. The revised version was given there on August 2, 1774, and was very favorably received. The melodic charm of the work is great; of all the operas of Gluck it is the one most frequently revived today. The story is of course derived from the well-known Greek myth.

Benjamin Louis Paul Godard

BORN Paris, August 18, 1849
DIED Cannes, France, January 10, 1895

WORKS ARRANGED FOR BAND:

Suite, SCÈNES POÉTIQUES (F
DANSE DES BOHÉMIENS (C
Berceuse from JOCELYN
WALTZ, MAZURKA & INTERMEZZO (F

GODARD was a successful romantic composer who enjoyed a great reputation during his lifetime. An elaborate dramatic symphony, with soloists and chorus, won for him a prize offered by the City of Paris in 1878, and from that time on many of Godard's compositions were popular at Paris concerts. His salon music was extremely fashionable; many numbers are still popular today. They are characterized by a Parisian elegance and polish. Godard's operas were performed with some success but, except for isolated numbers, are now forgotten. The *Berceuse* (Lullaby) from the opera *Jocelyn,* founded on Lamartine's romantic poem, is the best-known of all Godard's compositions, and is played in many arrangements.

Jocelyn was first produced in Brussels in 1888.

The suite, *Poetic Scenes,* received its first performance at a concert of the Châtelet Orchestra in Paris in 1879.

Edwin Franko Goldman

BORN Louisville, Kentucky, January 1, 1878

ORIGINAL WORKS FOR BAND:

Grand Marches: AMERICA (F
UNIVERSITY (F
and more than seventy marches,
including: ON THE MALL
CHEERIO
PRIDE OF THE LAND, etc., etc.
Intermezzi, waltzes, etc.

EDWIN FRANKO GOLDMAN comes of one of the most famous musical families in America. It was thus not difficult for him to choose his career. As a boy his ambition was to become a great cornetist. By the time he was fourteen he had successfully passed the examination for a scholarship at the National Conservatory of Music. There he studied composition under the Conservatory's famous director, Antonin Dvořák. A year later, Jules Levy, then the world's greatest cornetist, accepted him as a free pupil.

At seventeen Goldman became solo cornetist of the Metropolitan Opera House Orchestra, playing under Toscanini, Mahler, Mancinelli and other illustrious conductors. He left the Metropolitan after ten years in order to lead his own band and orchestra concerts and to teach cornet and trumpet. At that time he had visions of founding a band which should be on a level with the finest orchestras of the world. The story of the Goldman Band is familiar to all those interested in the band movement. The summer concerts given since 1918 by that organization are a national institution.

Besides forming and directing his own band, Dr. Goldman was founder and first active president of the American Bandmasters' Association, which has been influential in raising the standards of bands and band music in America. He is now Honorary Life President of that body. Dr. Goldman's work has been recognized by many honors and distinctions. Besides New York, many other cities and civic bodies have conferred honors upon him. Philips University (1934) and Boston University (1936) have awarded him the honorary degree of Doctor of Music. He has been decorated by the governments of France, Italy and Czechoslovakia. In addition he holds honorary positions in more organizations than can be here enumerated. In 1932, John Philip Sousa's favorite baton was presented to him by Mrs. Sousa at one of the Goldman Band Concerts in Central Park. In a moving speech Mrs. Sousa said that she felt sure that her husband would have wanted this baton to go to Dr. Goldman.

Dr. Goldman's many marches are too well known to require comment. They are played throughout the world. The whistling and singing trios which he has incorporated into many of them give them an added attraction for all audiences.

Grand March, America: Dr. Goldman's second grand march was composed in May, 1935, for the occasion of the thousandth free concert given by the Goldman Band. The march had its first performance at that concert, which took place in Central Park on July 10, 1935.

America is written in $4/4$ time. It is broad in style and has several fanfare passages. In the finale, the hymn *America* is heard in the trombones and baritones as a counter-melody. This work is dedicated to President Franklin D. Roosevelt.

Grand March, University: This march was written in February, 1932, in honor of the one-hundredth anniversary celebration of the founding of New York University. It is dedicated to the late Chancellor Elmer Ellsworth Brown, The Trustees and Faculty of the University.

The march is dignified in character and has several fanfare passages. In the finale, the melody of *Auld Lang Syne* is heard in the trombones, baritone and euphonium against the leading melody of the trio.

Carl Goldmark

BORN Kesathely, Hungary, May 18, 1830
DIED Vienna, January 2, 1915

WORKS ARRANGED FOR BAND:

Overtures: SAKUNTALA (F; Ru
IN SPRINGTIME (Ba
Ballet Suite from THE QUEEN OF SHEBA (F
Processional March from THE QUEEN OF SHEBA (AMP
Symphonic Poem: RUSTIC WEDDING
Mvts. 2, 3, 4, 5 (B&H
Mvts. 2, 3, 4 (F

GOLDMARK's works are thoroughly representative of the romantic tendencies of the nineteenth century. Although not all of his music falls into the category of "program-music," most of it is poetic or descriptive in character, and reveals a dependence on literary suggestion rather than structural strength. He composed a number of operas, many of which were successful in his time, but he is best known for his colorful and melodious overtures. Goldmark was for a time a critic on a Vienna paper, and was one of the earliest to express an admiration for Wagner.

Overture, Sakuntala: It was this work which first established Goldmark's fame. Hanslick, the famous Viennese critic, recognized it as a work of great talent and spoke highly of its wealth of orchestral coloring. Goldmark was very fond of Oriental and semi-Oriental effects, a fondness nowhere better exhibited than in this overture. The composition is founded on the classic Hindu poem of Khalidasa (Sixth Century, A.D.). The hunting theme descriptive of the King and the love theme associated with the heroine may readily be recognized as the first and second themes of the overture. The work had its first performance in Vienna in 1865.

Overture, In Springtime: Whereas a great number of Goldmark's works show a love of exotic color, the overture *In Springtime* is a simple bit of nature-painting. It opens with a vigorous subject suggestive of the freshness of Spring, and continues to a quieter theme over which the songs of birds are heard. In the middle section there is an episode descriptive of a storm. The overture concludes with a long coda, in which the bird imitations are heard after new episodic material, the whole ending in brilliant and spirited fashion.

Processional March from *The Queen of Sheba:* Goldmark devoted ten years to the composition of his first opera, *The Queen of Sheba,* which was first performed in Vienna in 1875. The libretto is founded on the incident of the Queen's famous visit to King Solomon, but makes use of much purely imaginative material. The music makes frequent and skillful use of Oriental color, and is notable for its wealth of brilliant and sensuous melody. The processional march occurs at the entrance of the Queen, and is a fine example of effective pageanty.

Symphony, A Rustic Wedding
I. Wedding March (B&H
II. Bridal Song (B&H; F
III. Serenade (B&H; F
IV. In the Garden (B&H; F
V. Dance (not published for band

Although Goldmark called this work a symphony, it is more accurately described as a suite describing various phases of a country wedding. The five movements are clearly characterized by their titles; they are in the composer's most pleasing and melodious vein. The *Wedding March* is not in march form; it is a theme with thirteen variations. The second and third movements are in simple song-form, while the fourth is evidently intended to suggest a duet between the newlyweds. The rustic dance which concludes the suite is broken off by a recurrence of the duet theme, after which it resumes. It concludes with a broader passage, unmistakably suggesting the singing of a hymn by the assembled guests.

Antonio Carlos Gomez

BORN Compinas, Brazil, July 11, 1839
DIED Pará, Brazil, September 16, 1896

ARRANGED FOR BAND:

Overture: IL GUARANY (F; ABC; Ru
Selection: IL GUARANY (B&H

GOMEZ, perhaps the foremost composer South America has ever produced, was born in Brazil of Portuguese parents. He was sent to Italy at the expense of the Brazilian government and studied at the Milan Conservatory. His first stage work was performed at Rio De Janeiro when he was twenty-two years of age, and he achieved his first European success six years later. The production of *Il Guarany* at La Scala in 1870 established his fame. It was later produced in various opera houses of Europe, but has never been given in North America. The overture, however, is frequently played. In it may be heard melodies based on the music of the Amazon Indians. These are effectively introduced and lend an interesting color to the work.

Charles François Gounod

BORN Paris, June 17, 1818
DIED St. Cloud, France, October 17, 1893

WORKS ARRANGED FOR BAND:

FAUST: *Prelude* (D
Ballet Music (F; D
Kermesse (F
Fifth Act (F
Soldiers' Chorus (SF; CB; F
Waltz (F; CB
Selections (C; D; F; Ba; Fil
ROMEO AND JULIET: *Selections* (F; B&H; CB
Ballet Music (C
QUEEN OF SHEBA: *Ballet Music* (D; F
Grand March (C; F; B&H
MIREILLE: *Overture* (F
Selections (B&H
PHILEMON AND BAUCIS: *Selections* (F; B&H
Unfold, Ye Portals from THE REDEMPTION (F; SF
FUNERAL MARCH OF A MARIONETTE (B&H; F
SALTARELLO (B&H
SANCTUS from SOLEMN MASS (St. Cecilia Mass) (B&H; F
Bach-Gounod: AVE MARIA (B&H; F; Ba

THE success and influence enjoyed by Gounod during his lifetime are almost without parallel in the history of music. His dramatic and sacred compositions placed him from the very beginning of his career in the very front ranks of nineteenth-century composers. And although today his influence is no longer great, many of his works retain their enormous hold on the public. Probably no other opera ever written has had as many performances as *Faust.*

Gounod won the Prix de Rome in 1839. Of a profoundly religious turn of mind, Gounod devoted himself at this time to sacred composition, and even considered taking ecclesiastic orders. As late as 1849, a number of his compositions were published under the name of "the Abbé Charles Gounod." In 1851 an article appeared in London and Paris, proclaiming that in Gounod's works there was "a genius at once true and new"; this article, among other things, decided Gounod to come out of his retirement and resume his career as a composer. From that time on, he produced a series of operas, almost all of which were tremendous successes. During the last years of his life Gounod's religious turn of mind once more dominated him, and he devoted himself to the composition of several large and elaborate sacred works. He was made a Grand Officer of the Legion of Honor in 1880.

In Gounod's work the lyric element predominates, although dramatic force is certainly not lacking. Gounod's melodies almost always have a polish and a grace which lend them distinction. His harmonies are rich, sometimes original, but never forced. On the whole, his music may be said to have all of those qualities which make for enduring popularity.

✓ ✓ ✓

Faust: Faust was originally produced at the Théâtre Lyrique in Paris on March 9, 1859. Its triumphal success established Gounod as the leading operatic composer of the time, although there were critics who felt at first that the score was too greatly developed. As originally produced, the singing parts of *Faust* were interspersed with spoken dialogue; it was not until 1869 that the dialogue was replaced by recitatives and the work was produced as a grand opera. In its final form *Faust* has been played in all countries and translated into all languages.

The libretto does not follow the great drama of Goethe, but merely makes use of the episode dealing with Faust and Marguerite. The lyric and dramatic passages of the work reveal Gounod at his best, and are by turns sensuous, poetic and mystical in character.

A.) *Waltz.* The delightful *Waltz* occurs in the second act of the opera, during the Kermesse scene. The Kermesse is the name given to a village fair; the *Waltz* is sung by the assembled villagers.

B.) *Soldiers' Chorus.* The *Soldiers' Chorus* is one of the most famous portions of Gounod's opera. It occurs at the opening of the fourth act, when the victorious soldiers return from the war. Gounod wrote the number for an earlier opera, but later incorporated it in *Faust.*

C.) *Ballet Music.* The ballet of *Faust,* which is an essential part of the French production, is often omitted when the opera is given in America. It is interpolated in the last act. Mephistopheles conjures up the vision of a great palace, wherein are recreated the most beautiful courtesans of history. Faust beholds Cleopatra, Helen of Troy, Aspasia, Phryné and others, who with their attendants, perform dances for him. There are seven movements in the ballet, which concludes with a bacchanale. The apparition of Marguerite finally causes the scene of attractive sinfulness to vanish.

Romeo and Juliet: Romeo and Juliet is, after *Faust,* the greatest and most popular of Gounod's operas. Many people prefer it to the earlier work. The music of *Romeo and Juliet* is full of charming passages. The libretto, by Barbier and Carré, is patterned after Shakespeare's play. The work was first produced in Paris in 1867, and was well-received from the outset.

Queen of Sheba (*Ballet Music* and *March*): The success of *Faust* in 1859 led the public to expect great things of Gounod, but his opera *The Queen of Sheba,* produced in 1862, was rather a disappointment. Although the libretto was written by Gérard De Nerval, one of the outstanding literary figures of the time, it was not altogether suitable for the stage. Consequently the opera is hardly ever performed, and little of the music, aside from the ballet scenes and the choral march, has survived. The ballet music has great elegance and is quite popular, while the march by reason of its splendor is a general favorite with bands.

Overture, Mireille: The failure of the grand opera, *The Queen of Sheba,* led Gounod to turn his attention to lighter and more lyrical subjects for his next theatrical work. *Mireille,* which he brought out in 1864, is founded on the celebrated Provençal poem by Frédéric Mistral. Unfortunately the adaptation was badly made, and despite the very delightful music the opera was not a success. In 1876 *Mireille* was revived in abridged form and was well received. The overture, which like the opera is of a pastoral nature, has always kept its place in the repertory.

Selections from *Philemon and Baucis: Philemon and Baucis* was produced following *Faust* in 1860. It was a rewritten and elaborated version in three acts of a much earlier one-act opera written by Gounod. The work was inspired by La Fontaine's treatment of the famous myth. Unfortunately the libretto was rather a pastiche. The score, however, contains some of the most charming music Gounod wrote. It is in a much lighter vein than *Faust,* but exhibits the same elegance of detail and cleverness of treatment.

Unfold, Ye Portals, from *The Redemption:* On the title page of the sacred trilogy, *The Redemption,* Gounod wrote: "the work of my life." The composition is a product of Gounod's last period, after he had renounced the stage to devote himself to religious music. The work is characterized by a simplicity of style, although it occasionally borders on the sensuous and dramatic. The excerpt "Unfold, Ye Portals" is the best-known choral number. *The Redemption* was first performed at Birmingham, England, in 1882.

Sanctus from *St. Cecelia Mass* (*Solemn Mass*): The *St. Cecelia Mass* was first performed in Paris in 1858. As a whole it is not one of Gounod's most inspired works, being rather monotonous and repetitive in character. The *Sanctus*, however, is on a level with Gounod's finest sacred compositions, and has survived the oblivion to which the rest of the mass has been consigned.

Ave Maria (*Bach-Gounod*): Gounod's famous melody is written over the Prelude in C major from Bach's *Well-Tempered Clavichord*. In many European conservatories students are assigned this particular task, but certainly no other melody to this prelude has ever attained a fraction of the fame of this one.

Funeral March of a Marionette: This composition, originally written for orchestra, is an effective bit of serio-comic program music. An introductory fortissimo phrase denotes the breaking of the puppet. The following adagio portrays expressions of regret. The march proper, a grotesque allegretto in 6/8 time, then begins. It is interrupted by a fortissimo D major chord, which is the signal for the mourners to stop and refresh themselves. The episode ends with the return of the march for the homeward procession.

Saltarello: This *Saltarello* was composed by Gounod as an independent orchestral number. It was first performed in London in 1871. The Saltarello is a lively Roman dance, either in $3/4$ or $6/8$ time. The derivation of the name (from *saltare,* to leap or hop) gives sufficient indication of the character of the dance. (The spelling usually seen on concert programs is that given, although Petrocchi's Italian Dictionary lists "Salterello" as preferable.)

Percy Aldridge Grainger

BORN Melbourne, Australia, July 8, 1882

ORIGINAL WORKS FOR BAND:

(Including works arranged by Mr. Grainger from his own compositions.)

IRISH TUNE FROM COUNTY DERRY (F
SHEPHERD'S HEY (F
COLONIAL SONG (F
Irish Reel, "MOLLY ON THE SHORE" (F
LINCOLNSHIRE POSY
March, "THE LADS OF WAMPHRAY" (F
SPOON RIVER

FOR MILITARY BAND AND PIANO:

THE GUM-SUCKERS MARCH (S
March, "OVER THE HILLS AND FAR AWAY" (S

FOR MILITARY BAND AND PIPE ORGAN:

IRISH TUNE FROM COUNTY DERRY (S
THE NIGHTINGALE AND THE TWO SISTERS (S

WORKS ARRANGED FOR BAND:

(Other than those arranged by the composer.)
COUNTRY GARDENS (S

BACH-GRAINGER:

BLYTHE BELLS
(Also see introduction.)

PERCY GRAINGER began his musical career as a piano virtuoso, and as such ranks with the greatest artists of his time. He commenced his pianistic studies in Australia, and gave his first concerts when he was but ten years of age. His further studies were pursued in Germany, and his early concert activities took place there and in other countries of Europe. Although composing steadily, Grainger determined that he would not have his works published or performed until he had attained a position of comparative independence. Fortunately for him, his extraordinary success as a pianist (greatly stimulated by the sponsorship of Edvard Grieg) soon enabled him to satisfy this requirement.

It was also largely due to the inspiration of Grieg that Grainger became interested in English folk music. Grainger's arrangements of folk tunes are brilliantly original and form the best-known portion of his work. Many of his original tunes, while exceedingly characteristic, clearly show the influence of his studies in folk music.

Grainger settled in the United States in 1915 and became an American citizen. He served with the Army Bandmasters' School during the war, and while there had an opportunity to further his familiarity with the wind band and its various instruments, a predilection for which he had already shown in early compositions such as the *Hill-Songs* (1902-1907). In recent years Mr. Grainger has done invaluable work in composing and arranging for the band; no other musician of his stature has done more towards the enrichment of the band's resources, nor has approached the problems of the band with so thoughtful and constructive an outlook. American bands and bandmasters are under a constantly increasing debt to him.

Mr. Grainger's attitude toward the band and his theories in regard to its potentialities are set forth in some completeness both in the following notes and in his own foreword to this volume. The reader can do no better than to dwell on these ideas in Mr. Grainger's own words.

✓ ✓ ✓

Irish Tune from County Derry: This famous and beautiful melody is also known as *The Londonderry Air.* It was heard and noted down in the middle of the last century by

Miss Jane Ross, of New Town, Limavady, Ireland. Grainger's arrangement for band makes exquisite use of little-explored tonal combinations.

Shepherd's Hey (*Morris Dance Tune*): The origin of the Morris Dance is still a subject for dispute, although it is said to have been introduced into England from Spain by John of Gaunt. It was extremely popular in the time of Henry the Eighth, and apparently was of a sufficiently frank character to cause its suppression by the Puritans. In various forms, the Morris Dance has survived in provincial England until the present day. The tunes used are generally eighteenth-century airs.

Children's March, "Over the Hills and Far Away": In this work the composer has carried into practice certain theories of his own with regard to scoring for band. Mr. Grainger is of the opinion that it is in the lower octaves of the band and from the deeper, larger members of the reed family that the greatest expressiveness is to be sought. Consequently, we find in his *Children's March* a more liberal and highly specialized use of such instruments as the bassoon, English horn, bass clarinet, contra bassoon, and the lower saxophones, than is usual in writing for band. So far as is known, this work is the first to be written expressly for piano and band.

This work received its first performance at a concert of the Goldman Band on the green of Columbia University on June 6, 1919, with Mr. Ralph Leopold at the piano and the composer conducting.

Gumsucker's March: "Gumsucker" is a nickname for Australians hailing from Victoria, the home state of the composer. Botanically speaking, a "Gumsucker" is a small chute or sucker of the gum (Eucalyptus) trees which abound in Australia.

Spoon River: The tune called *Spoon River* was heard and noted down by Captain Charles H. Robinson, who heard it played by a fiddler at a country dance at Bradford, Ill., in 1857. When Edgar Lee Masters' *Spoon River Anthology* appeared in 1914, Captain Robinson was struck by the similarity of the title to that of the old tune, and sent the latter to Mr. Masters, who passed it on to Mr. Grainger. The tune is archaic in character, typically American, yet reminiscent of certain Scotch and English dance-tunes types.

Mr. Grainger's setting, completed in 1929, aims at preserving a pioneer blend of lonesome wistfulness and sturdy persistence. It bears the following dedication: "For Edgar Lee Masters, poet of pioneers." The band arrangement received its first performance, under the direction of the composer, at a Goldman Band concert on June 22, 1933.

Blythe Bells: This composition is described as a free ramble on Bach's aria *Sheep May Graze in Safety Where a Goodly Shepherd Watches over Them,* from the secular cantata *Was mir behagst ist nur die muntre Jagd* (*The Joyous Hunt Delights Me*). The ramble is inspired by the thought that Bach, in writing the melody in thirds with which the number opens and closes, may have wished to give a suggestion of the sound of sheep bells. *Blythe Bells* was written at the suggestion of Dr. Goldman for the annual convention of the American Bandmasters' Association in Boston, 1931, where it had its first performance under the composer's direction.

Colonial Song: In this composition the composer has expressed feelings aroused by the scenery of his native country, Australia. It was originally written as a piano solo and dedicated to Mr. Grainger's mother. The band arrangement was made by Mr. Grainger in 1919, and received its first performance at a concert of the Goldman Band at Columbia University on June 6 of that year, under the direction of the composer.

Irish Reel, "Molly on the Shore": This composition is based on two Cork reel tunes from "The Complete Petrie Collection of Ancient Irish Music" edited by Charles Villiers Stanford. The tunes are known as *Molly on the Shore* and *Temple Hill.* The origin of the reel has never been accurately established; the dance is found in Scandinavia as well as in Scotland and Ireland, with considerable variations from place to place. The *Irish Reel* is in two-fourth or common time and is livelier than the other versions.

Country Gardens: This well-known composition is based on a Morris Dance tune, collected by Cecil J. Sharp, whose researches in the field of English music have brought to life immense numbers of old songs and melodies.

(For information on the Morris Dance see note on *Shepherd's Hey*, above.)

A Lincolnshire Posy:

(a) Dublin Boy (A Sailor's Song)
(b) Harkstow Grange (The Miser and his Murderer)
(c) Rufford Park Poachers (A Poaching Song)
(d) Lord Melbourne (War Song)
(e) The Lost Lady Found (A Dance Song)

The above tunes were collected by Percy Grainger with the aid of the phonograph, by which method the folk-song singing habits, dialect pronunciations and personal idiosyncrasies of individual singers are preserved in all their details. This little suite of "musical wildflowers" (hence the title), was composed by Grainger direct for the band. In his foreword the composer writes as follows: "Although these tunes all had words (narrative verse) associated with them, it is not the plot, events, meanings of the verse that I have wished in most cases to express in my band settings. Rather, I have striven to create musical portraits of the old folk singers who sang the melodies to me. These countryside men, often leading hard and tragic lives, and many of them inmates of workhouses in their latter years, were great artists in their own field and some of the strongest and sweetest personalities I have ever met. Joseph Taylor (who sang me 'Rufford Park Poachers') was the perfect type of an English yeoman; sturdy and robust, yet the soul of gentleness and sweetness. At the age of 74, his ringing tenor voice (one of the loveliest I have ever heard) was as fresh as a young man's and he was a past master of graceful, birdlike vocal ornament. 'Harkstow Grange' was sung by a most remarkable personality, George Gould Thorpe, whose typical Lincolnshire looks revealed their original Scandinavian origin. His had been a hard, pitiful life that had left its mark on his gaunt, worn-out appearance. But his native sweetness of nature and a certain grand generosity of mood never deserted him. These characteristics I have tried to express in the setting. 'Lord Melbourne' is a real war song (of the Marlborough period); a rare thing amongst genuine folksongs in England. 'The Lost Lady Found' is a real dance song—a survival from the days when voices, rather than instruments, held village dancers together. It was sung by an old woman who danced in iron pattens on the brick floor of her kitchen as she sang it; in fact, she was incapable of singing it unless she danced: 'Dublin Boy' was collected under rather amusing circumstances. When I first met its singer (Mr. Deane, of Hibbaldstowe), he was in a workhouse in Brigg. I started to note down 'Dublin Boy,' but had soon to desist, as his heart was very weak and the singing of the old melody (which he had not sung for forty years) made him burst into tears. A year or so later, when I had acquired a phonograph, I returned to get Mr. Deane's 'Dublin Boy,' alive or dead. I thought he might just as well die singing it as die without singing it. But I found him in the hospital ward, with a great wound in his head (he having fallen downstairs) of which he was very proud, but far too weak to record his song, as he himself told me. 'All right, Mr. Deane,' I said to him, 'you needn't sing yourself; but I would like you to hear some records made by other singers in these parts.' He had not heard half a record through before he said, impulsively, 'I'll sing for you, yoong mahn.' So the phonograph was propped up on his bed, and in between the second and the third verse he spoke these words into the record: 'It's pleasin' me.' Which shows how very much folksinging is part of the genuine folk-singer's *natural* life."

March, Lads of Wamphray: This march, composed originally for band, is based on some melodies written by Grainger in a choral setting of a Scottish Border Ballad text, *The Lads of Wamphray,* hence the title of the march. No folk songs or other traditional musical material of any kind are used in the composition in which the composer has wished to express the devil-may-care dare-devilry of the cattle-raiding, swashbucklering "Border folk" in the Middle Ages.

Enrique Granados

BORN Lerida, Spain, July 29, 1867
DIED at sea, March 24, 1916

WORKS ARRANGED FOR BAND:

Intermezzo from GOYESCAS (S

THE career of Granados, one of the most gifted of modern Spanish composers, was tragically ended when the steamer on which he was returning to Europe was torpedoed during the World War. Although he was best known as the composer of the opera *Goyescas,* Granados was primarily a composer for pianoforte; like most of the Spanish composers he based much of his work on definitely Spanish forms and rhythms. No composer of his time did more to spread the fame of Spanish music.

The *Goyescas* were originally written as a set of pieces for pianoforte solo, and later expanded into the form of an opera. The work was inspired by paintings and drawings of the artist Francisco Goya (1746-1828), famous for his brilliant originality and bizarre imagination. The opera was first produced at the Metropolitan Opera House, New York, in 1916. The beautiful *Intermezzo* was written about ten days before the première, the entire composition of it occupying the composer under an hour. It was interpolated into the opera just before the scene of *The Candle-Lit Ball.*

Edvard Hagerup Grieg

BORN Bergen, Norway, June 15, 1843
DIED Bergen, Norway, September 4, 1907

WORKS ARRANGED FOR BAND:

PEER GYNT SUITE #1 (F; C
PEER GYNT SUITE #2 (F
Suite: SIGURD JORSALFAR (F; B&H
Triumphal March from SIGURD JORSALFAR (F; Ru; B&H
Two Elegiac Melodies: HEART WOUNDS (F
THE LAST SPRING (F
NORWEGIAN DANCES (Various ones by F; B&H; J
DANCE CAPRICE (F
EROTIK (F
WEDDING DAY AT TROLDHAUGEN (F
MARCH OF THE DWARFS (S
IN THE MOUNTAINS (F
GAVOTTE (F
Anitra's Dance from PEER GYNT (J

GRIEG's importance as a composer lies in the manner in which he combined the feeling of Norwegian folk music with a strong individualism and a thoroughly sound musicianship. He studied composition under Gade, at Leipzig, but on his return to Norway revolted against what he considered "the effeminate Mendelssohn-Gade Scandinavianism," and joined the Norwegian composer Nordraak to form a genuine Norwegian school. Grieg gained prominence with the performance of his piano concerto in 1879, and in 1894 he received the honorary degree of Doctor of Music, at Cambridge. Most of his life was spent in seclusion near Bergen.

Although Grieg based his music on the folk tunes of his country, he did not hesitate to modify this material in accordance with his own strong individuality. Except for his piano concerto and several sonatas, he composed in small forms. His talent was lyrical rather than dramatic, and he was at his best in simple pieces to which his expressive melodic idiom and novel harmonies lent great distinction.

Peer Gynt Suite #1:

I. Morning
II. Asa's Death
III. Anitra's Dance
IV. In the Hall of the Mountain King

The incidental music for Ibsen's fantastic drama is probably the most popular work of Grieg. From that music Grieg made two suites, of which the first is the better-known. Both suites were originally published as piano duets and later arranged for orchestra.

The first number of this suite, *Morning,* occurs in the original as the prelude to the fourth act. The second number accompanies the scene of the death of Ase, Peer Gynt's mother. *Anitra's Dance* takes place in Africa. The oriental character of this number is a far-cry from Grieg's usual use of Scandinavian material. The last number of the suite, *In the Hall of the Mountain King,* describes Peer's visit to the cavern of the gnomes. The gnomes dance around Peer in a grotesque orgy until finally the sound of bells from a distant church causes the destruction of the Mountain King's Hall.

Peer Gynt Suite #2:

I. Abduction of the Bride (Ingrid's Lament)
II. Arabian Dance
III. Peer Gynt's Homecoming (Stormy Evening on the Coast)
IV. Solvejg's Song
V. Dance of the Daughter of the Mountain King

Like the first Peer Gynt suite, the second is arranged for concert use and the sequence of the numbers bears no relation to the order in which they occurred in Ibsen's drama.

The following note is prefaced to Grieg's original score: "Peer Gynt, the only son of poor peasants, is drawn by the poet as a character of a morbidly developed fancy. . . . He had many wild adventures. He comes, for instance, to a peasant's wedding, where he carries off the bride up to the mountain peaks." This is the subject of the first number of this suite. "He then enters the kingdom of the Mountain King, whose daughter falls in love with him and dances to him." The music to this scene forms the fifth number. After leaving the Kingdom, he wanders to foreign countries. He appears as a prophet in Morocco, and is greeted by Arab girls, who also dance for him. This dance is the third number of the suite. Following many more adventures, he returns home as an old man, having survived a shipwreck just as he approached the coast.

Suite, Sigurd Jorsalfar (Sigurd the Crusader):

I. Introduction
II. Intermezzo (Borghild's Dream)
III. Huldigungsmarsch (Triumphal March)

Sigurd Jorsalfar is the title of a popular drama by Björne Björnson, for which Grieg wrote the incidental music. The play has the character of a folk epic, and although not one of Björnson's greatest, has enjoyed a wide popularity in Scandinavia. Grieg's original score called for male chorus, solo and orchestra. The three numbers of this concert suite were later arranged for orchestra alone. They are considered among the finest things Grieg ever wrote.

Two Elegiac Melodies, Heart Wounds and *The Last Spring:* These two characteristic numbers were originally written for string orchestra. Those familiar with the piano pieces of Grieg will realize how similar they are to his *Lyric Pieces.* The nostalgic melodies, the subtle harmony and the intensity of expression in a small medium, make these two pieces rank high among Grieg's shorter works.

Norwegian Dances: Grieg's love for the music of his own country was apparent in almost everything he wrote, but was nowhere more characteristically expressed than in the Norwegian dances. These were directly inspired by the melodic and harmonic characteristics of Norwegian folk music. Grieg arranged a number of them for the pianoforte, two hands and four hands; some of these were made into orchestral pieces. Among the dance forms used were the *Halling* and the *Springer.*

Erotik, March of the Dwarfs, Wedding Day at Troldhaugen, etc. (*From Lyric Pieces for Pianoforte*): Grieg wrote nine books of lyric pieces for the pianoforte. Included among these are numbers of almost every conceivable character, ranging from the sentimental to the grotesque and from the tragic to the comic. There are few volumes of piano music more original or more colorful. Most of the numbers are short and of no great technical difficulty. Probably for this reason pianists seldom include them on concert programs; amateurs, however, have always delighted in them.

In the Mountains: This pleasing and characteristic piece is an arrangement of the first of a set of three Humoresques for pianoforte known as *Pictures from Folk-Life,* Opus 19. In its simplicity, sturdiness and freshness of harmonic idiom, it is a typical expression of Grieg's fondness for the native characteristics of Scandinavian music.

Ferde Grofé
(Ferdinand von Grofé)

WORKS ARRANGED FOR BAND:

On the Trail from GRAND CANYON SUITE (Rob
Mardi Gras from MISSISSIPPI SUITE (LF

FERDE GROFÉ comes of a musical family, and his first musical studies were undertaken at home. His instruments were the violin and viola. At the age of seventeen he became a member of the Los Angeles Symphony Orchestra, where he remained for ten years. With the emergence of a new group of American composers, of whom Gershwin was the leader, Grofé became interested in what is known as "symphonic jazz," soon achieving fame through his remarkable arrangements and orchestrations. In his original compositions, Grofé's avowed intention has been to describe America in music.

Mardi Gras: Grofé's *Mississippi Suite* is descriptive of an imaginative journey along the Father of Waters, a journey involving time as well as space, since it recalls past days and legendary characters. The finale, however, is altogether contemporary, being a colorful portrayal of carnival time in New Orleans. The music of the suite is full of clever suggestions and displays the ingenious rhythms and novel harmonies for which the composer is famous.

On the Trail: In this number from the *Grand Canyon Suite,* Grofé attempts to describe in music the jogging gait of a pack-laden burro as it moves along. The humorous qualities of the music will be readily appreciated, as well as the sound musicianship and ingenious skill through which the effects are attained.

Henry K. Hadley

BORN Somerville, Massachusetts, December 20, 1871
DIED New York, September 6, 1937

WORKS WRITTEN FOR BAND:

Overture, YOUTH TRIUMPHANT (F
FESTIVAL MARCH (Fitz

WORKS ARRANGED FOR BAND:

Overtures: IN BOHEMIA (S
HEROD (F
ALMA MATER (Birch
CONCERT OVERTURE (S
Suites: SILHOUETTES (F
BALLET OF THE FLOWERS (F
THREE CHARACTERISTIC NUMBERS (F
Song of the Marching Men (D
Festival March, THE BOHEMIANS (F
Prelude from SUITE ANCIENNE (F
Ballet Airs, PIERROT AND PIERRETTE (F

HENRY HADLEY was one of the most distinguished of contemporary American composers and conductors. His musical education was received both here and abroad. At the New England Conservatory he studied under Stephen Emery and George W. Chadwick. After achieving success in Europe, he returned to America, where he became conductor of the Seattle Symphony Orchestra and subsequently of the San Francisco Orchestra, the Philharmonic Orchestra and the Manhattan Symphony Orchestra, the last of which he himself organized.

His compositions, which include works in every form, have received innumerable awards. Hadley's music is characterized by great native energy, careful thought and scholarly knowledge, as well as by melodic freshness and ingenuity of invention. His operas, which have been presented by the Metropolitan Opera Company and the Chicago Opera Company, are considered by many critics to be the finest yet produced by an American composer.

Mr. Hadley was always keenly interested in bands. He appeared as guest conductor of the Goldman Band and in addition to composing several original works, supervised the arrangement of many of his compositions for wind instruments.

✓ ✓ ✓

Overture, Youth Triumphant: This overture is an expression of Mr. Hadley's interest in bands and band-music. It was conceived and written specially for the modern concert band at the request of Edwin Franko Goldman. *Youth Triumphant* is in the classical overture form; its themes are consciously adapted to the qualities and capacities of band instruments. It is full of a joyful holiday spirit, typically youthful, energetic and gay.

The overture received its first performance at the concert of the American Bandmasters' Association in Boston, on April 12th, 1931. It is dedicated to the Association.

✓

Overture, In Bohemia: This overture, one of the most popular of Mr. Hadley's compositions, was written in 1900 for the Bohemian Club of San Francisco. It received its first performance in Pittsburgh, under the direction of Victor Herbert. The work is dedicated to Victor Herbert and the Bohemian Club. The "Bohemia" of the title is that universal but wholly imaginative one which is supposed to be the abode of artists. The overture is full of the happy and carefree spirit which is characteristic of "Bohemian" life. The music has a freshness and gaiety which give it instant appeal. It is in regular overture form.

✓

Overture, Alma Mater: This overture is one of Mr. Hadley's lighter works written for orchestra. It is founded on several well-known American college songs, including *Goodnight, Ladies; Upa-dee, Upa-dee; The Quilting Party; Good Old Yale* (Drinking Song); and *Fair Harvard* (*Believe Me If All Those Endearing Young Charms*).

Overture, Herod: This overture formed part of the incidental music written by Mr. Hadley in 1902 for the production of *Herod,* a romantic drama by Stephen Philips.

Festival March: The Festival March was completed in 1936. Like the overture, *Youth Triumphant,* it was conceived and written directly for band, and reflects the composer's great interest in bands and band-music. The first performance of the march took place at Milwaukee, Wisconsin, on March 7, 1937, as a special feature of the concert given by the American Bandmasters' Association. The work is dedicated to Edwin Franko Goldman.

Suite, Ballet of the Flowers: The twelve short numbers of this suite are divided into three parts. Each number bears as title the name of some flower. The music is of a light and graceful nature, as befits the subject.

Song of the Marching Men: This composition is taken from Mr. Hadley's ode for chorus and orchestra, *The New Earth,* written in 1917. In its band arrangement it makes a highly effective number, full of vigor and energy.

Suite, Silhouettes:

I. Spanish
II. French

III. Italian
IV. American
V. Egyptian
VI. Irish

The six silhouettes of Mr. Hadley's suite are, as is evident from their titles, short instrumental sketches in various national styles. They were originally written for orchestra. Arranged for band, they were first brought out at a concert of the Goldman Band in 1919, under the direction of the composer. The imitation of national characteristics in the music is cleverly done.

Concert Overture: This little overture was written by Hadley for orchestra. It shows that exuberant and joyous spirit which is the principal characteristic of his music. The *Concert Overture* is in E flat, in lively 4/4 tempo throughout. Just before the end the tempo broadens slightly to provide an energetic and effective climax.

Jacques François Fromental Elias Halévy

BORN Paris, May 27, 1799
DIED Nice, France, March 17, 1862

WORKS ARRANGED FOR BAND:

Selections from LA JUIVE (F

HALÉVY was a brilliant composer and teacher whose talent for music revealed itself when he was a mere child. He competed for the Prix de Rome when he was seventeen but did not win it until two years later. His talents were devoted almost entirely to the composition of opera, but it was not until 1835 that he scored a great success with *La Juive.* The same year saw the composition of *L'Eclair,* the other work by which Halévy is best-known. These two works are so completely different that it is hardly believable that both were written by the same man.

Halévy composed a number of operas after *La Juive* and *L'Eclair,* but they did little to add to his reputation. At the same time he was professor of harmony, counterpoint and composition at the Conservatory and taught such distinguished pupils as Gounod and Bizet.

⸙ ⸙ ⸙

La Juive (*Selections*): The production of *La Juive* aroused wild enthusiasm and secured for its composer admission to the Institute. The music is intensely dramatic, brilliant and colorful. *La Juive* is remarkable for the delineation of the characters, in which respect it has seldom been surpassed.

Georg Friedrich Handel (Haendel)

BORN Halle, Saxony, February 23, 1685
DIED London, April 14, 1759

WORKS ARRANGED FOR BAND:

Oratorio, THE MESSIAH (complete) (B&H
Hallelujah Chorus from THE MESSIAH (F; AMP
March & Chorus from JUDAS MACCABAEUS (Bote & Bock
Dead March from SAUL (F; CB
Coronation Anthem, ZADOK THE PRIEST (B&H
"THE HARMONIOUS BLACKSMITH" (C
Air from RINALDO (B&H
Menuet from SAMSON (B&H
LARGO (B&H; F; Ba; CB; J
HOSANNAH (F
Hymn, SAXONY (F
"OCCASIONAL" OVERTURE (B&H
March from "OCCASIONAL" ORATORIO (N

IT WAS long the fashion to rank Handel with Bach as one of the fathers of modern music. From Handel's pen came some of the greatest music ever written, this being especially true of his choral works. The finest of Handel's music occurs in his magnificent oratorios. When the composer turned his hand to opera, in which the bulk of his work consists, he was apt to be influenced by the prevailing Italianized taste and by the demands of his singers for excessively florid airs. As an instrumental composer, Handel produced a number of beautiful concertos, sonatas, and suites, but these form a small portion of his work in comparison to his operas and oratorios.

Handel's first opera was produced at Hamburg in 1705. Shortly thereafter he visited Italy where he came under the influence of Carissimi, Scarlatti and others. He journeyed to London in 1710. In that city Italian opera had already arrived; Purcell had been dead for fifteen years and his successors were not gifted enough to combat the Italian influence. Handel thus found the stage already set for him. He set out on a career as a successful composer of the type of operas in vogue. It was not until his later years that Handel began to be preoccupied with the possibilities of oratorio. His great works in this field commence with the year 1739. From that time on he produced in rapid succession such masterpieces as *Israel in Egypt, The Messiah, Samson* and *Saul.* These works are on a scale much vaster than his operas and instrumental compositions, and it is on them that Handel's fame principally rests. The magnificent contrapuntal writing for chorus in these great oratorios has never been surpassed.

Hallelujah Chorus (from *The Messiah*): The *Hallelujah Chorus* is the triumphal climax of Handel's best-known oratorio. It is a fine example of that magnificent contrapuntal writing for voices which no later composer has ever equalled. The first time the *Hallelujah Chorus* was performed, in London in 1743, King George II rose to his feet to show his respect, and the entire audience followed his example. This has since become a custom which all audiences observe during the performance of this work.

March and Chorus from *Judas Maccabaeus* (*See The Conquering Hero Comes*): The oratorio *Judas Maccabaeus* was composed in 1746 to celebrate the return of the Duke of Cumberland after the victory at Culloden. The actual writing of the work occupied Handel but thirty-two days, yet despite this apparent haste, the oratorio has always been ranked with Handel's greatest. The famous *March and Chorus* occurs in the third part of the work. After a messenger arrives to announce the news of the victory of Judas Maccabaeus over the enemy, the young men and women go forth to meet him with this stirring music. The band arrangement follows the original construction of the number, which is sung first as a three-part chorus, then as a duet and finally by the full chorus and orchestra.

Dead March from *Saul:* The oratorio *Saul* was first sung in 1739 and was one of the first of Handel's great works in this form. The *Dead March* occurs as an instrumental interlude and is the best-known portion of the work. It is unique in the fact that, although it is a dirge both in name and in feeling, it is written in the Major mode.

Coronation Anthem, Zadok the Priest: Handel wrote four anthems for the coronation of King George II toward the end of the year 1727. This was soon after the musician had become an English subject. *Zadok the Priest* is the first of these hymns, and it is a typical example of the stirring choral music associated with the composer's name. This anthem has an instrumental introduction, in those days called a "symphony," which is followed by a chorus entitled, "And all the people rejoiced." This is followed by another stirring chorus, "God Save the King!"

Air from *Rinaldo:* The air which occurs in *Rinaldo* as *Lascia ch' io pianga* (*Let me weep*), was apparently a favorite of Handel, since he used it in no less than three operas. It is a melody of great beauty, one of the most unforgettable Handel ever wrote.

Rinaldo his first opera for London, written in 14 days, was produced in 1711. Splendidly staged, it was a great success. The story is based on an episode in the *Gerusalemme Liberata* of Torquato Tasso (1544-1595).

Largo (*Air* from *Xerxes*): The *Largo* is unquestionably the most frequently played of Handel's compositions. It has, of course, been arranged for almost every solo instrument as well as every combination of instruments. In its original form it was a tenor solo in the opera *Xerxes,* written in 1738. The accompaniment was scored for strings alone. The air occurs in the first scene of the first act, sung by Xerxes as he stands in the shade of a plane (sycamore) tree growing in a beautiful garden. The words (with an approximate English rendition) are as follows:

Ombra mai fù Di vegetabile Cara ed amabile Soave più.	(No shade of any growing thing was ever more precious, more peaceful or more pleasant.)

Strangely enough, although the melody has come to be known as the *Largo,* the tempo marking of the original was "Larghetto."

Air and Variations, The Harmonious Blacksmith: The famous air known as *The Harmonious Blacksmith* was written by Handel as the final movement of his fifth suite for harpsichord, in E major. The variations are five in number, and are quite simple in structure, the theme being always quite clearly discernible in the midst of the ornamentation. The name of "Harmonious Blacksmith" was not given the work by the composer, but was added at a later date. The air, it may be noted, was not original with Handel, having been published in Paris late in the sixteenth century.

Overture to the *Occasional Oratorio:* The occasion for which Handel wrote his *Occasional Oratorio* was the same that called forth his great *Judas Maccabaeus:* the victory of the Duke of Cumberland over the "young pretender"

Charles Edward, son of James Stuart, at Culloden in 1746. The oratorio as a whole does not rank in majesty and impressiveness with many of Handel's more famous works, but the overture is in his most elevated style. It is in the nature of a free prelude or what might have been called in Handel's day a *Symphony*. Four movements are clearly marked: Adagio—Allegro—Adagio—Allegro.

Minuet from *Samson: Samson* was written in 1741 and was first performed in London on February 18, 1743. It is thus one of the earliest of his great oratorios. The words were adapted from Milton's *Samson Agonistes*.

Franz Josef Haydn

BORN Rohrau, Austria, March 31, 1732
DIED Vienna, May 31, 1809

WORKS ARRANGED FOR BAND:

MILITARY SYMPHONY (Complete) (F
Andante from SURPRISE SYMPHONY (F
Finale from FAREWELL SYMPHONY (F
The Heavens Are Telling from THE CREATION (F; B&H; CB
GYPSY RONDO (C
OXEN MENUET (F; B&H

HAYDN was the first great master of the symphony and the string quartet, bringing these forms to a point of development at which Mozart and Beethoven were able to take them up. During his long life Haydn composed well over a hundred symphonies and almost uncountable string quartets, trios and sonatas for various instruments, yet throughout all of this work there is almost invariably a sense of freshness and spontaneity.

In the music of the eighteenth century (which has been called "the age of reason"), there is to be found no romantic or dramatic expression of man's struggles with his soul, no sentimental poeticism, and very little attempt to make music represent anything but itself. The ideal of classic music was to present music for its own sake in forms for which no extraneous explanation was necessary. That was the basis for the development of the sonata form, which had as its primary purpose the establishment of a perfectly transparent medium for the expression of purely musical ideas. Clarity, abstract beauty and economy of means were the objectives of eighteenth-century music.

Haydn's music realizes these ideals. His delightful symphonies and quartets do not paint pictures or tell stories;

their sparkling themes stand in relations determined solely by considerations of musical order and intelligibility. Except in his oratorios and songs, and a number of his occasional pieces, Haydn worked almost exclusively within the framework of the sonata form. All of his music is characterized by a certain vigor, directness and geniality. In regard to the pure musical beauty of his works, Haydn was surpassed by few composers. His works are as fresh today as they were when they were written.

Haydn enjoyed fame and success during his lifetime. Untroubled by financial worries, he was able to compose without interruption. From the year 1761 until the end of his life, he was musical director to Prince Nicholas Esterhazy, for whom he composed many of his finest works. Trips to Vienna and to London varied the routine of court life. On these trips Haydn achieved some of his greatest successes. Haydn was honored by honorary memberships in many academies and institutions, and received the honorary degree of Doctor of Music from Oxford University. Toward the close of his life his public appearances were occasions for impressive demonstrations, so great was the esteem in which the composer was held.

Military Symphony (*G Major*):

I. Largo—Allegro
II. Allegretto
III. Menuet
IV. Finale, Presto

On his second trip to London Haydn wrote a set of six symphonies for the impressario Salomon. The *Military Symphony* is the second of these. It was first played at a concert for the benefit of the composer. The work was given the name of "Military" because of its use of the percussion, considered very unusual at the time.

The first movement opens with a slow introduction of a broad and harmonious character. The principal theme is of that simple nature so often found in Haydn's compositions. It is repeated and answered in several voices before the introduction of the second theme. The whole movement has the regular rhythm and swinging melody of a march. The development is rather more extended than is usual in Haydn.

The *Allegretto* is based on an old French romance. The charming tune is punctuated by trumpet calls and the sounds of various percussion instruments. The music is military in character only in the sense that one might call it a pastoral army's marching-tune.

The *Menuet* and the *Finale* are little different from the corresponding movements of other Haydn symphonies so far as their formal or melodic characteristics are concerned. They are full of jollity, naturalness and the inexhaustible genius of the composer.

Surprise Symphony (*G Major*): The *Surprise Symphony* was written in 1791, during Haydn's first visit to London. It immediately became a great favorite. Haydn is said to have admitted his intention of startling the audience with the well-known sudden introduction of the drums in the *Andante*. In any case it is certain that the effect was introduced in a humorous spirit. It was, of course, from this famous passage that the symphony derived its name.

Farewell Symphony (*F♯ Minor*): Haydn wrote this famous work in 1772, as a delicate suggestion to his patron that he shorten his stay at Esterhaz. Haydn was on friendly terms with the musicians of his orchestra, and knew they wished to rejoin their families in Vienna. In the *Finale* of the *Farewell Symphony*, the musicians stop playing one after another and leave the stage, until only two are left. Prince Esterhazy found that the hint contained in this was unmistakable; as a result Haydn is said to have attained his object.

Oxen Minuet: The following story is told of this composition: A certain butcher of Vienna came to Haydn one day and expressed his appreciation of Haydn's music. Relying on the well-known amiability of the composer, he asked to have an entirely new minuet for the wedding of his daughter. Haydn was pleased at this novel homage and promised to give him the minuet within two days. The butcher returned and gratefully accepted the gift. Soon after, Haydn heard his new minuet being played on the streets. He went to the window and saw beneath his balcony a promenading orchestra grouped around a magnificent garlanded ox. The butcher entered the house and explained that he could think of no more suitable way of expressing his gratitude than by presenting the finest of his oxen to the composer. From that moment on, the Minuet was known throughout Vienna as the *Minuet of the Ox.*

The Heavens Are Telling from *The Creation:* Haydn worked with great ardor on the score of his greatest oratorio. He said that he was never so pious as when he was composing *The Creation.* The work was first performed privately in 1798, but with its publication in 1800 it was immediately performed everywhere. Its success and popularity were prodigious. The chorus, *The Heavens Are Telling,* is but one of the splendid numbers which make up this genial work. The poem used as a basis for this work was compiled and translated, with considerable alterations, from Milton's *Paradise Lost.*

Gypsy Rondo: This popular rondo is taken from Haydn's fifth string trio, in G. The title *Gypsy Rondo* does not seem to have been given the number by the composer, but like so many such subsequently given names has become a fixture. The rondo has been transcribed many times, and especially as a piano piece it has become a student classic.

Richard B. Hayward

BORN London

ORIGINAL WORKS FOR BAND:

Overture: THE CORSAIR'S BRIDE (F
Suites: IN A SPANISH CITY (F
THREE CHARACTERISTIC DANCES (F

CAPTAIN R. B. HAYWARD was graduated as Bandmaster from the famous Kneller Hall in London, and shortly thereafter became Bandmaster of the Royal Irish Rifles Band. At the beginning of the World War he was promoted to a combat commission, the only serving bandmaster in the long history of the British Army ever to receive that distinction.

In 1921 Captain Hayward came to Canada as Director of Music of the Queen's Own Rifles. Within fifteen months of assuming leadership he brought the band to a state of efficiency high enough to win the Canadian National Band Championship by a large margin. In 1926 he retired from the Army in order to organize the Toronto Concert Band, which has attained a high position in the Canadian musical world.

❦ ❦ ❦

Overture, The Corsair's Bride: This overture, published in 1937, was written for use by school bands. It opens with a short introduction, *andante pomposo,* in which the principal theme of the *allegro* is foreshadowed. The main section of the overture (E flat, 3/4 time) is of a bright and straightforward character. The contrasting section (C minor, 3/4 time) is an *andante.* The thematic material is completed by an episode in 9/8 time, *andante non troppo,* in which the treble and bass instruments alternate in carrying the melody. The overture ends with a spirited coda based on the first theme, followed by five fanfare-like measures in the full band.

Suite, In A Spanish City:

I. A Bull Fight
II. Vespers
III. Tarantella

This colorful suite consists of tonal descriptions of typical Spanish scenes. The first number follows the action of a bull fight from the entry of the Toreador to the triumphant review of the Picadors, Matadors and Toreador after the performance. The second number opens with the sound of evening bells. As the hour of prayer approaches, the sounds of a hymn of praise echo from the cathedral. An interlude follows, during which a bird is heard singing. The movement ends with a grandiose repetition of the hymn. The third number is a typical Tarantella, the lively Italian dance in 6/8 time, which is also popular in Spain.

Suite, Three Characteristic Dances:

I. Danse Gracieuse (France)
II. Vals Pequeño (Spain)
III. Jig (England)

Victor Herbert

BORN Dublin, Ireland, February 1, 1859
DIED New York, May 26, 1924

WORKS ARRANGED FOR BAND:

FESTIVAL MARCH (F
WESTERN OVERTURE (F
AMERICAN FANTASY (F
PAN-AMERICANA (W
IRISH RHAPSODY (W
Selections from: NATOMA (S
SWEETHEARTS (S
BABES IN TOYLAND (W
NAUGHTY MARIETTA (W
MLLE. MODISTE (W
and many others
Entr'Acte from MLLE. MODISTE (W
Entr'Acte from BABES IN TOYLAND (W
BADINAGE and other short pieces
Many marches, including: CENTENNIAL (LF
THE GOLD BUG (F
etc.

ALTHOUGH Victor Herbert was born in Ireland and educated in Germany, America proudly considers him an American composer. The greater part of his life was spent in this country and all of the works by which he is best-known were composed here.

Herbert was a grandson of Samuel Lover, the famous Irish novelist and poet. His musical education commenced when he was seven, at which time he was sent to Germany. The 'cello was his chosen instrument, and he became known as a fine player before he acquired renown as a composer. He came to America in 1886 in order to play as first 'cellist of the Metropolitan Opera House Orchestra. He remained at the Metropolitan for a short time, becoming known throughout the country both as 'cellist and conductor. For brief periods he played with the Theodore Thomas and Anton Seidl orchestras, being associate conductor of the latter. In 1894 he succeeded Gilmore as director of the 22nd Regiment band, and in 1898 he became conductor of the Pittsburgh Orchestra, retaining the latter position until 1904.

After leaving the Pittsburgh Orchestra, Herbert devoted himself to composition. His comic operas quickly won their way into the hearts of the public, and his grand opera, *Natoma,* was produced at the Metropolitan with considerable success. It is by such delightful works as *Naughty Marietta, The Fortune Teller* and others of his long list of light operas, however, that he is best remembered. The motion-pictures have presented several of them; others are still performed on the stage. The best-known excerpts from them have never diminished in popularity, and are "household music" all over America.

Festival March: This spirited and unusual march was written for the Pittsburgh Exposition of 1900, at which Herbert and his orchestra were a star attraction. The number was always a great favorite of the composer, and was included by him on all programs of a gala nature. It was never performed by any orchestra other than Herbert's own during his lifetime, and it was only after many years that it was published. The march has a splendid swing and the typical Herbert melodiousness. It introduces that old favorite, *Auld Lang Syne,* at the conclusion.

American Fantasie: The *American Fantasie* was originally written for orchestra, and is one of the most popular works of the popular composer. It includes a number of well-known tunes which no listener can fail to recognize, blended together with Herbert's customary skill.

Pan-Americana: This number was composed by Victor Herbert for the Pan-American Exposition in Buffalo in 1903, where the Pittsburgh Orchestra, under the composer's direction, was a stellar attraction.

Pan-Americana embodies the idea which inspired the exposition. It appears in the Indian-like character of the first part, the Southern idiom of the second part and the Spanish South-American melodies of the third part of the composition.

Irish Rhapsody: The *Irish Rhapsody* is possibly the most brilliant of all Herbert's compositions for orchestra. It is his one composition which has maintained its place in the symphonic repertory. The work was published in 1910, and was dedicated to the Gaelic Society of New York. Based on a number of fine old Irish tunes, including the well-known *Garry Owen, St. Patrick's Day, The Rocky Road to Dublin, Believe Me If All Those Endearing Young Charms, Erin, O, Erin* and others, the *Irish Rhapsody* contrasts the spirit of jig and the reel with the tender melodies of the Irish love-songs. The composition opens *allegro molto* (6/8), with the theme of *Garry Owen.* The tempo changes to *lento,* and the tune of *Believe Me If All Those Endearing Young Charms* is introduced. The third section is *allegro feroce* (9/8). The work develops to a dynamic climax, with the themes of *Garry Owen* and *Erin, O Erin* brilliantly combined.

Selections from *Natoma: Natoma* was the first, and the most successful, of Herbert's grand operas. It was first performed in Philadelphia on February 25, 1911, with John McCormack and Mary Garden in the leading roles. The story deals with life in California in the days of Spanish domination, about 1820. The heroine, *Natoma,* is an Indian girl whose devotion to an American naval lieutenant forms the main theme of the plot. Herbert's music is unusually tuneful, and although the opera is seldom heard, many excerpts are popular. Among the most frequently heard sections of the opera is the *Dagger Dance* from Act II, which is often played separately.

Western Overture: This work, which is a fantasy rather than an overture, was composed by Herbert during one of his engagements with his orchestra at Willow Grove Park, near Philadelphia. Briefly, the work follows the settling of the West, from the time when the Indians roamed the plains through the successive arrivals of the New England pioneers, the Army, the railroad and so forth. The defeat of the Indians in followed by the "Chant of the Races that have won the West." The work concludes with a dressed-up version of *America.* Among the tunes which are heard in this "overture" may be mentioned *Hold the Fort, The Seminole Love Song, There'll Be a Hot Time Tonight, For He's a Jolly Good Fellow* and a few national melodies.

Louis Joseph Ferdinand Hérold

BORN Paris, January 28, 1791
DIED Les Ternes, France, January 19, 1833

WORKS ARRANGED FOR BAND:

Overtures: ZAMPA (F; B&H; D; CB
LE PRÉ AUX CLERCS (F

HÉROLD was one of the most brilliant of the entire school of French comic-opera composers. A pupil of Méhul, he won the Prix de Rome in 1812, and his early compositions show that he could have succeeded as a symphonic composer had he chosen. In France at that time, however, the stage was the surest way to success, and Hérold soon began to produce a number of lively and charming operas.

His style was graceful, polished and occasionally even moving. No musician summed up better than Hérold the qualities for which the French school is noted. Hérold died just as he felt that he was beginning to understand the requirements of the stage, and his two most famous works date from the closing years of his life.

Overture, Zampa: Zampa, or *The Marble Bride,* was a brilliant success. The libretto, by Mélesville, was both adroit and well-constructed; the music by turns vivacious and sentimental. The plot of the opera concerns the amorous adventures of the pirate Zampa and his eventual undoing through the intervention of the statue of the fiancée he has deceived. The overture is constructed on themes from the opera, and is more of a medley than a regular overture in form. It opens with a lively theme taken from the Pirates' Chorus in the first act, continues with the ballad from the second act. Three more themes are introduced. The material is skillfully put together to make a brilliant and delightful number which has enjoyed tremendous popularity in all parts of the world.

Overture, Le Pré aux Clercs: Le Pré aux Clercs was produced a year after *Zampa,* and enjoyed an equally great success. In France it is still the most popular of Hérold's works, and is regarded as one of the masterpieces of comic-opera. The libretto, by Planard, undoubtedly contributed to its success. The *Pré aux Clercs* (or *The Scholars' Meadow*) was a field near Saint-Germain-des-Près in Paris, which served both as a promenade and as a duelling-ground for the scholars of the old University of Paris. Many traditions are bound up with it; the reference to these unquestionably enhanced the opera's appeal for the Parisian public.

R. E. Hildreth

WORKS WRITTEN FOR BAND:

Overtures: CHICOT THE CLOWN (F
ONE BEAUTIFUL DAY (Fil
MYSTIC KNIGHTS (D
CARILLON (J
Forest Fantasy: SEQUOIA
and many others for school bands

R. E. HILDRETH was born in England but was brought to the United States at the age of twelve. While still very young, he became proficient on a number of instruments, and at the age of eighteen had appeared as conductor. His composing started in a modest way, but his talent for both composition and arranging was soon manifest. In both fields, Mr. Hildreth has been eminently successful.

Mr. Hildreth's interest was aroused by the school band movement almost as soon as it began to assume shape. He has composed a great deal of music especially designed for the capacities of school bands, and these works have the merit of being musical without being difficult. His arrangements of other works for school bands have brought him a considerable reputation.

Besides his work for school bands, Mr. Hildreth has written two operettas, numerous choruses and songs, a string quartet, a cantata and many other works in the larger forms for both band and orchestra.

Forest Fantasy, Sequoia: The composer provides the following note in connection with this work: "This composition is the result of a conversation with Dr. Goldman at one of his band concerts in August, 1936.

"The following couplet conveys the sentiment of the composition:

The giant trees point upward to the sky above
To that eternal home attained by faith and love.

"The fantasy opens with a long introduction depicting woodland sounds. There is then heard light, gentle breezes through the trees, which eventually assume stormy proportions. A sudden calm changes the atmosphere and this is followed by a choral:

Let all give thanks for living
To Him on high, for giving
The earth, the sea, to you and me;
God, hear our song in praise to Thee!

which re-echoes throughout the woods. A glorious repetition of the choral leads into a short coda suggestive of the feelings of exhilaration produced by the preceding."

Gustav Theodore Holst

BORN Chelton, England, September 21, 1874
DIED London, May 25, 1934

ORIGINAL WORKS FOR BAND:

FIRST SUITE IN E♭ (B&H
SECOND SUITE IN F (B&H

WORKS ARRANGED FOR BAND:

From the *Suite,* THE PLANETS: *Jupiter* (B&H
Mars (B&H

GUSTAV HOLST was one of the most prominent and original of modern English composers. His compositions cover a wide range, but in every sphere show a great technical command of material and a marked individuality. They fall more or less distinctly into different periods, during each of which the composer was pre-occupied with definite ideas. As a result, Holst had at one time a reputation for Orientalism, at another for spiritualism. The most abiding influence discernible in his work, however, is that of the English folk song. In this he was comparable to his friend and co-worker, Vaughan Williams.

Holst showed great interest in writing for wind instruments. He was a proficient trombonist, and during the war had charge of the army bands in Salonika. In addition to the two published suites, his works for band include the Prelude and Scherzo *Hammersmith,* and the *Moorside Suite* for brass band. He also composed some chamber music for wind combinations. (See introduction.)

The composer visited America in 1923 to conduct several of his works at the University of Michigan, and again in 1932. He was made an Honorary Member of the American Bandmasters' Association during his last visit.

First Suite for Band in E♭ (Opus 28-A):

I. Chaconne
II. Intermezzo
III. March

Holst's *First Suite for Band* was composed in 1909. It is thus one of the first works by an important modern composer written directly for band. Holst's use of the possibilities of the band is extremely striking and shows a profound knowledge of the qualities of the various instruments. Not being hampered by an orchestral tradition of scoring, Holst was able to accomplish a genuinely new coloring in this work.

The Chaconne is a dance form first used in the sixteenth century. It occurs frequently in the works of Bach and his contemporaries. It is stately in character, in triple time, and generally in a major tonality.

Second Suite for Band, in F (Opus 28-B):

I. March. (*Morris Dance, Swansea Town* and *Claudy Banks*)
II. Song without Words: *I'll Love My Love*
III. *Song of the Blacksmith*
IV. Fantasia on *The Dargason.* (Introducing *Green Sleaves*)

The *Second Suite for Band* written by Gustav Holst is founded on old English country tunes. It was written around 1911 and published in 1922. Perhaps even more than in his *First Suite,* Holst here revealed his genuine feeling for wind instrumentation; certainly no more delightful contribution has ever been made by a prominent composer to the band repertory.

The first movement is in the form of a march based on three folk tunes. It opens with the *Morris Dance,* followed by the tune of *Swansea Town,* both in 2/2 time. The middle section is based on *Claudy Banks,* in 6/8, and is followed by a repetition of the first part. The *Morris Dance* tune is from the collection of Cecil Sharp; *Swansea Town* and *Claudy Banks* were collected in Hampshire by Dr. G. B. Gardiner.

The *Song without Words* (Andante, 4/4) is based on another tune collected in Hampshire by Dr. Gardiner. This modal melody, exquisitely set, has a grave and pathetic beauty. It is first taken by the oboe, later repeated, over a more moving accompaniment, by the solo cornet and flute. The volume never rises above a *piano* throughout.

A lively contrast to the preceding movement is provided by the *Song of the Blacksmith,* founded on a tune likewise collected in Hampshire by Dr. Gardiner. Tremendous rhythmic energy and striking effects abound in this movement, in which the full tonal and percussive forces of the band are brought into play. The tempo is *Moderato e Maestoso,* the signature shifting frequently between 4/4 and 3/4.

The finale of the suite, the *Fantasia on the Dargason,* is almost identical with the finale of the *St. Paul's Suite,* written by Holst some years earlier for string orchestra. Hearing the *Fantasia* in its two forms, one cannot help feeling that it is richer and more rewarding in its band version. *The Dargason* is an ancient tune (allegro moderato, 6/8) to be found in many collections of English folk-music, and is obviously of the dance-song type. Twice during the *Fantasia,* Holst introduces the old tune of *Green Sleeves* * (in 3/4) against that of *The Dargason* (in 6/8), building up to a huge climax with extraordinarily happy effect.

Suite, The Planets: (Only *Mars* and *Jupiter* arranged for band.) Holst's most famous orchestral work was first performed in 1919. The original score calls for a huge orchestra and a chorus of women's voices. The entire work is large in

* *Green Sleeves* is a very well-known tune of considerable antiquity. It is found, among other places, in the score of *The Beggar's Opera* by John Gay.

conception. There are seven movements, named after the principal planets, with subtitles indicating their astrological significance. The length of the work is such that it is seldom given in its entirety.

The first movement is entitled *Mars—The Bringer of War*. This movement is written in 5/4 time and is full of rhythmic energy. There are three principal themes which may be distinguished. The development is elaborate and includes a number of climactic passages, which lead to the real climax of the movement. This is a passage of great power, using the full resources of the band. It is followed by fanfare passages in the brass.

Jupiter—The Bringer of Jollity is the fourth movement of the suite. Like the other movements, it is somewhat irregular in form and lends support to the theory that the composer attached some astrological significance to the music. It opens with a cheerful tune, which gives way to the emergence of a strong rhythmic idea. The time shifts between 2/4 and 3/4, with a good deal of episodic material introduced. The movement ends rather unexpectedly with a return to the material of the opening.

Engelbert Humperdinck

BORN Siegburg, Germany, September 1, 1854
DIED September 27, 1921

WORKS ARRANGED FOR BAND:

Selections: HANSEL AND GRETEL (F
DIE KÖNIGSKINDER (B&H
March from DIE KÖNIGSKINDER (B&H
Suite, THE MIRACLE (B&H

ALTHOUGH HUMPERDINCK composed much music of a very high order, his reputation rests almost entirely on his opera *Hänsel and Gretel.* Its composition took place almost casually, and this is reflected in the spontaneity and grace of the music. The composer's sister had arranged the well-known fairy-tale of the brothers Grimm in dramatic form to amuse her own children. Humperdinck intended to write a few simple melodies to accompany this diversion, but was so taken with the idea that he determined to use it as the basis for a complete opera. In the music to this child's tale, Humperdinck used the musical methods of his master, Richard Wagner.

The production of *Hänsel and Gretel* at Weimar in 1893, immediately made Humperdinck famous throughout Europe. The opera was greeted with acclaim as a change from the weightiness of Wagner and the turgid melodrama of the Mascagni school. An air of wholesome charm is notable in the entire work. The music itself is simple and captivating, very close in spirit to the beautiful old folk songs of Germany.

Humperdinck's three-act opera *Die Königskinder* (*The King's Children*) was first brought out at the Metropolitan Opera House in New York under Alfred Hertz in 1910. The opera was fashioned from a play of the same name to which

Humperdinck had written the incidental music. Much of this music, which was composed in 1895-96, was used in the opera version. The story tells of a legendary episode in the Hellaforest, where two King's children, a Prince and a Princess, are the victims of exile and witchcraft. In its folk-like quality, the opera is similar to *Hänsel and Gretel.* The music has the same charm and spontaneity, and much of the same homely and unpretentious substance.

ɾ ɾ ɾ

Suite from *The Miracle:*

1. Prelude
2. Procession and Children's Dance
3. Banquet
4. March of the Army—and Death Motif
5. Xmas Scene—Finale, First Act

Among the last commissions undertaken by Humperdinck was that for the incidental music to Max Reinhardt's production of *The Miracle*. Humperdinck's score was admirably suited to the atmosphere of the drama and greatly enhanced the effect. The concert suite extracted from the incidental music includes some of Humperdinck's most expressive pages. *The Miracle* was produced in New York in 1922.

Mikhail Mikhailovitch Ippolitov-Ivanov

BORN Gatchina, Russia, November 19, 1859
DIED Moscow, January 28, 1935

WORKS ARRANGED FOR BAND:

Suite, CAUCASIAN SKETCHES (F; Aff
I. In the Mountains
II. In The Village
III. In the Mosque
IV. Procession of the Sirdar

IPPOLITOV-IVANOV was a pupil of Rimsky-Korsakov. Early in his career he became conductor of the Symphony Orchestra at Tiflis in Georgian Russia. While there he made a careful study of the music of the Caucasus and of Georgia. His well-known suite, *Caucasian Sketches,* written in 1895, shows the result of that study, being based almost entirely on native music. The numbers themselves are straightforward in character and admirably descriptive of the scenes suggested by their titles. The last number is remarkable for its alternation between *forte* and *piano,* suggestive of the music's being carried one way and then another by the wind.

Edvard Armas Jaernefeldt

BORN Viborg, Finland, August 18, 1869

ARRANGED FOR BAND:

PRAELUDIUM (B&H*

AFTER SIBELIUS, JAERNEFELDT is probably the best known composer of Finland. His musical training was received in his native land, in Berlin and in Paris. In 1898 he became conductor of the orchestra of Viborg, later becoming director of the musical institute of Helsingfors. Although Jaernefeldt has composed many symphonic works, his fame rests upon his many songs and upon the ever popular *Praeludium*, which has been arranged for almost every possible combination of instruments.

* In U. S. A.: (M

Albert W. Ketelbey

BORN Birmingham, England

WORKS ARRANGED FOR BAND:

IN A PERSIAN MARKET
IN A MONASTERY GARDEN
and some twenty more descriptive pieces, Valses, etc.
(All published by Bosworth*)

A. W. KETELBEY (pronounce with accent on second syllable) showed his disposition for music at an early age. One of his boyhood compositions was highly praised by Sir Edward Elgar; he won the Queen Victoria Scholarship at Trinity College, and was awarded many medals for his excellence in his musical studies.

He performed frequently as pianist and organist, eventually becoming conductor of a light-opera company. His compositions soon acquired a wide popularity, and it is on them that his reputation rests.

Almost all of Ketelbey's works which have been arranged for band are of a nature which needs no analysis. Many of them are printed with synopses presumably written by the composer, while others have quotations scattered throughout the music itself. Others have words to be sung, and these, of course, give a more than adequate interpretation of the music.

* In America: Boosey-Hawkes-Belwin.

Karl King

WORKS WRITTEN FOR BAND:

Overtures: FOUNTAIN OF YOUTH (Ba
THE GOLDEN DRAGON (Ba
SUNNY SPAIN (King
THE WANDERER (King
and many others, mostly grades 2&3
Over 200 marches, waltzes, serenades, novelties etc.
(pub. by King, Ba; Fil)

KARL KING is one of the most active of American bandmasters and composers. His early band experience was acquired with traveling circuses, among which may be mentioned Buffalo Bill's Wild West Show and the Barnum and Bailey Circus. He later became director of the Grand Army Band at Canton, Ohio, retaining that position until he was called to Fort Dodge, Iowa, in 1920. He has been director of the Fort Dodge Municipal Band since that date. Under his leadership the band has become well and favorably known through its many successful appearances. Mr. King is a member of the American Bandmasters' Association and Past President of the Iowa Bandmasters' Association. He has also served as President of the A. B. A.

Mr. King's compositions are of a light and spirited nature. Many of them are designed for young bands or bands of intermediate proficiency. All of his works have titles which are more or less suggestive of their characters. One of his best known marches is *Barnum and Bailey's Favorite,* which was written while Mr. King was with that company.

Mayhew Lester Lake

BORN Southville, Massachusetts

WORKS WRITTEN FOR BAND:

Overtures: AMERICANA (F
Fantasias: THE EVOLUTION OF DIXIE (F
THE EVOLUTION OF YANKEE DOODLE (F
Grand Marches: THE PILGRIM (F
DEMOCRACY (ABC

Many medleys, novelties, descriptive numbers, marches, etc.

MAYHEW LAKE is known as one of the most gifted band arrangers in America, and is also famous for his many original compositions. He has been associated with bands and band music during his entire career. His compositions are for the most part of a light and pleasing nature, although he has written works of a more serious nature as well. Mr. Lake received his musical education in America. He has made special arrangements for Victor Herbert, Maurice Ravel, John Philip Sousa, Henry Hadley, Edwin Franko Goldman and many others.

Overture, Americana: This overture was written in the fall of 1918 and received its first performance at a concert of the Goldman Band at Columbia University on June 20, 1919. It is dedicated to Henry Hadley. One of the principal themes of the overture is the old melody, *Old Zip Coon;* the other is an original melody in the style of a Negro chant. They are developed with the composer's customary skill, and built up to make an original and effective number.

Fantasia, The Evolution of Dixie: This popular fantasia is based on the original idea of taking a well-known tune and imaginatively depicting its evolution from a primitive state to the shape in which it has become famous. Mr. Lake takes the tune, *Dixie,* and develops it from "The Creation" to an "Aboriginal Dance," then to a "Minuet," and finally to its usual form. He then follows the development out further by presenting the tune as a waltz, as ragtime and as grand opera.

Grand March, The Pilgrim: This march was composed in 1928. It is an impressive number, written with a great deal of the composer's characteristic rhythmic strength and instrumental skill, and is very popular on band programs.

Victor Antoine Edouard Lalo

BORN Lille, France, January 27, 1823
DIED Paris, April 22, 1892

WORKS ARRANGED FOR BAND:
NORWEGIAN RHAPSODY (F; S

LALO was of Spanish origin but spent his entire life in France. The distinction of his work entitles him to recognition as one of the foremost French composers of the nineteenth century. His melodies are generally original and incisive and he had great skill in orchestration. His best-known works are the opera, *Le Roi d'Ys,* and his *Symphonie Espagnole* for violin and orchestra. Lalo was awarded the Legion of Honor in 1880.

The *Norwegian Rhapsody* was arranged for orchestra from a *Norwegian Phantasy* written for violin solo and orchestra. As an orchestral number it was first performed with great success at one of the Colonne concerts in Paris in 1879. It makes use in an effective manner of characteristic Norwegian themes.

Eduard Lassen

BORN Copenhagen, Denmark, April 13, 1830
DIED Weimar, Germany, January 15, 1904

ARRANGED FOR BAND:

Overture: FESTIVAL (F

ALTHOUGH LASSEN was born in Denmark, he received his musical education in Belgium, and after winning the Prix de Rome in 1851 established himself in Weimar. In 1861 he succeeded Liszt as conductor of the opera there. He composed several operas, two symphonies, and many smaller works, of which this *Festival* overture is perhaps the best-known. It is founded on German (Thuringian) folk songs.

Ernesto Lecuona

BORN Cuba

WORKS ARRANGED FOR BAND:

MALAGUEÑA (M
ANDALUCIA (M

ERNESTO LECUONA is probably the leading contemporary composer of Cuba. He manifested musical talent at a very early age, composing several pieces during his eighth year. His formal studies were pursued in Spain under De Falla and Turina. On his return to Cuba he entered upon the career of a virtuoso pianist and conductor, appearing with great success throughout Latin America as soloist and as conductor of the Symphony Orchestra of Cuba.

The work by which he is best known is the suite *Andalucia,* composed for piano solo. The *Malagueña* and the number entitled *Andalucia* from this suite have attained great popularity in a variety of arrangements.

Ruggiero Leoncavallo

BORN Naples, Italy, March 8, 1858
DIED Montecatini, Italy, August 9, 1919

ARRANGED FOR BAND:

I PAGLIACCI:
Prologue (F
Intermezzo (F
Fantasie (S

I Pagliacci had its first performance at Milan in 1892, and was the first of the composer's operas to receive a hearing. It scored a great success, as a result of which some of Leoncavallo's earlier works were produced. Neither these nor any of his later compositions were well received, but his reputation has endured solely on the basis of *I Pagliacci,* which is in the repertory of probably every opera house in the world. Leoncavallo wrote his own libretto for this work, revealing a talent for the dramatic which is further illustrated in the music. The story, as is well-known, deals with an episode in the career of a troupe of traveling artists.

Erik W. G. Leidzén

BORN Stockholm, Sweden, 1894

WORKS WRITTEN FOR BAND:

Overtures: SPRINGTIME (S
DEBONNAIRE (F
HOLIDAY (F

AUTUMN (S
NORDIC MARCH (F

ERIK LEIDZÉN, known as one of the outstanding composers and arrangers for band in America, received his musical education at the Royal Conservatory of Music of Stockholm. He came to the United States shortly after reaching his twentieth year, and is an American citizen. He was active for many years as pianist, composer and teacher, and became interested in the band field through a meeting with Dr. Edwin Franko Goldman. He is now principal arranger for the Goldman Band as well as for several publishing houses, and has become well-known through his splendid original works for band.

Mr. Leidzén was conductor of the famous Swedish Glee Club of Brooklyn for six years, bringing that organization to an eminent position among choral groups. He was conductor-in-chief at the Gustavus Adolphus tercentenary in New York, and won the St. Erik prize for orchestral composition in 1921. He has been the recipient of many other awards for his compositions. His *Fugue with Chorale* was performed by the Rochester Civic Symphony under Howard Hanson, with great success.

In addition to his creative and editorial activity, Mr. Leidzén is head of the theoretical department of the Ernest Williams School of Music, in Brooklyn, where his work has attracted wide attention.

Overture, Springtime: The *Springtime* overture was written in 1935, in response to a request for an original band work from Mr. Leidzén's pen. Although the overture bears a title, it follows no particular program; indeed it was conceived purely as music and the title was added as an afterthought. The composer has pointed out, however, that the different themes may, if it is held desirable, be taken to represent the varying aspects of Spring, and has supplied the following outline:

"The introduction is based on the secondary theme appearing first at 4. This 'song-theme' should be played so as to represent the sweetness, romance and poetic yearning incident to the awakening of Nature after the sleep of winter. The restless *Allegro* typifies the busy growth and restless evolution of the period. The trumpeting figure at 3 (which also serves as an accompaniment to the 'song-theme') may be imagined as the bugle-call of the heralds of Spring, while the more pompous strains at 6 may be the approach of her majesty itself. The codetta at 7 gives the bubbling over of joyousness which I believe all healthy minds feel in Springtime. The development which follows may readily be interpreted with the aid of the given suggestions, but it should be noted that when the 'song-theme' occurs again (at 13), it is in a plaintive minor, for, alas, Springtime is short. But gladness soon takes the upper hand again and at 16 the three principal themes are united, the 'song-theme' predominating and this time again in the major."

The overture is dedicated to Dr. Edwin Franko Goldman, at whose concerts it had its first performance.

Overture, Holiday: This lively overture was completed early in 1937 and had its first performance at the convention of the American Bandmasters' Association in Milwaukee,

Wisconsin, on March 5-7 of that year. It is dedicated to the association.

The work is in rapid 6/8 tempo. It has no particular program except that suggested by the gay carnival spirit of the music. The musical contrast of the themes is skillfully handled without changing the mood of the overture as a whole. Near the end the tempo changes to 3/4 time, and the music takes on a broader, more impressive aspect just before the finale.

Overture, Debonnaire: This overture was composed in 1937, in response to the great demand for an easy yet thoroughly musical work for young bands. The atmosphere of the overture is one of graceful gaiety. With the exceptions of the introduction and the finale, this mood pervades the entire composition. *Debonnaire* is dedicated to the National School Band Association.

Overture, Autumn: This melodious overture was written especially for younger bands, and with a regard to the problems of massed-band performance. The contrapuntal element is not as highly developed as in most of Mr. Leidzén's other works. The *Autumn* overture is in the key of D minor, and is in 3/4 time throughout. The main theme is somewhat plaintive, while the second theme is a little brighter and gives interesting passages for various solo instruments. The work is dedicated to the Pennsylvania School Music Association.

Nordic March: This grand march is built entirely on thematic material taken from famous Scandinavian tunes. The introduction uses the closing phrase of *Du gamla, du fria,* which in Sweden corresponds to our *America.* The first strain introduces *Kong Kristian,* the Danish national anthem. This vigorous and martial air melts into the minor refrain of

Suomi's Song (Finnish), which in turn is followed by the opening bars of the pompous *Ja, vi elsker* (the Norwegian national anthem) thundered out by the basses and trombones. Then follows *Du gamla, du fria,* this time complete. The trio returns to the minor, and consists of an arrangement of the Swedish tune, *Ack, Värmeland, du sköna!*

Anatol Konstantinovich Liadov

BORN St. Petersburg, May 11, 1855
DIED Novgorod (Russia), August 28, 1914

WORKS ARRANGED FOR BAND:

Valse Badinage from A MUSICAL SNUFF-BOX (B&H

ANATOL LIADOV began the study of music at an early age under the tutelage of his father, a well-known musician of St. Petersburg. Later he enrolled in the St. Petersburg Conservatory, from which he was graduated in 1877. At the Conservatory he studied under Rimsky-Korsakov, and was considered by that inspired teacher to be among the greatest talents he had ever known. From 1878 on, Liadov taught at the Conservatory.

The second generation of the St. Petersburg school of composers counted Liadov among its most valued members. Like others of the school, Liadov excelled in orchestration, and like them gave much of his music a national character. In his work the latter tendency was, however, less pronounced than in the cases of Moussorgsky or Rimsky-Korsakov. Liadov was perhaps more essentially a composer for the pianoforte than others of the group, yet he distinguished himself in almost every branch of composition.

A Musical Snuff-Box (*Une Tabatière à Musique*): The *Musical Snuff-Box,* Opus 32, is a collection of characteristic pieces written for the pianoforte, and is perhaps the most famous work of the composer. Various pieces from the set have been arranged in many forms, the composer himself having made several arrangements of the *Valse Badinage* (see introduction). The set shows the composer in a light and charming vein, yet with all the elegance and refinement for which his music is noted.

Franz Liszt

BORN Raiding, Hungary, October 22, 1811
DIED Bayreuth, Germany, July 31, 1886

WORKS ARRANGED FOR BAND:

Symphonic Poems: LES PRELUDES (F; AMP
TASSO (AMP
MAZEPPA (F
HUNGARIAN RHAPSODIES, No. 1 (C; F
2 (F; B&H; AMP
3 (F; B&H
4 (F
6 (F
LIEBESTRAUM No. 3 (F; B&H; Brg
SECOND POLONAISE (F; AMP
RAKOCZY MARCH (D; J

LISZT was one of the great figures of nineteenth-century music. His place in history is secure not only by reason of his achievements as pianist, composer and conductor, but also on account of the encouragement and assistance he gave to Wagner and innumerable other contemporaries. During the twelve years Liszt was at Weimar, that small city was the center of musical life in Germany. Musicians and amateurs gathered there to hear the new works which Liszt introduced and championed. The unselfishness of Liszt was proverbial; he was a great and powerful personality as well as the most influential musician of his day.

Liszt's own music is completely romantic in conception and rather unequal in inspiration. His original works and transcriptions for piano were for the most part written as virtuoso pieces, although many of them have a direct and natural poetic quality. His orchestral works, such as the symphonic poems, are more operatic than symphonic in quality, and were considered revolutionary when first performed.

They carried "program music" to its furthest development before the time of Richard Strauss.

Symphonic Poem, Les Préludes: Liszt composed *The Preludes* while he was at Weimar. The first performance of the work took place in that city in 1854. The programmatic basis of this symphonic poem is the following passage, condensed from Lamartine's *Poetic Meditations:* "What is life but a series of preludes to that unknown song whose initial solemn note is tolled by Death? The enchanted dawn of every life is love; but where is the destiny on whose first delicious joys some storm does not break?—a storm whose deadly blast disperses youth's illusions, whose fatal bolt consumes its altar. And what soul thus cruelly bruised, when the tempest rolls away, seeks not to rest its memories in the calm of rural life? Yet man allows himself not long to taste the kindly quiet which first attracted him to Nature's lap; but when the trumpet gives the signal he hastens to danger's post, whatever be the fight which draws him to its lists; that in the strife he may once more regain full knowledge of himself and all his strength."—(Translated by Huneker.)

Symphonic Poem, Tasso (*Lament and Triumph*): The second of Liszt's symphonic poems was conceived in 1840 as a pianoforte work. It was orchestrated in 1848, and produced as the introduction to Goethe's drama *Tasso* at Weimar in 1849. Like the drama, Liszt's work is founded on the life and works of Torquato Tasso, the great Italian poet of the Renaissance whose most famous work is the epic *Jerusalem Delivered.*

Symphonic Poem, Mazeppa (*Finale*): The story of Mazeppa, the hero of the steppes, has been made familiar by

Byron's poem. Liszt, however, took as the foundation of his composition the treatment of the same subject by Victor Hugo. It is the sixth of the composer's set of symphonic poems, and like several of the others was originally conceived for pianoforte. It was orchestrated in 1858.

The *Finale* opens with a tremolo in the lower instruments, following which a sharp theme is announced by the brass. The music becomes stronger and more animated until a fiery climax tells of Mazeppa's rescue and glorification.

Hungarian Rhapsodies: Liszt composed fifteen Hungarian rhapsodies for the piano. These became so popular that the composer, in collaboration with Franz Doppler, arranged six of them for orchestra. The rhapsodies are perfectly free in form and development and are based on national Magyar melodies and rhythms.

Rhapsody No. 1: The first Hungarian rhapsody for orchestra corresponds to the fourteenth of the piano set. The themes used in this composition were such favorites with the composer that he also used them in his Hungarian fantasy for piano and orchestra.

Rhapsody No. 2: The second Hungarian rhapsody (for orchestra) is the most popular of the set. It opens with a slow movement patterned after the "Lassen," a Magyar dance, and continues with the rapid "Friska," taken from the "Czardas," the national dance of Hungary.

Rhapsody No. 3: The third Hungarian rhapsody (for orchestra) is dedicated to Count Apponyi, and is the sixth of the piano set.

Rhapsody No. 4: This rhapsody is known as the twelfth of the original edition, and is dedicated to Joseph Joachim, the renowned violinist.

Rhapsody No. 6: The sixth rhapsody, one of the most

popular, is also known as *The Carnival of Pesth.* It is the ninth of the piano set. This rhapsody, as suggested by its alternate title, is prevailingly joyous in mood, the slower middle section occurring between a spirited *presto* and a vivacious *allegro.*

The Second Polonaise: Liszt's *Second Polonaise* compares in popularity with his second Hungarian rhapsody. It was originally composed for the pianoforte. The *Polonaise* is adapted from a Polish dance form; it is in 3/4 time and usually majestic in character.

Liebestraum: (No. 3) (Dream of Love): This ever-popular composition is one of a set of three nocturnes written for the piano. All three of these nocturnes are adaptations of songs previously composed by Liszt. The third has completely overshadowed the other two in popularity.

Henry Litolff

BORN London, February 6, 1818
DIED near Paris, August 6, 1891

ARRANGED FOR BAND:

Overture, MAXIMILIAN ROBESPIERRE (F

LITOLFF studied piano under Moscheles and gained a considerable reputation in Europe as a pianoforte virtuoso. Later in his life he settled in Germany and went into the music-publishing business. He composed prolifically, his works including operas, oratorios and compositions in smaller forms. His overture *Maximilian Robespierre* is an old favorite in the band repertory. It is very dramatic in content, and is a good example of standard program music. The introduction is intended to depict the background of the turbulent French Revolution. The Robespierre motif soon emerges; its gradual dominance of the music is the musical counterpart of the hero's role in the Revolution. At length a trumpet signal proclaims Robespierre's approaching doom, and the overture ends with a tonal picture of his execution.

Gustav Albert Lortzing

BORN Berlin, October 23, 1801
DIED Berlin, January 21, 1851

WORKS ARRANGED FOR BAND:

Overtures: CZAR AND ZIMMERMANN (F
UNDINE (F; D
THE ARMOURER (D; B&H; AMP
VOICE OF NATURE (F
FEST OVERTURE (F

Selections: CZAR UND ZIMMERMANN (F

LORTZING spent the first forty years of his life following the career of an opera singer. At the same time he composed a number of comic operas and some instrumental music. His music is natural and pleasing, and at its best is characterized by a freshness of melody and an abundance of humor.

Czar und Zimmermann: Lortzing's comic opera, *Czar und Zimmermann,* was produced in 1839 and was warmly greeted. It is still a general favorite in Germany. It has been produced in English under the title of *Peter the Shipwright.*

Undine: Lortzing became conductor of the Leipzig opera in 1844 but resigned after a short time. Reduced to poverty, he wandered from city to city in Germany, and in 1845, at Hamburg, brought out his opera, *Undine.* The production was a success and served to re-establish him temporarily. His works fell into neglect, however, and the last years of his life were spent in bitter poverty.

Edward Alexander MacDowell

BORN New York City, December 18, 1861
DIED New York City, January 24, 1908

WORKS ARRANGED FOR BAND:

Suites: WOODLAND SKETCHES (B&H
SEA PIECES (B&H

MACDOWELL was the first American composer to achieve a considerable European reputation, and he undoubtedly takes rank as the foremost American composer of his time. His musical education was received in France and Germany; the German influence was pronounced throughout his career. MacDowell composed many large works, but is best-known by his short and charming pieces for piano. MacDowell's romanticism is reflected in the poetic titles which he gave to most of these pieces.

MacDowell was appointed Professor of Music at Columbia University in 1896 and held that position until 1904.

✓ ✓ ✓

Suite, Woodland Sketches:

I. To a Wild Rose
II. Will o' the Wisp
III. At an Old Trysting Place
IV. In Autumn
V. From an Indian Lodge
VI. To a Water Lily
VII. From Uncle Remus
VIII. A Deserted Farm
IX. By a Meadow Brook
X. Told at Sunset

The *Woodland Sketches* were written for the pianoforte and in that form have attained immense popularity. The descriptive titles of the pieces give a good idea of the moods the composer wished to evoke. In the fifth piece, *From an Indian Lodge,* MacDowell made use of an authentic Indian melody. MacDowell's interest in American Indian music was reflected in some of his larger compositions, but nowhere more effectively than in this sketch.

Suite, Sea Pieces:

I. To the Sea
II. From a Wandering Iceberg
III. A. D. MDCXX
IV. Starlight
V. Song
VI. From the Depths
VII. Nautilus
VIII. In Mid-Ocean

Like the more famous *Woodland Sketches,* the *Sea Pieces* were originally composed for pianoforte. They have not become quite as popular as the former, possibly because they are on a slightly larger scale. There is a real majesty and impressiveness in many of these *Sea Pieces,* notably the first, the sixth and the last. The third piece, *A. D. MDCXX,* commemorates the landing of the Pilgrims at Plymouth Rock.

Heinrich August Marschner

BORN Zittau, Saxony, August 16, 1795
DIED Hanover, Germany, December 14, 1861

WORK ARRANGED FOR BAND:

Overture: HANS HEILING (F

MARSCHNER abandoned the study of law to pursue that of music, and was more successful as a composer than he possibly would have been as a lawyer. His early operas were greeted with such acclaim that he became joint director with Weber and Morlacchi of the Dresden Opera in 1823. Later he became *Kapellmeister* at Leipzig and at Hanover; in the latter position he remained for twenty-eight years, until he was forced to retire for expressing too liberal opinions. The most famous of his many operas, *Hans Heiling*, was written while he was at Hanover, but the work was first produced at Berlin in 1833. It was an enormous success and is still in the regular repertory of many German opera companies. Little of the music, with the exception of the overture, is familiar in this country.

Marschner's style derives from that of Weber, although in some respects he anticipated the early operas of Wagner.

Pietro Mascagni

BORN Leghorn, Italy, December 7, 1863

WORKS ARRANGED FOR BAND:

CAVALLERIA RUSTICANA: *Intermezzo* (F; CB
Selections (F

IRIS: *Introduction* (B&H
Selections (B&H

MASCAGNI spent his early years in obscurity and want. It was not until his one-act opera, *Cavalleria Rusticana* (Rustic Chivalry), won a prize offered by the publisher Sonzogno that the composer scored a success. The work was produced in Rome in 1890 and the next day Mascagni was famous. The libretto was based on a story of Sicilian life by Giovanni Verga. The success of the opera was due largely to the quick and direct action of the story and the dramatic emotional appeal of the music. *Cavalleria* started a vogue for sensational "realistic" operas, but nothing the composer wrote subsequently achieved anything like the success of this work.

✓ ✓ ✓

Intermezzo from *Cavalleria Rusticana:* The *Intermezzo* which is played between the first and second parts of *Cavalleria* made an immediate appeal to opera-lovers, and it is still one of the most popular operatic excerpts known. In the opera itself it comes as a welcome contrast after the turbulent drama of the Church scene.

✓

Iris (*Selections*): The opera *Iris* was produced in Rome in 1898, but in spite of several pleasing passages was not a success. The setting of the opera is Japanese, and the story is one of those remarkable melodramas possible only on operatic stages.

The introduction to the first act is the most popular portion of the opera. It pictures the breaking of day in the garden of Iris, the young and innocent girl who is the heroine of the opera. As the sun rises, the music works up from a delicate *pianissimo* to a fuller and brighter sonority. When day is fully revealed, Iris appears in the garden and makes her daily obeisance to the sun.

Jules Massenet

BORN near St. Etienne, France, May 12, 1842
DIED Paris, August 13, 1912

WORKS ARRANGED FOR BAND:

Overture, PHÈDRE (F; B&H; D
Suites: SCÈNES PITTORESQUES (F; D
SCÈNES NAPOLITAINES (F; B&H
SCÈNES ALSACIENNES (B&H
THE FURIES (LES ERINNYES) (C
Selections: MANON (F
LE CID (B&H
HÉRODIADE (F; D
DON CÉSAR DE BAZAN (F
THE LAST DREAM OF THE VIRGIN (F
Meditation from THAÏS
PARADE MILITAIRE (F
ELÉGIE (F; ABC
Aragonaise from LE CID (F
AUBADE (F
Angelus from SCÈNES PITTORESQUES (J

THE FAME AND POPULARITY of Massenet's music are due more to the composer's gift for pleasing melody than to any startling originality or dramatic power. Massenet's ability to please the public taste enabled him to win success and honors during his lifetime. As Professor of Composition at the Paris Conservatory, he taught, and to a certain extent influenced, such well-known composers as Bruneau, Leroux, Pierné and Charpentier. Massenet wrote about forty works for the theatre and a variety of orchestral and vocal music. In 1878 he was elected to the Academy of Fine Arts, the youngest man ever to be so honored. In 1899 he was made a Grand Officer of the Legion of Honor.

Overture, Phèdre: When the conductor and impresario, Jules Pasdeloup, commissioned Massenet to write an orchestral work for the Pasdeloup Concerts, the composer responded with this overture, inspired by the famous tragedy of Racine, the greatest of the classic French dramatists. The *Phèdre* overture is strictly programmatic, following in a general way the action of the drama, which may be roughly summarized as follows: Phèdre, wife of Theseus and daughter of Minos, is consumed by passion for her step-son, Hippolytus. He, however, repulses her. Phèdre, with the proverbial fury of a woman scorned, poisons the mind of Theseus against his son. Theseus recalls a promise of assistance made to him by Neptune, and commits Hippolytus to the vengeance of the god. Hippolytus seeks to escape, but Neptune sends for a sea monster which terrifies the horses of the unfortunate youth, and he is dragged to his death. Phèdre, overcome by remorse, commits suicide.

The overture begins with a gloomy passage which leads into a theme associable with Phèdre's love for Hippolytus. Her declaration of her passion is presented with great intensity and leads directly to the music descriptive of the flight of Hippolytus. The development of these themes reaches an energetic climax which depicts the death of Hippolytus, after which the sombre music of the opening section returns as a lament.

Suite, Scènes Alsaciennes:

I. Sunday Morning
II. At the Tavern
III. Under the Linden Tree
IV. Sunday Evening

Massenet's *Alsatian Scenes,* written not long after the close of the Franco-Prussian War, may well be termed "propaganda music," designed to remind the French public of the charm of a lost territory. A thoroughly patriotic synopsis standing at the head of the score explains that the composer recalls with happiness the Alsatian village, with its good people and pleasant life. The scene is that of a peaceful Sabbath in the days before the war.

Suite, Scènes Pittoresques:

I. March
II. Angelus
III. Fête Bohème

Between 1872 and 1877, Massenet temporarily abandoned the stage and composed many works for orchestra. These were very well received and this particular suite has become exceptionally popular. The march is piquant and pleasing. The *Angelus,* often played separately, is more specifically descriptive than the other movements. There are passages suggestive of church choirs and there is likewise a suggestion of the Angelus bells, produced by four horns in unison. The *Fête Bohème* is opened by a fanfare in the brass, and proceeds with music suggestive of colorful merrymaking.

Suite, Scènes Napolitaines:

I. The Dance
II. Procession and Improvisation
III. The Fête

The *Scènes Napolitaines* is the fifth of Massenet's orchestral suites. The first movement is patterned on the Tarantella, a lively Italian dance of colorful character. The *Procession and Improvisation* is a musical picture of the bustling life of Naples, contrasting typically religious strains with the careless performances of street musicians. The third movement presents a gay public carnival, with all of the vividness associated with the famous Italian city.

Suite, The Furies (*Les Erinnyes*) and *Elégie:*

I. Entr'Acte

II. Religious Scene

III. Finale

In 1873 Massenet wrote the incidental music for *Les Erinnyes,* a tragedy in Greek style by Charles Leconte de Lisle (1818-1894). This drama in verse was inspired by the last part of the *Oresteiad* of Aeschylus, likewise entitled *The Furies* (*Eumenides*).

Massenet, doubtless realizing that so lofty a drama would have little vogue in the theatre, later arranged portions of his music in a suite for concert performance. In this form it has become popular. The music is not entirely Hellenic in character, but it has a great deal of elegant charm. The *Religious Scene,* which forms the second number of the suite, was originally written to accompany the funeral ceremony at the tomb of Agamemnon, murdered by his wife Clytemnestra, and her lover, Aegisthus. The second section of this movement is the famous *Elégie,* which Massenet later arranged as a song, and which has become popular as a separate number. It was played during the drama while Elektra poured a libation on her father's grave. The *Finale* of this suite is in the form of a series of lively dances, offering a decided contrast to the preceding movement.

Selections from *Manon: Manon,* first produced at the Opéra Comique in Paris on January 19, 1884, is generally considered to be Massenet's masterpiece. It is founded on the novel by the Abbé Prévost (1697-1763) which had already served as subject for Halévy, Auber and Balfe, and which was later to be used by Puccini. In this opera, Massenet made use of leading themes in the manner of Wagner, although of course neither his melodic vein nor his orchestral coloring resemble those of the German master. *Manon* has retained its great popularity and is frequently performed. Many of its arias are great favorites with singers and audiences, among these being, *Ah Fuyez, Douce Image!* (*Depart, Sweet Vision!*), which was a favorite number of Caruso, and *On L'Appelle Manon* (*She is Called Manon*).

Selections from *Le Cid:* This opera followed the same composer's *Manon* by about a year; it has never attained the success of the latter outside of France, however. The libretto is freely based on the play by Pierre Corneille (1606-1684), but it is decidedly lighter in treatment. The hero of the opera is Don Rodrigue Diaz de Bivar, the great Spanish hero of the eleventh century who was known as "El Cid Campeador" ("The Fighting Chief"), and who led his armies against the Moorish chief Boabdil.

The best-known portions of Massenet's opera are those making up the ballet music in the second act. The *Aragonaise,* superficially based on the native dance rhythms of the Spanish province of Aragon, is extremely well known and has been arranged in many forms.

Selections from *Hérodiade:* Massenet's five-act Biblical opera was first produced at Brussels in 1881. The librettists based their work on the novelette by Flaubert, but needless to say did not succeed in preserving the remarkable atmosphere of the great writer's story. The opera itself does not rank in popular esteem with the same composer's *Manon,* but there are a number of airs which are general favorites. Among these are *Il est doux, il est bon* (*He is good, he is kind*), sung by Herod in Act II. These airs, and much of the music throughout the opera, have the grace and expressiveness characteristic of the composer.

The Last Dream of the Virgin: This well-known selection is taken from *The Virgin,* a sacred legend in four scenes written by Massenet and produced at the Paris Opera in 1880. In its original form this excerpt is the prelude to the fourth scene. It was originally scored for string orchestra.

Meditation from *Thaïs:* Massenet's opera *Thaïs* is based on the novel by Anatole France. It deals with the successful struggle of the monk Athanaël to lead the courtesan Thaïs back to a life of virtue. (The librettists gave the name of Athanaël to the character known in France's novel as Paphnuce.)

In its original form the *Meditation* occurs as a violin obbligato between the third and fourth scenes of the opera. It depicts the all-night vigil of Athanaël outside the house of Thaïs, where he has vowed to remain until she repents.

Felix Mendelssohn
(Jacob Ludwig Felix Mendelssohn-Bartholdy)

BORN Hamburg, Germany, February 3, 1809
DIED Leipzig, Germany, November 4, 1847

WORKS ARRANGED FOR BAND:

Overtures: FINGAL'S CAVE (*Hebrides*) (F; B&H
RUY BLAS (F; B&H; C
CALM SEA AND HAPPY VOYAGE (F
SON AND STRANGER (F; B&H

From A MIDSUMMER NIGHT'S DREAM:
Overture (F; B&H
Nocturne (F; D
Wedding March (F; B&H; CB

From ATHALIE:
Overture (F
Selections (B&H
War March of the Priests (F; B&H

From "ITALIAN" SYMPHONY:
Pilgrim's March (F; B&H; C
Saltarello (C

"SCOTCH" SYMPHONY: Part I (B&H
FUNERAL MARCH IN A MINOR (AMP
CORNELIUS MARCH (B&H
RONDO CAPRICCIOSO (F
SONGS WITHOUT WORDS (various selections and publishers)

ORIGINAL WORK FOR BAND:

MILITARY OVERTURE IN C, OPUS 24 (F; AMP

MENDELSSOHN, like Mozart, gave evidence of his remarkable musical gifts at a very early age. At nine he made his debut as pianist; at eleven he was already a prolific composer. His talents were fostered by the intelligent direction of his family and by the atmosphere of refinement which prevailed in their home.

Mendelssohn's most remarkable exhibition of precocity

was his composition of the overture to *A Midsummer Night's Dream* when he was seventeen. This overture shows as complete a mastery of every aspect of composition as do the works he wrote at the end of his career. His musical training and intelligence were, indeed, so complete that in 1829, when a young man of twenty, he succeeded in having the *St. Matthew Passion* of Bach produced at Berlin—the first performance of that work since Bach's death. Thus he associated himself with the revival of interest in Bach's music in a distinguished manner; throughout his lifetime he continued his propaganda for the music of the great master.

From 1830 on, Mendelssohn's career was one of distinction. He made nine trips to England, where he felt at home and where his works were accorded enormous favor. In Germany, he organized concerts, gave benefits, encouraged the growth of music organizations and did much, by his inspiration and example, to add to the glory of German music. He organized the Domchor of Berlin and established the fame of the Gewandhaus Orchestra of Leipzig, which he conducted from 1845 on. These are but a few of his accomplishments, in recognition of which, it may be added, the present German government has forbidden the performance of his works and removed his statues from public places.

Mendelssohn's music has a character quite its own, whether in its smaller aspects, such as the songs and the *Songs Without Words,* or in the larger forms, such as the symphonies and the two oratorios, *St. Paul* and *Elijah,* the greatest of their kind since the time of Handel. It is music distinguished by a perfection of finish, a polish of phrase; by a serenity of feeling and a perfect adaptation to the medium chosen. Writing for orchestra, for piano or voice or violin, Mendelssohn was equally at home and wrote in an equally idiomatic manner. It is said that he wished to win fame as a dramatic composer, but that is the one field in which he produced nothing great; his talents were not of a dramatic order. For a time the music of Mendelssohn suffered neglect, by reason of the sheer weight of Wagner and Brahms. Today, however, there is a certain revival of interest, which is no more than justice to one of the purest talents of the last century.

Overture, Fingal's Cave (Hebrides): In the summer of 1829, after a successful concert season in London, Mendelssohn made a trip through Scotland, during which he visited Fingal's Cave in the Hebrides Islands. He was greatly impressed by this visit, and jotted down a few bars of music which he sent to a friend. During the rest of that year he was preoccupied with the idea of developing these bars into a finished composition. The result, completed in 1830, was the present overture, one of the most justly celebrated in the whole orchestral repertory.

Overture, Ruy Blas: Mendelssohn wrote the *Ruy Blas* overture in two days, as the result of an appeal from the theatrical pension fund in Leipzig. Victor Hugo's drama, for which the overture was written, did not appeal to the composer in the slightest, but the overture is nevertheless on a level with his best works. It is said that he insisted on calling it an "Overture to the Pension Fund." *Ruy Blas* was composed and performed in 1839, and was published posthumously as Opus 95.

Overture, Calm Sea and Prosperous Voyage: This overture was written shortly after the more famous *Fingal's Cave,* and was brought out in Berlin in 1832. As is true of most of Mendelssohn's works, the title is more for purposes of reference than for anything else, for the music is not in the least bit programmatic. It is said that Mendelssohn resented Schumann's attempt to discover diverse pictures and images in his music; it is evident that Mendelssohn believed that the beauty of the music should far out-weigh all other considerations.

Overture, Son and Stranger (Heimkehr aus der Fremde): Son and Stranger is the title of a one-act musical play written in 1829 by Mendelssohn for the silver wedding of his parents. In spite of the dramatic ability which it revealed, it was neither published nor performed again until after the composer's death. The overture, evidently written in a short time, is a charming piece which has maintained its popularity.

Overture, Midsummer Night's Dream: Mendelssohn's famous overture was inspired by the reading of Shakespeare's play. Written when the composer was seventeen years of age, it is one of the most astonishing accomplishments in the history of music. It is completely original in conception, admirably solid in form and structure and of a character truly inimitable. The overture was not used in conjunction with the play until seventeen years after its composition, at which time Mendelssohn composed the remainder of the incidental music.

Scherzo, Nocturne and *Wedding March* from *Midsummer Night's Dream:* These numbers were written for a performance of Shakespeare's play in Berlin in 1843, and it is not hard to believe that they were greeted with enthusiasm. There is no difference in spirit between them and the overture which Mendelssohn had composed seventeen years earlier. All of them are characterized by the same joyousness, the same perfection of finish and the same brilliance of orchestration. It is hard to imagine any other music capable of so admirably capturing the spirit of the comedy.

Athalie: Overture and War March of the Priests: The incidental music to Racine's tragedy was commissioned in 1843 but not completed until 1845. During those years Mendelssohn was so busy filling commissions in Berlin and London that he had to engage someone to take his place as conductor of the orchestra in Leipzig. Listening to the music Mendelssohn wrote during this time, however, it is hard to imagine that any of it was composed under pressure. The music for *Athalie* includes a number of choruses and vocal solos, but these are not nearly as well-known as the overture or the purely instrumental pieces.

"Italian" Symphony in A (Pilgrim's March and Saltarello): Mendelssohn's "Italian" Symphony was composed for the Philharmonic Society of London. It was begun when the composer was in Italy in 1830, but not completed until 1833. Mendelssohn had written more than a dozen symphonies during his early youth, but the "Italian" Symphony is one of the first which shows his full maturity. Mendelssohn himself modestly admitted that it showed progress. It has been, with the possible exception of the "Scotch" Symphony, the most popular of Mendelssohn's works in this form. Highly original in content, simple and transparent in form, it is one of the most characteristic expressions of Mendelssohn's genius.

"Scotch" Symphony in A Minor: Between 1833 and 1842, Mendelssohn completed no symphonies, although he had begun work on his A Minor Symphony ("Scotch") as early as 1830. This work, like the *Hebrides* overture, was undoubtedly inspired by his trip to Scotland in 1829, but the

score was not finished until 1842. The "Scotch" Symphony is the largest of Mendelssohn's works in this genre; like the "Italian" Symphony, with which it shares popularity, it is an expression of Mendelssohn's great individuality. It is supposed to be played through without pause, although it is divided into the conventional movements. Only the first part has been arranged for band.

Songs without Words: Probably no piano pieces are as well-known or universally loved as Mendelssohn's six books of *Songs without Words.* Written at various times during his life, they show a simplicity and charm which few imitators have been able to achieve. The idea of calling these diverse pieces *Songs without Words* was Mendelssohn's own. Each number bears a short title suggested by its character; most famous perhaps is the *Spring Song,* though others are at least as deserving of fame. Many of these have been arranged for band, and indeed for a variety of other instrumental combinations. It is safe to say that Mendelssohn's name is best-known by these intimate little pieces, so many of which were dashed off at a single sitting.

Giacomo Meyerbeer

BORN Berlin, September 5, 1791
DIED Paris, May 2, 1864

WORKS ARRANGED FOR BAND:

Selections from: THE HUGUENOTS (F; B&H; CB
ROBERT LE DIABLE (C; F
IL CROCIATO (B&H

Overtures: THE NORTH STAR (F
EMMA OF RESBURG (B&H
MARGUERITE OF ANJOU (B&H
THE HUGUENOTS (B&H

Coronation March from THE PROPHET (F; B&H; J

Benediction of the Swords from THE HUGUENOTS (F; B&H

Shadow Dance from DINORAH (F

Indian March from L'AFRICAINE (F

SCHILLER MARCH (B&H

TORCH DANCE (F; B&H; ABC; D; SF

GIACOMO MEYERBEER was the adopted name of Jacob Liebmann Beer, an extremely talented composer whose influence on nineteenth-century opera was very great. His early works were in the Italian style of the period, written under the influence of Rossini, and were favored with considerable success. Meyerbeer, however, felt keenly the dramatic limitations of such works and the need of a more grandiose or spectacular type of work for the stage.

The production of *Robert Le Diable* in Paris in 1831 marked a new period in the history of opera. Its mixture of dramatic force, scenic splendor, elaborate staging and novel instrumentation made it an unparalleled success. Five years later *The Huguenots* carried this new magnificence a step further, and established Meyerbeer as the leading operatic composer of Europe until the advent of Richard Wagner.

Selections from *The Huguenots: The Huguenots* was produced at the Paris Opera in 1836. It was conceived on a grand scale and may be said to have created the grandiose style of historical opera. The action of the opera centers about the massacre of the Huguenots on St. Bartholomew's Day in 1572; the romantic counterplot is of course not missing. *The Huguenots* securely established Meyerbeer's fame, and held the stage for many years. It is seldom performed today, for its novelty has somewhat worn off, and it is not of sustained interest through the extreme length of its five acts. Portions of the opera, which contains some of Meyerbeer's greatest music, are, however, still among the favorites of the operatic repertory.

Selections from *Robert le Diable: Robert le Diable* was the first of Meyerbeer's great successes. Its first performance at the Paris Opera in 1831 not only was an operatic sensation, but practically made the fortune and the reputation of the opera itself. The vigor and vividness of the work struck an entirely new note, in strong contrast to the melodious but hopelessly unexciting Italian operas of the day. Scribe's libretto was highly melodramatic, and Meyerbeer did full justice to it in his music, which abounds in what were for that time brilliant and unlooked-for effects. The opera's extreme length makes it unwieldy to produce today, but portions of it have maintained some popularity.

Selections from *Il Crociato: Il Crociato* was the last of the operas Meyerbeer wrote for the Italian stage. It was produced at Venice in 1824. The reception accorded it was almost without parallel; scenes of wild enthusiasm culminated with the calling of the composer to the stage to have a crown set upon his head! In *Il Crociato,* which is all but forgotten today, Meyerbeer made his first attempts toward the development of his famous dramatic style, so fully set forth in *Robert the Devil* seven years later.

Selections from *Emma di Resburgo: Emma di Resburgo* is one of the early operas of Meyerbeer, written in the Italian style. It was produced, with great success, in Venice in 1820.

Selections from *Marguerite of Anjou:* This early opera of Meyerbeer was written for La Scala of Milan, where it was produced in 1820. It is said to be the best of the Italian operas of the composer, but its fame has been eclipsed by the reputation of the composer's later works.

Overture, The North Star: The North Star was Meyerbeer's attempt to compete with the French comic-opera composers on their own ground. It was not altogether successful, the opinion apparently being that Meyerbeer's melodramatic style was hardly suited to the character of his libretto. The work was produced in Paris in 1854. The overture has always been a popular one, although the opera itself is seldom played today.

Shadow Dance from *Dinorah:* The opera *Dinorah* was known originally as *The Pardon of Ploërmel,* and at one time enjoyed considerable popularity. In contrast to Meyerbeer's more famous works, *Dinorah* is not a historical opera. It was first produced in 1859 at the Opéra Comique in Paris. Much of the music is very agreeable and is still played, notably the famous *Shadow Dance* which occurs at the beginning of the second act. The libretto of the opera, unfortunately, is such a tissue of absurdities as to justify the work's exile from the stage.

Coronation March from *The Prophet: The Prophet* was a product of Meyerbeer's full maturity and is thoroughly representative of all the qualities which made his reputation. Melodramatic action, sensational effects, original instrumentation and elaborateness of scale contributed to its success. It was first performed in Paris in 1849. The libretto deals with the Anabaptist uprising led by John of Leyden in 1543. The *Coronation March,* which occurs at the end of the fourth act, is one of the few portions of the opera frequently performed today.

Indian March from *L'Africaine:* The opera *L'Africaine* was written over a period of twenty-six years (1838-1864) and was not performed until after the composer's death. It is in many ways the finest of Meyerbeer's works, but its excessive length (six hours) keeps it from the stage. The *Indian March* occurs in the fourth act during a scene of great magnificence, in the course of which the Indian Princess, Selika, is welcomed home by her people.

Torch Dance: Meyerbeer composed three Torch Dances for "brass orchestra" in honor of the weddings of the King of Bavaria (1846), Princess Charlotte of Prussia (1850), and Princess Anne of Prussia (1853), respectively. The first of these is the one which has become the most popular and most frequently played. The Torch Dance (*Fackeltanz*) in itself is a survival of a medieval custom dating from the days of tournaments; it still formed a part of certain German court ceremonies in the nineteenth century. The music is similar in character to the Polonaise.

Schiller March: The *Schiller March* was composed in 1859 for the Schiller Centenary Festival in Berlin. It is a Grand March, pompous in character and grandiose in style.

Stanislaw Moniuszko

BORN Lithuania, May 5, 1820
DIED Warsaw, Poland, June 4, 1872

ARRANGED FOR BAND:

Overture, HALKA (F

AFTER CHOPIN, STANISLAW MONIUSZKO was perhaps the most famous Polish composer of the nineteenth century. He wrote prolifically in almost all forms, but little of his music is known outside of Poland. His fifteen melodious operas, all of a decidedly national character, won for him the esteem and enthusiasm of his compatriots. *Halka*, produced at Warsaw in 1846, was the first of these, and probably the best known.

In 1858 Moniuszko became director of the Opera at Warsaw and professor at the Conservatory. His works were edited after his death by a society especially formed for the purpose.

Moritz Moszkowski

BORN at Breslau, August 23, 1854
DIED Paris, March 8, 1925

WORKS ARRANGED FOR BAND:

Suite, FROM FOREIGN LANDS (F; B&H
Inauguration March & *Malagueña* from BOABDIL (F
VALSE CÉLÈBRE (S
SERENADE (B&H; J
SPANISH DANCES (one or several pub. by F; D; B&H

MOSZKOWSKI was famous both as pianist and composer, and was the teacher of a number of famous artists. His compositions are characterized by imitativeness of various national styles, and reflect a taste for the exotic which was quite characteristic of late nineteenth-century salon-music.

✓ ✓ ✓

Suite, From Foreign Lands (*Aus Aller Herren Länder*):
Part I: Russia. Germany. Spain.
Part II: Italy. Poland. Hungary.

This suite of characteristic pieces bears the Opus No. 23, and was originally written for pianoforte duet. The numbers are not actually based on the folk music of the different countries, but merely represent the composer's conception of the national styles.

✓

Inauguration March and *Malagueña* from *Boabdil:* Moszkowski's opera, *Boabdil* or *The Last King of the Moors,* was produced at Berlin in 1892. It was the composer's only effort in this form and was a dismal failure. The march and some of the ballet music have survived. The *Malagueña* is the first movement of the ballet and the best-known. The Malagueña is a dance of slow and languorous character, Spanish in origin.

Serenade: Moszkowski is best remembered by his salon-music for piano. This *Serenade,* which belongs in that category, embodies the elegance and grace which made Moszkowski's work popular.

Spanish Dances: Moszkowski wrote two books of Spanish Dances for pianoforte, four hands. It was these compositions that brought the composer's music in vogue. The dances are not based on authentic Spanish tunes, but merely reflect Moszkowski's idea of the general characteristics of Spanish music.

Modeste Petrovitch Moussorgsky

BORN Pskov, Russia, March 28, 1839
DIED St. Petersburg, March 28, 1881

WORKS ARRANGED FOR BAND:

BORIS GODOUNOV: *Coronation Scene* (F
Suite: PICTURES AT AN EXHIBITION (F
Hopak from THE FAIR AT SOROTCHINTSI (B&H
Persian Dance from KHOVANTCHINA (C

MOUSSORGSKY was an altogether exceptional genius: a composer who had little formal training in music, but who succeeded better than all his learned and gifted contemporaries in conveying the spirit and the earthiness of old Russia in his music. He was an army officer in his youth, but became a pupil of Balakirev, the inspirer of the neo-Russian school of composition. All of this group, which included Borodin, Cui and Rimsky-Korsakov, believed firmly in the creation of a national music based on the folk music of the Russias. Their harmonies, rhythms, and melodic concepts developed from this starting-point; what little they took from the classic German tradition appears insignificant beside their own individualism.

Moussorgsky's works gained acceptance slowly, for he departed even more radically than the others from the accepted paths. His harmonies are bolder, his use of folk tunes more frank and less stylized, his rhythms and color more earthy. He knew little about instrumentation, but benefited by the collaboration of Rimsky-Korsakov in many of his works. His works are mainly dramatic; operas and songs take up the greater part of the list. At his death he left a number of unfinished works which were edited and completed by others.

✓ ✓ ✓

Coronation Scene from *Boris Godounov:* Moussorgsky's most famous opera is founded on the great poem of Pushkin, dealing with the dramatic career of Boris Godounov, who usurped the throne of Kiev in the thirteenth century. This colorful episode of Russian history was an ideal basis for Moussorgsky's vividly national music. The opera was first performed in 1874 at the Imperial Opera of St. Petersburg. The originality and power of the work can be better appreciated if one recalls that at that time in Europe, the dominant opera-composers were Wagner, Verdi and Gounod.

The *Coronation Scene* occurs in the first act. It is a scene of great splendor and impressiveness, honestly achieved. The music is strong and full of color. The chimes of the bells are worked into the music in an unusual manner; there is something almost primitively real about them. The choral which runs throughout the scene is an old Russian one, one of many such folk-melodies used in the opera. This one is known as *Slava Bogu* (*Glory be to God*). It may be found in the second volume of Rimsky-Korsakov's collection of Russian folk music.

Suite, Pictures at an Exhibition:

I. Promenade
II. The Old Castle
III. Tuileries (Children quarreling at play)
IV. Bydlo
V. Ballet of the Unhatched Chickens
VI. Market Place at Limoges (French Market-women quarreling)
VII. Catacombs
VIII. Hut of Baba-Yaga
IX. The Great Gate at Kiev

This suite was written for pianoforte, inspired by an

exhibition of paintings and drawings by Moussorgsky's friend Hartmann. In the original form, most of the numbers are separated by the recurrence of the "Promenade" theme, which serves not only to indicate the composer's wandering about the gallery from picture to picture, but also as a means of modulating from key to key. The suite was brilliantly orchestrated by Maurice Ravel, and is unquestionably more effective in orchestral form.

The titles of the pictures give a sufficient key to the character of the music. Many of them are essentially fantastic, some even grotesque. But in all of them may be noted a boldness of outline and of harmony, a kinship to Russian folk music, a richness of imagination.

The "Promenade," with its alternating 5/4 and 6/4 measures, is intended to describe the changing gait of one wandering more or less aimlessly through the picture-gallery; stopping now to admire a painting, walking on to another, retracing his steps, starting and then stopping. *Bydlo* is the name of a Polish type of wagon, a lumbering affair with solid wooden wheels; the composer attempts to reproduce its heavily slow progress in the piece of that name. *Baba-Yaga* is a fabled witch of Russian folk-lore. The other numbers of the set have titles which are more or less self-explanatory. There are ten numbers in the suite, but one of these has not been arranged for band.

Hopak: This lively dance occurs in the third act of Moussorgsky's opera, *The Fair at Sorotchintsi.* This opera, unfinished at the composer's death, is, like *Boris Godounov* and *Khovantchina,* purely national in character, but differs from them in that it is light, vivacious and non-epic in conception.

The Hopak is a spirited dance in 2/4 time. In *The Fair at*

Sorotchintsi it is performed during a festival in a small Russian village.

Persian Dance from *Khovantchina: Khovantchina,* an opera in five acts, is even more grand in conception than *Boris Godounov.* Moussorgsky completed the piano score during his lifetime, but entrusted the instrumentation to Rimsky-Korsakov.

Wolfgang Amadeus Mozart

BORN Salzburg, Austria, January 27, 1756
DIED Vienna, December 5, 1791

WORKS ARRANGED FOR BAND:

Overtures: DON JUAN (F; B&H
THE MARRIAGE OF FIGARO (F; B&H
THE MAGIC FLUTE (F; B&H
COSÌ FAN TUTTE (B&H
IDOMENEO (B&H

Menuet from DON JUAN (F
Menuet from SYMPHONY IN E♭ (D
TURKISH MARCH (F
Sanctus from MASS IN G (F
From the TWELFTH MASS: *Agnus Dei* (CB
Credo (CB
Gloria (CB; F
Kyrie (CB
Sanctus (CB

AT THE age of three, with a precocity that has seldom been rivalled, Mozart already played the harpsichord and had begun to compose minuets. The promise of these early days was more than amply fulfilled. Mozart became one of the most famous virtuosi of his day and developed into a composer who ranks with the great of all times. His career was an extraordinary one; he knew the heights of success and he endured bitter poverty, yet throughout everything he continued to create some of the most beautiful music that has ever been given the world.

All that has been said about classic style in connection with Haydn applies equally to Mozart. The latter, however, with his indubitably greater genius, brought a far wider range to the clear and well-defined forms which Haydn had in a way created for him. Mozart's melodies have infinitely greater variation than those of his predecessor, his instrumentation is richer, and his sense of form is, if anything, more highly developed. But the same spontaneity seems to pervade the works of Mozart and Haydn; in the case of Mozart even his most elaborate contrapuntal writing seems to come naturally, effortlessly and inevitably.

Mozart's compositions include over forty symphonies, innumerable sonatas, concertos, quartettes and operas. For sheer versatility Mozart was extraordinary; in every field he touched he left the mark of his own genius. In him the "classic" style marked its purest development.

(Mozart's expert knowledge of wind instruments is shown not only by the way he used them in his orchestral works, but especially in his delightful divertimenti and serenades for wind instruments alone. These were written for outdoor performance; many of them are slight, but some are on the level of his best work. Present-day bandsmen can still learn much from Mozart's individualized and idiosyncratic handling of wind instruments; each is given a part suited to its own qualities and characteristics, each appears to the best possible advantage.)

Overture, The Marriage of Figaro: Beaumarchais' famous comedy, adapted by Lorenzo da Ponte, served as libretto for the first of Mozart's greatest series of operas. The combination of Da Ponte's witty text and Mozart's sparkling music was irresistible, and the opera, when produced in 1786, was an immediate success. The adventures of the resourceful barber (who appears again in Rossini's *Barber of Seville*) are illustrated by some of the most delightful music Mozart ever wrote. The overture, which is in one tempo throughout, is a pure gem of spontaneous melody and skillful design.

Overture, The Magic Flute: The Magic Flute was the last

of Mozart's operas. Written when the composer was already suffering severely, it was not produced until two months before his death. It is more varied in style than any of Mozart's other operas, and contains examples of almost every form of writing from the lied to the fugue. Beethoven considered *The Magic Flute* to be Mozart's greatest work; Goethe was also one of its admirers. The libretto, by Emanuel Schikaneder, contains a number of Masonic allusions; it is fantastic and sometimes puzzling, but nevertheless effective on the stage. The overture is a masterpiece of inventiveness and skill, containing a fugue which displays an ease of which only Mozart was capable.

Overture, Don Giovanni (Don Juan): The success of *Don Giovanni,* produced in Prague in 1788, moved the Austrian Emperor to appoint Mozart his "chamber-composer," a rather belated recognition of Mozart's genius, and a not too generous one. Mozart did not long retain the position, but relied on being able to do better by composing for the public. His financial troubles increased rapidly from that date; he died, as is well known, in poverty.

Don Giovanni, like *The Marriage of Figaro* and *Così Fan Tutte,* had the advantage of a libretto by Da Ponte. The opera overflows with grace and wit. It contains some of the most admirable concerted numbers Mozart ever wrote, as well as a number of brilliant arias. The music does not illustrate; rather it seems to breathe the very spirit of the gay hero's adventures with his ladies and with his altogether remarkable servant. The overture is a masterpiece by itself.

Overture, Così Fan Tutte (Women Are All Alike): Così Fan Tutte was composed in 1790 at the order of the Austrian Emperor. The libretto, a topical comedy, was supplied by

Da Ponte, with whom Mozart collaborated so successfully. The music of this opera-buffa abounds in lovely melodies and subtle humor. Its scope is not as great as that of *Don Giovanni,* but within its own dimensions it is a masterpiece. It was successfully revived a few years ago at the Metropolitan Opera House, where it delighted all who heard it.

Overture, Idomeneo: Idomeneo was the first of the last great series of operas Mozart composed. It was composed for the Munich Carnival of 1781 and was first performed at Munich in January of that year. The opera was on a much grander scale than any of Mozart's previous dramatic works, and it is said that the composer himself attached great value to it. For the first time, he had arrived at a modification of the inconsequential Italian style, and achieved an intensity of effect equal to that attained by Gluck. The overture, in its brilliance and force, was superior to anything of its kind the composer had previously attempted, and remains a splendid example of his genius.

Turkish March: This popular and pleasant piece is taken from the Piano Sonata in A (K. 305), of which it is the final movement. The sonata was composed in 1778. This movement is headed *Alla Turca,* and is actually a gay bit of eighteenth-century fantasy.

Sanctus, from *Mass in G* (*K. 49*): The *Mass in G* was Mozart's first composition in that form. Written in 1768, when the composer was twelve years of age, the work shows Mozart's amazing development, his stylistic maturity and his grasp of form. The *Mass in G* hardly ranks in originality or inspiration with his later and greater masses, but shows that Mozart had more than mastered the idiom of the eighteenth century. The mass was commissioned for the consecration of a new church in Vienna, and was first performed, under the composer's direction, on December 7, 1768.

Twelfth Mass, in C (K. 262): Mozart's *Twelfth Mass* was written at Salzburg in 1776, a year in which a good part of his energy was devoted to sacred composition. The *Twelfth Mass,* being on a slightly larger scale than the four other masses dating from that year, is known as a Grand Mass. It follows the customary divisions of the form, and is not distinguished in any remarkable way from its companion works, although it has enjoyed a greater renown and is more often performed.

Minuet from *Symphony No. 39, in E♭ (K. 543)*: After the production of *Don Giovanni* at Vienna in May, 1788, Mozart's financial difficulties seemed to increase. A period of depression set in, but despite this the composer wrote within six weeks the three symphonies which are almost universally accepted as his orchestral masterpieces. The E♭ Symphony was the first of these, and with the others, may be said to mark the high point of the "classic" symphony. In purity of form, wealth of invention, in transparency and subtlety, these symphonies remain unsurpassed. The *Minuet* from the E♭ is one of the most perfectly developed examples of that much-used dance form.

Ethelbert Woodbridge Nevin

BORN Edgeworth, Pennsylvania, November 25, 1852
DIED New Haven, Connecticut, February 17, 1901

WORKS ARRANGED FOR BAND:
Suite, A DAY IN VENICE (P

IN HIS BRIEF CAREER NEVIN established himself as a favorite among American composers. His graceful piano pieces and attractive songs quickly gained a popularity which they have continued to hold. It is safe to say that no songs by American composers are better known than *The Rosary* or *Mighty Lak a Rose.*

Nevin began his musical studies in Pittsburg, continuing them in New York, in Boston, and finally in Germany. His early death cut short a career which gave promise of contributing significantly to American music.

/ / /

Suite, A Day In Venice: (*Un Giorno In Venezia*)

I. At Dawn
II. Venetian Love Song
III. The Gondoliers
IV. Good Night

The poetic idea underlying the music of this popular little suite is that of a day spent in tranquil enjoyment of the picturesque Italian city. Beginning at dawn with an Aubade, or morning song, and closing with a Serenade, the suite paints four miniature tone-pictures of the Venetian scene. The suite was originally written for pianoforte, but soon became so popular that it was arranged for many instrumental combinations.

Carl Otto Ehrenfried Nicolai

BORN Koenigsberg, Prussia, June 9, 1810
DIED Berlin, March 11, 1849

ARRANGED FOR BAND:

Overture, THE MERRY WIVES OF WINDSOR (F; B&H; D

NICOLAI was a much traveled composer and conductor whose talents were highly appreciated in his day. He composed prolifically, occupied many important posts as opera and symphony conductor, and was founder of the Vienna Philharmonic Orchestra. His death occurred just after the first performance of his most brilliant success, the opera *The Merry Wives of Windsor.*

This rollicking work was produced in Berlin on March 9, 1849, and soon achieved popularity throughout Europe. It long held its place in the German comic-opera repertory, while the overture, with its humor and beauty, is still a universal favorite. The opera was adapted from Shakespeare's comedy, and Nicolai's handling of the material invites comparison with Mendelssohn's treatment of the *Midsummer Night's Dream.* The overture to *The Merry Wives of Windsor* does not follow the action of the opera, but makes use of themes which are easily associable with the characters.

Jacques Offenbach

BORN Cologne (Köln), Germany, June 21, 1819
DIED Paris, October 5, 1880

WORKS ARRANGED FOR BAND:

Overture, ORPHEUS IN THE UNDERWORLD (F; B&H; D; CB

Selections from: TALES OF HOFFMANN (F; B&H
THE GRAND DUCHESS OF GEROLSTEIN (D
BEAUTIFUL HELEN (C; B&H
THE DRUM MAJOR'S DAUGHTER (F; B&H
and others rarely, if ever, now performed

Barcarolle from THE TALES OF HOFFMANN (F; B&H; Ru; CB; J

OFFENBACH, although born in Germany, is identified exclusively with French comic opera, into which he introduced a new spirit. He came to Paris while very young, studied 'cello and composition there, and soon joined the orchestra of the Opéra Comique. He became conductor at the Théâtre Français in 1849, and during the rest of his lifetime was constantly associated with various theatres, including one of his own, as conductor and producer.

His career as composer began with small pieces and the incidental music to de Musset's comedy, *The Chandelier*. From 1853 on, he produced operettas and comic operas one after another, arriving at the truly impressive total of 102. His feeling for the public taste was unfailing, but he had more than merely that: he really created a new type of comic opera, more satirical and more robust than those, say, of Adam or Boieldieu. Offenbach's music, in his best works, follows his sometimes burlesque stage-situations with exceptional cleverness; a lively sense of humor saved him, in most instances, from falling into melodic clichés or sentimental trivialities. His works were enormously popular in their day and many of them are still played.

Overture, Orpheus in the Underworld: From 1855 to 1866, Offenbach had his own theatre known as the *Bouffes Parisiens* (*Parisian Jests*). Here many of his favorite works, including *Orpheus,* were produced. Offenbach's burlesque version of the Greek myth is truly Gallic, with a Parisian Orpheus who is not too sure that he is unwilling to leave his Eurydice in the hands of Pluto, and an assortment of gods who are exceedingly involved in domestic troubles. The music is full of charm and mock-heroic humor. That time has not greatly dulled the appeal of the score or the libretto is indicated by the successful revival of the opera in Paris in 1932, where, brought up to date with a few contemporary political allusions, it ran for many months to packed houses.

Selections from *The Tales of Hoffmann:* Offenbach's most popular comic opera, generally considered his masterpiece, was first performed in Paris on February 10, 1881. Since that time it has been more or less constantly in the repertories of the world's leading opera houses. The libretto is curious and interesting. The historical Hoffmann was Ernest Theodore Amadeus Hoffmann (1776-1822), a German novelist and musician famous for his extravagant imagination and his delightful fantasy. Offenbach's opera, in three acts with prologue and epilogue, is concerned with a purely imaginary episode in the life of the poet Hoffmann. Entering a tavern, he proposes to relate his three love affairs: the first, with a doll—the second with a woman of the world—and the third, with a young and innocent singer. The acting out of these three affairs forms the three acts of the opera. At the end, Hoffmann draws the moral for his listeners in the tavern;

having experienced three types of love (and having been deceived in each), he resolves to devote himself to the Muse. Whether the allegorical significance of the story led Offenbach to compose music of a higher order than that in some of his other operas is a matter for debate. Suffice it to say that the music of *The Tales of Hoffmann* is of great charm.

Barcarolle from *The Tales of Hoffmann:* The famous *Barcarolle* occurs in the second act of Offenbach's opera, which has its setting in Venice. The *Barcarolle* is sung by Hoffmann and the Lady Giulietta; later it is played as an orchestral intermezzo. No single number from an opera has achieved greater popularity than the *Barcarolle.*

Charles O'Neill

ORIGINAL WORKS FOR BAND:

Overtures: THE KNIGHT ERRANT (Ru
THE SILVER CORD (S
BUILDERS OF YOUTH (F
Entr'actes: CLAIR DE LUNE (Waterloo Music Co.
MLLE. COQUETTE (F
Selection: SOUVENIR DE QUEBEC (F
Many marches, cornet solos, serenades, etc.

UNTIL 1937 Captain Charles O'Neill was the senior bandmaster of the Canadian Army; he had been director of music of the Royal 22nd Regiment, Quebec, since 1910. In addition to his work as bandmaster, Captain O'Neill was the founder and conductor of the Quebec Symphony Orchestra. He received his musical training at the famous Kneller Hall in London, graduating as bandmaster in 1909. McGill University awarded him the degree of Doctor of Music in 1924. In 1937 Captain O'Neill became Professor of Music at the University of Wisconsin.

Captain O'Neill has been one of the leading figures in the band movement of the United States and Canada. As past-president of the American Bandmasters' Association, as adjudicator of many of the most important contests and festivals, as composer and lecturer, he has added much to the prestige of bands and band music.

Besides his works for band, Captain O'Neill has composed numerous pieces for orchestra, many songs, and two cantatas for tenor solo, chorus and orchestra. He is likewise well known for his symphonic band transcriptions.

✓ ✓ ✓

Overture, The Knight Errant: Concerning this popular overture, the composer writes as follows: "In my younger days tales of Gallant Knights held a peculiar fascination for me (as no doubt they did and do in the case of most boys) and I often visualized myself as a Knight of Old in search of adventure. Maturer years arrived and the fancy struck me to attempt to depict in tone colors the quest of a *Knight Errant* for excitement.

"*Knight Errant* Overture was conceived and written for wind band. While following in general the lines of classical form, the distinctive voice and technique of the concert band was constantly kept in view during its writing.

"All the material from which the overture is constructed is contained in the two introductory sections of five measures each with which the work opens. The triplet figure forms the basis of the first subject of the overture proper, and is much used throughout. The two staccato chords in measures three and four form the motive from which the *Ben Marcato* section is constructed. A feature of the overture is the cadenza leading to the recapitulation. It will be noted that the cadenza is distributed to three instruments in different octaves and that it touches on both subjects of the overture."

Overture, The Silver Cord: The composer gives the following descriptive note concerning this overture: "The *Silver Cord Overture* was written specially as a contest number for High School Bands. It is a well balanced composition, symphonic in outline and treatment and intended to develop well rounded musicianship in young players.

"The name should suggest that the several movements of the work are bound together by *The Silver Cord,* which is not an inflexible rope, but, as the name implies, a cord that will hold and at the same time allow of some freedom of movement.

"The first four measures contain the germs from which the whole of the Overture is constructed. The connection between the first two and the last six measures of the composition is obvious. The figure allotted to the horn, alto saxophone and third clarinet in measures three and four dominates the entire work. From it is developed the cornet solo, and later (by inverse movement), the trombone solo. The canonic figure which opens the *Allegro* is identical with measures six and seven of the cornet solo. Thus is the *Silver Cord* exemplified."

Overture, Builders of Youth: Builders of Youth was written expressly for concert and symphonic band, mainly to add to the literature suitable for performance by the better bands in the School Music Movement. The work is dedicated to the School Music Directors of the United States of America.

The composition is written in strict form with an introduction which is a complete movement in itself.

The main theme can be easily traced throughout the work. The first subject proper is the exposition of a fugue in five voices, derived from material of the introduction.

Amilcare Ponchielli

BORN Cremona, Italy, August 31, 1834
DIED Milan, Italy, January 16, 1886

WORKS ARRANGED FOR BAND:

Selections from LA GIOCONDA (F; B&H
Dance of the Hours from LA GIOCONDA (F; D

AT ONE TIME PONCHIELLI was considered second only to Verdi in the sphere of Italian opera. His works, during his lifetime, attained tremendous success in his own country. Of them all, however, only *La Gioconda* has actually enjoyed continued fame.

Ponchielli pursued his studies at the Milan Conservatory, and shortly after leaving that institution became a bandmaster. He began bringing out operas with almost unbroken success, reaching the high point of his career with the productions of *The Lithuanians,* in 1874, and *La Gioconda,* in 1876. Both were performed at La Scala. In 1881 Ponchielli became *maestro* of Piacenza Cathedral, and from that time on composed mainly sacred music.

The Dance of the Hours, which is the best-known excerpt from *La Gioconda,* occurs in the third act. It is purely incidental in character, having nothing whatsoever to do with the action of the opera. It is produced for the entertainment of Alvise's guests at a banquet in his magnificent palace. The dance takes its name from the fact that the dancers are costumed to represent the hours of the day and night.

(For purposes of record it may be mentioned that the story of *La Gioconda* has nothing to do with either Leonardo da Vinci or his famous painting. The libretto was fashioned by Arrigo Boito (q. v.), writing under his acrostic name of Tobia Gorrio. Taken from a melodrama of Victor Hugo, it may safely be termed "operatic" in the most unflattering sense of the word. Stabbings, poisonings, stranglings and suicides follow one another with sufficient regularity to satisfy the most jaded taste.)

Sergei Sergeievitch Prokofiev

BORN Ekaterinoslav, Russia, April 11, 1891

ARRANGED FOR BAND:

March and *Scherzo* from THE LOVE OF THREE ORANGES (B&H

WRITTEN FOR BAND:

SPARTAN MARCH (Aff

PROKOFIEV, one of the most distinguished of present-day Russian composers, studied under Rimsky-Korsakov, Liadov and Tcherepnin, winning the Rubinstein award in 1910 with his first piano concerto. He is well-known as pianist and conductor.

Prokofiev's music makes use of every legitimate device which has been explored by contemporary musicians. It is solid, colorful and original, entirely unromantic but extremely energetic and forceful. He has written in all forms, including opera, his best-known work in the latter field being *The Love of Three Oranges,* which was produced in Chicago in 1921. The libretto, written by the composer himself, is taken from one of the satires of Carlo Gozzi, an eighteenth-century Venetian. The march from this opera, with its great originality and exuberant vitality, has become extremely popular, as has the scherzo.

Prokofiev has made frequent trips to America. His most recent appearance (as this goes to press) was in the early part of 1937, when he conducted a first performance of his *Romeo and Juliet* in Chicago and his Fourth Symphony in Boston. He lives at present in Moscow.

Giacomo Puccini

(Giacomo Antonio Domenico Michele Secondo Maria Puccini)

BORN Lucca, Italy, June 22, 1858
DIED Brussels, Belgium, November 29, 1924

WORKS ARRANGED FOR BAND:

Selections from: MADAME BUTTERFLY (B&H
TOSCA (B&H
LA BOHÊME (B&H
MANON LESCAUT (B&H
THE GIRL OF THE GOLDEN WEST (B&H

PUCCINI was descended from a family of musicians, and had little difficulty in choosing his own career. He studied under Ponchielli at the Milan Conservatory and very quickly demonstrated his unusual talent. Even his earliest works aroused interest, for in addition to melodic inventiveness, they possessed a remarkable feeling for the theatre. These qualities distinguish almost all of the later works by which Puccini is best-known. While few of his libretti had any literary worth, his handling of them was always theatrical and his music was always appropriate. In richness of harmony, sensuousness of melody and in dramatic effectiveness, Puccini's operas represent a great advance over those of Verdi; they are, however, different in conception and hardly compete with those of "the grand old man" on their own ground.

Puccini experimented with the harmonic innovations of Debussy to some extent, and also made use of what he could from Wagner. He made his own idiom out of these elements, however, so that in no sense could he be termed an imitator. He had a fondness for exotic and highly dramatic subjects, and in some instances tried to impart a local flavor to his operas by the use of national tunes. In this one respect he was not altogether convincing; *The Star-Spangled Banner* in

Madame Butterfly, while justified from the point of view of the story, is handled rather clumsily with regard to the rest of the music. Puccini was at his best in his lyrical and dramatic scenes, where he could give free scope to his abundant melodic gifts.

Verdi is said to have called Puccini the most promising of his successors. Certainly the favor in which Puccini's operas are held throughout the world has confirmed that estimate.

✓ ✓ ✓

Excerpts from *Madame Butterfly:* When *Madame Butterfly* was first produced at La Scala in 1904 it received a cool reception, due possibly to the novelty of the setting and story. It was an immense contrast to the wild enthusiasm which had greeted Puccini's previous works. The opera soon took hold after its initial failure, however, and now ranks as one of the most frequently played and generally admired of all Puccini's operas.

The libretto is based on Belasco's dramatization of John Luther Long's novel. It tells of the devotion of Cio-Cio-San ("Madame Butterfly") to the American naval officer who marries and then deserts her. Puccini, as in almost all his operas, shows rare theatrical skill in handling the situations, extracting from them every possible bit of pathos and drama. American and Japanese tunes are used through *Madame Butterfly* to give color, but these detract rather than add to the effect of the composer's impassioned original melodies. Many of these arias, such as *O quanti occhi fisi* (Duet in Act I), *Un bel dì vedremo* (Act II), and others, are among the best Puccini ever wrote.

✓

Excerpts from *Tosca:* With the production of *Tosca* in Rome in 1900, Puccini arrived at that fully robust and passionate style which has made his works fixtures in all operatic repertories. The work, more than any earlier one, revealed his fine sense of theatrical effect, his ability to lend conviction to otherwise melodramatic scenes, and his gift for creating compelling melodies. *Tosca* was received with wild enthusiasm, and within two years had been performed in almost every country which boasted an opera house.

The story is taken from an extremely sensational melodrama of Sardou, dealing with the love of Floria Tosca, a singer, and Mario Cavaradossi, a painter. Through the arrival of a political refugee, who throws himself on Mario's mercy, and through the jealous treachery of Scarpia, the police chief, the drama proceeds to the murders of Scarpia and Mario and the suicide of Tosca. These grim happenings are handled with remarkable skill by Puccini, and illumined by some of the most stirring arias in operatic literature.

Excerpts from *La Bohême: La Bohême,* produced at Turin in 1896, was the first opera which fully showed Puccini's genius and announced to the world that a worthy successor to Verdi had been found. More than some of his later works, *La Bohême* is lyrical rather than sensational in character; it is an almost unbroken succession of poignant and memorable melodies, but like the composer's later works, it shows a marked ability to make the most of any given scenes in a theatrical sense.

The story is based on a few episodes from Henri Murger's famous novel, *La Vie de Bohême* (*Bohemian Life*), which is a highly romanticized account of the struggles and joys of four young artists in the Paris of 1830. The libretto emphasizes the love affairs between Marcel, the painter, and Musetta, and between Rudolf, the poet, and pathetic little Mimi. The arias and duets in the love scenes have a passionate tenderness which is inimitably Puccini's contribution to Italian opera. Parts of several of these may be heard in this selection.

Excerpts from *Manon Lescaut: Manon Lescaut* was the third opera composed by Puccini, but the first one which was really successful. It was first performed in Turin in 1893.

The libretto was written by Puccini with the assistance of a group of friends, and was adapted from the famous romance of the Abbé Prévost which had already served as inspiration for Halévy, Auber, Balfe and Massenet. It tells the story of the elopement of Manon with the handsome Chevalier des Grieux, her abandonment of him, and her return. Sentenced to deportation as an undesirable character, Manon is shipped to Louisiana whence Des Grieux follows her. Manon dies "in a desert near New Orleans" (sic!), alone except for the faithful Des Grieux.

Excerpts from *The Girl of the Golden West:* After *Madame Butterfly*, Puccini resolved to work on another Belasco drama and selected *The Girl of the Golden West*, a story of the American frontier. The opera received its first performance in New York on December 10, 1910. Its ephemeral success in this country was not duplicated elsewhere; today it is one of the few operas of Puccini that is hardly ever played. Puccini experimented in the score with new ideas which were not altogether realized; the opera has a few fine arias in the composer's characteristic style, but the work as a whole is weak. The "frontier melodies" interpolated in the score sound out of place. The best of the opera is to be heard in concert arrangements such as the present one.

Sergei Vassilievich Rachmaninov

BORN Government of Novgorod, Russia, April 1, 1873

WORKS ARRANGED FOR BAND:

PRELUDE IN C SHARP MINOR (F; B&H; J
PRELUDE IN G MINOR (F; B&H

SERGEI RACHMANINOV, one of the most eminent composers, pianists, and conductors of our time, received his musical education at the St. Petersburg and Moscow Conservatories. He studied pianoforte under Siloti and composition under Taneiev and Arensky. His career has been a brilliant one; possibly no other musician of today has exhibited such versatility. His compositions include symphonies, operas, piano concertos and works in almost all the smaller forms. He is best-known, of course, by his shorter piano pieces.

Prelude in C# Minor: This prelude definitely suggests the famous bells of Russia. The thundering chimes imitated by the opening theme are answered by the counter-chimes of the smaller bells. The prelude builds up to a tumultuous climax, which is broken by the crash of a cymbal. After this the sound of the chimes returns, becoming softer and softer until the end.

Prelude in G Minor: Prelude in G Minor is almost as popular as the composer's *Prelude in C# Minor*. It is equally original in character and just as fundamentally Russian. Its great energy and stirring rhythms give it an irresistible appeal.

Maurice Ravel

BORN Ciboure, France, March 7, 1875
DIED Paris, December 28, 1937

ARRANGED FOR BAND:

BOLERO (EV

RAVEL was one of the outstanding composers of recent times. In many ways he was the inheritor of the tradition of Debussy, though he brought to this tradition a striking originality. Each score of Ravel reveals the experimenter and the craftsman; none surpassed him in his superb use of instrumental combinations or his sure sense of musical appropriateness. All his works are characterized by an exquisite, finished quality; the polish of music truly French.

✓ ✓ ✓

In *Bolero,* Ravel took a lively Spanish dance-form in three-quarter time, and elaborated it into a brilliant orchestral tour-de-force. The effect of the different instrumentations used for each repetition of the theme is startling and original. The continued crescendo and strongly accented rhythm produce a movement which is almost primitive in character. Few hearers can escape the sheer physical effect of this work; perhaps for that reason it has become one of the most popular of all contemporary compositions.

Ottorino Respighi

BORN Bologna, Italy, July 9, 1879
DIED Rome, April 18, 1936

ORIGINAL WORK FOR BAND:

HUNTING-TOWER BALLAD (R, American Edition

WORKS ARRANGED FOR BAND:

THE PINES OF ROME (R, Italian Edition
THE FOUNTAINS OF ROME (R, Italian Edition
ROMAN FESTIVALS (R, Italian Edition

UNTIL HIS DEATH IN 1936, RESPIGHI was unquestionably the most significant of modern Italian composers. It may be said that Respighi's orchestral works were the first major compositions outside the realm of opera to be penned by any Italian within recent memory. Respighi studied composition under Martucci in Italy, under Rimsky-Korsakov in Russia and under Max Bruch in Germany. He thus acquainted himself with styles other than the Italian, although he always retained the characteristically Italian conception of melody as well as a powerful dramatic quality.

He is best-known in America by his symphonic works, *The Pines of Rome* and *The Fountains of Rome*, which were brought out by Toscanini. He made several visits to the United States, among them one to supervise the production of his opera *The Sunken Bell*, at the Metropolitan Opera House.

The *Hunting-Tower Ballad* was written specially for band at the request of Dr. Edwin Franko Goldman on behalf of the American Bandmasters' Association. The score was completed in February of 1932. The title is derived from the name of a town in Scotland where Respighi sojourned. A Scotch theme is introduced in the middle section. The work shows the composer at his best, and is a good example of that harmonic richness and melodic inventiveness which have made him famous. It is extremely well adapted for band and shows the possibilities which may be realized by a skillful composer. The work is short and ends with a huge climax.

The *Hunting-Tower Ballad* received its first performance at a concert given by the American Bandmasters' Association during its convention in Washington, D. C., in April, 1932. The score bears the following dedication: "To Edwin Franko Goldman and the American Bandmasters' Association."

Nicolai Andreievich Rimsky-Korsakov

BORN Government of Novgorod, Russia, March 18, 1844
DIED St. Petersburg, Russia, June 21, 1908

WORKS ARRANGED FOR BAND:

Suite, SCHEHERAZADE (B&H
CAPRICCIO ESPAGNOLE (F; B&H
Song of India from SADKO (F; B&H
Hymn to the Sun from THE GOLDEN COCKEREL (F; B&H; ABC
Dance of the King and Princess from THE GOLDEN COCKEREL (F
Procession of Nobles from MLADA (F
Polonaise from A MAY NIGHT (B&H
Dance of the Tumblers from THE SNOW MAIDEN (B&H; W
The Flight of the Bumble-Bee from TSAR SALTAN (F; B&H; Ru
Many others in arrangements for Russian bands (Aff)

RIMSKY-KORSAKOV manifested his talent for music at an early age, but since he came of a good family with a position to maintain, he was prepared for a career in the Imperial Navy. While at the Naval Academy, however, he managed to devote his spare time to musical studies; toward the close of his training period he met Balakirev, and from that time on determined to pursue the career of a musician. While on a three-years' cruise, Rimsky-Korsakov found time to complete his first large work, a symphony. Balakirev, to whom it had been sent for criticism, had it performed in 1865 at a concert in St. Petersburg. Rimsky-Korsakov remained in the Navy until 1873, by which time he had acquired a considerable reputation. He had already written an opera and the symphonic poem, *Sadko,* and had been appointed Professor of Composition at the Conservatory. After his retirement from the Navy, he recommenced his musical studies for the purpose of grounding himself more thoroughly in every branch of music. By this intensive work he enabled himself to perform enormous services to Russian music, for his technical knowledge was brought to the assistance of Moussorgsky, Borodin and others of his fellow-artists.

As composer and conductor, Rimsky-Korsakov was the most brilliant figure of the entire neo-Russian school. Believing firmly in the principles enunciated by Balakirev, and shared by Moussorgsky, Borodin and Cui, he based his music on the national traditions of Russia, and did much to speed the acceptance of this music throughout the world. As a teacher, he was extremely influential; the list of his pupils includes Liadov, Glazounov, Ippolitov-Ivanov and Stravinsky, to name but a few. He conducted the Russian Symphony in St. Petersburg, as well as many other orchestras in Russia and abroad, and was exceptionally gifted in this field as well as others.

Rimsky-Korsakov's work was divided between the stage and the symphony. All but one of his fifteen operas are based on Russian subjects and all are set to music entirely Russian in its characteristics. Rimsky-Korsakov made a careful study of the folk-music, not only of Russia proper, but also of the central Asiatic districts. Much of this Eastern color is apparent in his compositions. All of the native material is handled with extreme skill and individuality; Rimsky-Korsakov was one of the really great masters of orchestration, a distinguished craftsman and a sensitive artist.

⸙ ⸙ ⸙

Symphonic Suite, Scheherazade:

I. The Sea and Sinbad's Ship
II. The Story of the Kalendar
III. The Young Prince and Princess
IV. Festival at Bagdad

Rimsky-Korsakov's most popular symphonic work was completed in 1888, with the full title, *Symphonic Suite,*

Scheherazade, after The Thousand and One Nights (better known to American readers as *The Arabian Nights*). Prefaced to the original score was the following legend:

"The Sultan Schahriar, convinced of the infidelity of women, had sworn to put to death each of his wives after the first night. But the Sultana Scheherazade saved her life by entertaining him with stories which she told him during a thousand and one nights. Overcome by curiosity, the Sultan put off from day to day the death of his wife, and at last entirely renounced his bloody vow.

"Many wonders were told to Schahriar by the Sultana Scheherazade. For the stories the Sultana borrowed the verses of poets and the words of popular romances, and she fitted the tales and adventures one within the other.

"I. The Sea and the Vessel of Sindbad. II. The Tale of the Prince Kalendar. III. The Young Prince and the Young Princess. IV. Feast at Bagdad. The Sea. The Vessel is Wrecked on a Rock on which is Mounted a Warrior of Brass. Conclusion."

The four movements of the suite really compose a symphony in free form. Few compositions ever written have more innate color, more suggestiveness or more glamour than *Scheherazade*. The richness of texture, brilliance of orchestration and melodic sweep of the music have gained it a place in the hearts of all concert audiences.

Spanish Caprice (*Capriccio Espagnole*)

I. Alborado
II. Theme and Variations
III. Alborado
IV. Scene and Gypsy Song
V. Asturian Fandango

Like his predecessor Glinka, Rimsky-Korsakov was occasionally attracted by the characteristics of national music other than his own. Though not a profound scholar of Spanish music, Rimsky-Korsakov succeeded in this composition, better than most European composers, in capturing the spirit of Iberia. The work is a masterful example of Rimsky-Korsakov's brilliant and original orchestration, and as such was greatly admired by Tchaikovsky.

The *Alborado* is the morning counterpart of the Serenade, the latter being in its original meaning an evening-piece. (Cf. Ravel's *Alborado del Gracioso.*) The first and third movements of the *Spanish Caprice* are virtually identical except for a change of key. The second movement is a typical Spanish theme with five variations; the fourth is fiery in character, opening with a striking passage for brass and concluding with lively Gypsy dance-song measures. The last movement, the *Fandango,* is a version of one of Spain's national dances, similar in character to the Bolero; Rimsky-Korsakov took this material from Asturias, a province in northern Spain.

A Song of India from *Sadko:* Rimsky-Korsakov's operas have never attained the world-wide circulation they deserve. Their essential nationalism is a possible cause for their exclusion from foreign stages. *Sadko,* perhaps better-known than most of the others, is like them founded on a Russian subject: an old story from Novgorod of a merchant-poet who catches miraculous fish with the supernatural connivance of a sea-king. The opera was produced privately at Moscow in 1897. Much of the music was adapted from an earlier symphonic poem of the same name, composed while Rimsky-Korsakov was still a naval officer.

The *Song of India* is the one excerpt from the opera which is universally known.

Hymn to the Sun and *Dance of the King and Princess* from *The Golden Cockerel* (*Le Coq d'Or*): *The Golden Cockerel* was Rimsky-Korsakov's last opera and the one which has gained the widest circulation. It was not performed until 1910, two years after the composer's death. Conceived as an opera, and not too successful in that form, *The Golden Cockerel* was rewritten as an "opera-pantomime" for the famous Diaghilev ballet. The brilliant performances of that group, with the singers concealed, did much to spread the fame of the work. The music is highly original, with a strong tinge of Asiatic coloring in both the melodic outline and in the instrumentation.

Dance of the Tumblers from *The Snow Maiden* (*Snegourotchka*): *The Snow Maiden* was the third of Rimsky-Korsakov's operas. It is a charming legend of Winter and Spring, set in an imaginary province of Russia. The character of the music is simple and lyrical; many of the airs and dances are popular outside of Russia. The opera itself, except for occasional performances, has never become well-known abroad. The Metropolitan Opera House presented the work some years ago.

The Flight of the Bumble-Bee from *Tsar Saltan*: *The Tale of Tsar Saltan*, founded on a Russian story, was produced in Moscow in 1900, but has never been heard in America. Parts of it, such as the *Warrior's March*, and this characteristic fantasy have, however, become familiar. *The Flight of the Bumble-Bee* is an extremely clever bit of writing, illustrating Rimsky-Korsakov's great facility in achieving onomatopoetic effects. It makes a very difficult, but effective number for bands.

Procession of Nobles from *Mlada:* During the season of 1869-1870, the Director of the Imperial Theatres of St. Petersburg conceived the idea of staging an elaborate "Opera-Ballet" based on a subject from the Slavic mythology. For this work, to be known as *Mlada,* he commissioned music from Cui, Borodin, Moussorgsky and Rimsky-Korsakov, the leading representatives of the new Russian school. The project was never realized, however, and most of the music which the composers had written found its way into other of their works.

Not until twenty years later did Rimsky-Korsakov decide to use the subject for an "Opera-Ballet" of his own. His *Mlada* was begun in 1889, completed in 1892, and produced at the Mariinsky Theatre in 1893. It was not a pronounced success. Nevertheless it is said to be an extraordinary combination of music, dance and spectacle. From the standpoint of orchestration, the score represents Rimsky-Korsakov at the height of his powers. Later the composer arranged a suite of five numbers from the music of the opera, the last number being the colorful and exuberant *Procession of Nobles.*

Polonaise from *A May Night: A May Night,* based on a tale by N. V. Gogol (1809-1852), was the second of Rimsky-Korsakov's fifteen operas. In it for the first time the composer attempted and achieved an almost purely lyrical style, although in the opera, as in almost all his other works, a strongly national flavor is preserved. *A May Night* was begun in 1878, and was produced in St. Petersburg in 1880.

Gioacchino Antonio Rossini

BORN Pesaro, Italy, February 29, 1792
DIED Paris, November 13, 1868

WORKS ARRANGED FOR BAND:

Overtures: BARBER OF SEVILLE (F; B&H; SF
WILLIAM TELL (F; (B&H; D; CB
ITALIAN IN ALGIERS (F; B&H
LA GAZZA LADRA (B&H
SEMIRAMIDE (F; B&H; D
TANCRED (F; B&H; CB
THE SIEGE OF CORINTH (B&H
OTHELLO (B&H
THE LADY OF THE LAKE (P

Selections from the above plus:
CINDERELLA (B&H; CB
MOSES IN EGYPT (B&H
ZELMIRA (B&H

STABAT MATER (complete) (B&H
Grand March & *Chorus* from SEMIRAMIDE (F
Ballet Music & *Soldiers' March* from WILLIAM TELL (F
(Rossini-Respighi: LA BOUTIQUE FANTASQUE) (C

ROSSINI's career was an extraordinary one in many ways. Unusually gifted by nature, he stopped studying the moment his teacher assured him that he knew enough to write operas (but not enough to write church music), began to turn out theatrical works in rapid succession, achieved fame and financial success, and ceased to compose shortly after he reached the age of thirty-five. He traveled from Venice and Rome to Vienna, London and Paris, harvesting acclaim in each city, and spent the latter part of his life in a villa near Paris, enjoying his pleasures and surrounded by devout admirers.

The rapidity with which he composed was exceptional, and he unquestionably could have produced greater things had he catered less to the public taste. His dependence on the public is illustrated by the strengthening of his resolution not to compose, after the great success of Meyerbeer in Paris. Yet Rossini had attained a definite place in operatic circles and it is improbable that any newcomer could have displaced him. He had, he claimed, taught the singers how to sing; and he had unquestionably taught the audiences to revere him.

The musical content of his operas is interesting. A good many of these works are considerably padded, and Rossini was never above using a good tune, even though another composer had used it before him. Many of the works he produced in Paris were but rewritten versions of his early Italian operas, or pastiches of several operas which had not been successes. There can be little gainsaying the fact that his facility was his greatest liability. He wrote, nevertheless, a great number of sparkling and delightful tunes, showed a ready wit and verve in his music, and established himself as the dominant Italian opera composer of his period.

He was almost deified during his lifetime, and his funeral was one of the most spectacular of the century. He was a Grand Officer of the Legion of Honor, a commander in innumerable Orders, possessed honorary positions by the dozens, and last, but not least, had endeared himself to the world by his amiability, his genius and his wit. His statue was placed in the Opera in 1846.

✓ ✓ ✓

Overture, The Barber of Seville: The Barber of Seville, Rossini's most popular opera and one of the finest comic-operas in the repertory, was produced in Rome in 1816 as *Almaviva, or the Useless Precaution.* The libretto was adapted from the famous comedy of Beaumarchais, already used by Mozart and Paisiello. It was due to the latter's employment of the same subject that Rossini's work was not a success at first, for Paisiello was a favorite of Roman audiences, and they resented the new opera as an impudence. It did not take long, however, before Rossini's opera attained a complete success not only in Rome but throughout Europe.

The music of *The Barber of Seville* is of an almost Mozartean purity. It is undramatic, but gay and charming, and is probably the most consistently inspired work Rossini ever composed.

Overture, William Tell: William Tell was Rossini's last opera and also the most serious and elaborate he ever attempted. Shortly after its première in 1829 Rossini made his famous resolution to compose no more, although the opera was greeted with great applause. It was played in reduced form after that year, until its revival in 1837 when it was an overwhelming triumph.

The story is based on the drama of Schiller, but is not well adapted to the stage. The overture, however, is second to none in its continued popularity. Its four sections are all descriptive in nature: the first pictures an Alpine dawn, while the second portrays a furious storm. The third part reproduces the piping of mountain shepherds after the storm, while the fourth brings the work to a close with a representation of the marching of Swiss troops.

Overture, The Italian in Algiers (*L'Italiana in Algeri*): *The Italian in Algiers*, an opera buffa, was the second of Rossini's works to achieve great success. It was produced in Venice in 1813. Like most of Rossini's works, *L'Italiana* is no longer played, but the sparkling melodies of the opera have made the overture a favorite on orchestra and band programs.

Overture, La Gazza Ladra (*The Thieving Magpie*): The overture to *La Gazza Ladra* is one of the most popular of

Rossini's many overtures. The opera itself, after an ephemeral success, is all but forgotten. It was written during Rossini's most productive period, hurriedly as was usual for him, and played at La Scala in 1817. Between 1813 and 1817, Rossini composed fourteen operas; to accomplish this without too great an effort, he openly transposed airs from one opera to another, defending the practice by pointing out that some of the operas had been failures. *La Gazza Ladra,* in spite of defects inevitable in such facile work, contains many fine passages.

Overture, Semiramide: Semiramide was the last work Rossini composed for the Italian stage. He had put more care into its composition than was generally the rule with him, and he was thoroughly disappointed by the lukewarmness of its reception when it was given in Venice in 1823. Rossini was, however, to be somewhat compensated for this, for in 1860 a French version of the opera under the title *Semiramis,* was triumphantly successful at the Paris Opera. Rossini was by that time very little interested in his own operas, and only reluctantly gave his permission for the revision, in which he had no hand. The overture is typical of Rossini at his best, and has survived the changing tastes in opera.

Overture, Tancred: Tancred was Rossini's first great success, and indeed was so great a success that Rossini was amazed. It was first performed in Venice in 1813; from that date on, Rossini was a feted celebrity. The airs of *Tancred* are catchy and simple, but dexterously handled.

Overture, The Siege of Corinth: Originally known as *Mahomet II,* this work was produced at Naples in 1820, just before the revolt of the Carbonari. Rossini had written it in his usual haste, but completed it with his usual success. Nevertheless for its production in Paris as *The Siege of Corinth,* the composer felt compelled to make considerable revisions and additions—a procedure which might have benefited others of his early works. The Paris production took place in 1826 and was completely successful. It has gone the way of almost all of Rossini's operas, into oblivion; but its overture, with its spontaneity and spirit, remains a favorite.

Stabat Mater: After announcing his resolution to give up operatic composition Rossini composed but little, and only in the field of sacred music. The *Stabat Mater,* by far the most famous of his sacred compositions, was written at intervals. The first six numbers were completed in 1832, the last four about 1840. The first complete performance was in Paris in 1842. The work is extremely melodious, but can hardly be said to be deeply religious in spirit. Its immediate agreeableness have kept parts of the music in constant use up to the present time.

Overture, The Lady of the Lake: The Lady of the Lake was composed in 1819, and had its first performance in Naples on October 4 of that year. The première was a great disappointment to Rossini, for the Napolitans seized the opportunity to demonstrate their hostility to the manager of the opera house, and hissed incessantly. The second performance, however, was a typical Rossini success; the audience had apparently given up hissing the manager as a bad job. The opera was produced in a revised version, with many additions, in Paris in 1824, Rossini following his usual practice of saving the good numbers from his unsuccessful works by incorporating them in others. The opera as a whole does not rank with Rossini's masterpieces, but the overture, like many of the composer's others, holds an independent place.

Albert Roussel

BORN Tourcoing, France, April 5, 1869
DIED Paris, August 24, 1937

WRITTEN FOR BAND:

A GLORIOUS DAY (EV

THIS work was composed specially for band at the request of Edwin Franko Goldman. It is dedicated to Dr. Goldman and the American Bandmasters' Association. Roussel himself provided the following note: "As the title indicates, I wanted to express in this work the joy and rhythm of a holiday. This composition interprets the sentiments of gaiety of those who are part of a big celebration. It must be performed with 'gusto.' I think that 'A Glorious Day' will take the place of a real march to accompany school festivals and University celebrations, and all other ceremonies where a band will add to their joyous festivities."

Roussel served for many years in the French Navy before definitely deciding to follow a musical career. He was one of the first pupils of Vincent D'Indy at the Schola Cantorum in Paris. His subsequent work, in various forms, showed a distinctive originality and a skillful craftsmanship. He was considered among the most important of contemporary French composers.

A Glorious Day received its first performance at a concert of the Goldman Band in Central Park, New York City, on June 19, 1933.

Anton Gregor Rubinstein

BORN Wechwotynetz, Russia, November 28, 1830
DIED Peterhof, Russia, November 20, 1894

WORKS ARRANGED FOR BAND:

TRIUMPHAL OVERTURE (F; C
TOREADOR AND ANDALOUSE (B&H; F
ROYAL TAMBOUR AND VIVANDIÈRE (B&H; F
Torchlight Dance from FERAMORS (F
Dance of the Bayaderes from FERAMORS (F; D
Rève Angélique from KAMMENOI OSTROV (F
MELODY IN F (F; D; J
ROMANCE IN E♭ (F; J

ANTON RUBINSTEIN's career was one of the most brilliant in the musical annals of the nineteenth century. As a piano virtuoso his only rival was Liszt, while as a composer he was esteemed throughout Europe. He traveled widely, giving recitals and appearing as conductor; in 1872-73 he toured America, but was not too well pleased with the artistic conditions then prevailing in the United States, and refused an offer to return. In 1862 he founded the St. Petersburg Conservatory. The Tsar recognized his services by elevating him to the nobility.

Rubinstein composed operas, symphonies, chamber music and songs, as well as the dozens of piano pieces by which he is best remembered today. These piano works derive somewhat from Mendelssohn in style. The larger compositions of Rubinstein are all but forgotten, but these short and unpretentious pieces are known in every musical household.

Triumphal Overture: Rubinstein's *Overture Triomphale* was written for the twenty-fifth anniversary of the wedding of Tsar Alexander II of Russia and Princess Marie of Hesse-Darmstadt in 1868. It is an "occasional piece" which in many ways anticipates Tchaikovsky's *"1812" Overture.* It too commemorates the invasion of Moscow in 1812 by the troops of Napoleon, and the victory of the Russians. It opens with a slow introduction depicting the terror of the inhabitants of Moscow. The Russian hymn is heard as the expression of the faith of the people. The principal portion of the overture portrays the flight of the Russians from Moscow, the defeat of the French and the final return of the Russians. The Russian hymn sounds triumphantly at the close to indicate the victory. As a mark of respect to the Princess Marie, and also because of the fact that the German arms were opposed to Napoleon, the national anthem of Germany is also heard throughout the work.

Toreador and Andalouse and *Royal Tambour and Vivandière* from *Bal Costumé, Opus 103:* These characteristic pieces are two favorites from a set of twenty written for pianoforte duet. They are quite typical of Rubinstein's elegant and tuneful salon music. Arranged for salon orchestra or for band, they have become widely known. All of the twenty pieces in this set are named for imagined characters at a masquerade.

Torchlight Dance and *Dance of the Bayaderes* from *Feramors:* The libretto of Rubinstein's opera *Feramors* was adapted from the famous poetic drama, *Lalla Rookh,* by Thomas Moore. It was produced in Dresden in 1863. The story concerns Lalla Rookh, an Indian girl who is on her way to Delhi to marry the Sultan. While traveling thither she falls in love with the poet, Feramors, who has recited his verses to her. All ends happily when she discovers that the Sultan she is to wed and the poet are one and the same person.

The opera as a whole was never a great success, but these

two numbers from the ballet music have always retained great popular favor.

Melody in F and *Romance in E♭:* Many of Rubinstein's shorter compositions for pianoforte have become universally popular and numbers of them have been arranged for band and orchestra. These pieces, while inviting comparison to Mendelssohn's *Songs Without Words,* have a character of their own. In most of them the melodies are flowing and the harmony simple.

Rève Angélique from *Kammenoi-Ostrov: Kammenoi-Ostrov* (literally, *Stony Island*), is the name of a suite of twenty-four "portraits" for pianoforte, Opus 10. Rubinstein took the title from that of a resort near St. Petersburg, where he often went for recreation. The *Rève Angélique* (*Angelic Dream*) is the twenty-second of this set. It is said to be an idealized tonal portrait of the composer's friend, Mlle. Anna de Friedbourg, to whom the piece is dedicated. The other numbers of the set are likewise connected with real or imaginary persons, but none are as well-known as *Rève Angélique,* which is one of the finest melodies Rubinstein ever wrote. The first theme is a flowing melody with an accompaniment suggestive of ripples on the water. In the course of the composition a few bars of a Russian church choral are introduced.

Antonio Mario Gaspere Sacchini

BORN near Naples, Italy, July 23, 1734
DIED Paris, October 7, 1786

ARRANGED FOR BAND:
Pantomime Suite from IL GRAN CID (F
I. March
II. Arietta
III. Finale
Overture: OEDIPUS AT COLONUS (S

SACCHINI was one of the most distinguished minor operatic composers of the eighteenth century. He was of extremely humble origin, but manifested a talent for music (it is said that he sang beautifully), and attracted the attention of the prominent Italian composer Durante. He was enabled to complete his musical studies, and early began to produce operas in the prevailingly superficial and florid style. By 1771, he had written over fifty such works. His success enabled him to travel; from 1772 to 1782 he lived in London, where he was well received. From London he went to Paris. This was a most important change for Sacchini, for in the latter center he was influenced to a certain extent by the work of Gluck (q. v.). His works from that time on have more substance.

Il Gran Cid (*The Great Cid*) was written while Sacchini was in London, and was brought out in a French version as *Chimène* in 1784. A typically eighteenth-century handling of an epic theme, Sacchini's opera is complete with ballets and delightful, if not too serious, airs. The *Pantomime Suite* contains some of Sacchini's best ballet writing, and is notable for its grace and piquancy.

Overture, Oedipus at Colonus: The opera *Oedipus at*

Colonus was by all accounts Sacchini's masterpiece. It was the composer's last work for the stage and exhibited a force and seriousness which showed plainly the influence of Gluck. *Oedipus at Colonus* was completed in 1785 and first performed at Versailles on April 4, 1786. Strong and dramatic choral writing marked the work, and an attention to dramatic effect set it apart from most of Sacchini's earlier compositions for the stage. Although Sacchini's death was hastened by the indifference shown to this work, it maintained a place in the repertory of the Paris Opera for many years. The overture, a striking example of Sacchini's best work, was edited by the late Sam Franko and revived by him at his famous concerts of old music. The band arrangement has been made from Mr. Franko's orchestral score.

Charles Camille Saint-Saëns

BORN Paris, October 9, 1835
DIED Algiers, December 16, 1921

WORKS ARRANGED FOR BAND:

Symphonic Poems: PHAËTON (F
THE YOUTH OF HERCULES (B&H
THE WHEEL OF OMPHALE (F; B&H
DANSE MACABRE (F; B&H
Overture to THE YELLOW PRINCESS (C; F
Prelude to THE DELUGE (F
Bacchanale from SAMSON AND DELILAH (F
Ballet from HENRY VIII (F
French Military March from ALGERIAN SUITE (F; Ru
HEROIC MARCH (F; B&H
THE SWAN (F
Selections from SAMSON AND DELILAH (F; C
Ballet Suite from ASCANIO (C

ORIGINAL WORKS FOR BAND:

March, ORIENT AND OCCIDENT (Durand, Paris)
March, ON THE BANKS OF THE NILE (Durand, Paris)

THE position held by Saint-Saëns in the history of French music can hardly be overestimated. By his example and influence he did much to revive French interest in serious symphonic music. His long career as composer and pianist began in his eleventh year, when he gave a piano recital in Paris. He took up the cause of progress in music at an early age, devoting himself to furthering all that was best in French music and aligning himself with such composers as Bizet and Berlioz rather than men of the stamp of Massenet.

His success was not immediate, but steadily became greater. He underwent the influence of Liszt in his symphonic poems, and of the classic German masters in his symphonies, but preserved a strong individuality which he combined with the traditional French ideals of polished craftsmanship. Dramatic composition interested him equally, and of his long list of successful operas, many are still performed. His sense of the dramatic was not powerful, but he had a genuinely refined lyric style.

Saint-Saëns made many tours as pianist and conductor, appearing twice in the United States, once in 1906 and again in 1915 for the Panama-Pacific Exposition. France honored him with the Legion of Honor and election to the Institute; Cambridge conferred upon him the honorary degree of Doctor of Music. The later years of his life were spent in continued activity and in the enjoyment of a great reputation. His influence on younger musicians became somewhat less marked after the emergence of Fauré, Franck and Debussy (q. v.), although it was still of considerable importance. But he had left his mark on the history of music in France, modifying both the teutonic influence of Wagner and the tendency to shallowness on the part of his own countrymen, restoring to French music its dignity and seriousness and promoting the development in France of formal instrumental music.

⸍ ⸍ ⸍

Symphonic Poem, Phaëton: The literary basis of this composition is found in a Greek myth. Phaëton, the son of Apollo, wished to take his father's place as driver of the chariot of the sun. With many misgivings, Apollo eventually consented. Phaëton started out bravely, but his strength was not equal to the task; the fiery steeds got out of his control and pulled the sun off its usual course, approaching nearer and nearer to the earth. Finally Zeus, in order to save the earth's inhabitants, launched a thunderbolt at Phaëton and took the chariot into his own hands.

Phaëton's wild career in the heavens is described in the music, which reaches its climax when Zeus intervenes. At the close, as a sort of coda, there is a short passage of lamentation for the too-ambitious youth. The composition was first performed in 1873 and is one of Saint-Saëns' most successful descriptive works.

Symphonic Poem, The Wheel of Omphale (*Le Rouet d'Omphale*): The first of Saint-Saëns' tone-poems, like the last, is concerned with the hero Hercules. *Le Rouet d'Omphale* tells the story of Hercules condemned, after the completion of his twelve labors, to serve as slave to a Lydian queen. Clothed in feminine attire, the unfortunate hero is compelled to operate the queen's spinning-wheel. His restiveness and the derision with which the queen treats him are depicted in the music, the principal theme of which is a characteristic imitation of the wheel. The composition is very short, and cast in a miniature sonata form.

Symphonic Poem, The Youth of Hercules (*La Jeunesse d'Hercule*): *The Youth of Hercules* was the fourth and last of the series of symphonic poems written by Saint-Saëns. It is not based on any of the familiar tales from Greek mythology, but represents a generalized symbolism. The program is set forth as follows, in a note to the score: ". . . Hercules on his entrance into life saw two roads open before him; that of pleasure and that of virtue. Insensible to the seductions of nymphs and bacchantes, the hero chose the path of struggle and great deeds, at the end of which, through the flames of the funeral pyre, he caught a glimpse of the reward of immortality." This program gives a good indication of what is to be found in the music. Two themes, representative of the two paths before Hercules, alternate in dominating the score, until at the end the theme typifying struggle triumphs in a stirring climax. The work was composed in 1877 and dedicated to Saint-Saëns' eminent contemporary, Henri Duparc.

Danse Macabre: The enormous popularity of this composition is undoubtedly due in a large measure to its fantastic originality. It is almost unique in its refined diabolism. Saint-Saëns based the work on a poem of Henri Cazalis. The poem describes Death playing a dance-tune in a cemetery, and enticing the skeletons from their tombs. The music begins with the sound of the midnight bell, immediately after which Death begins to tune his fiddle. The main portion of the work depicts the ghostly dance of the skeletons as they rattle and dodge about among the gravestones. At the first signs of dawn, the cock crows and the dancers return to their resting places.

Marche Militaire Française (*French Military March*) from *Suite Algérienne:* The subtitle of Saint-Saëns *Algerian Suite* is: "Picturesque Impressions of a Voyage to Algeria." Of its four movements, three are decidedly Oriental in coloring. The fourth, the "Military March," is by contrast quite French; it was intended to emphasize the contrast found at Algiers between the native and the French settlements. In a note to the score the composer emphasized the fact that he not only felt joyful at seeing French soldiers, but was conscious of the security he enjoyed under their protection.

Prelude to *The Deluge: The Deluge,* called by its composer a "Biblical poem," was written in 1874, but was not produced until 1876. It was the third attempt by Saint-Saëns to secure a place of honor on the operatic stage, but like the preceding ones was not entirely successful. The work is little known today outside of France, and even there is seldom performed. The prelude, however, is one of the most popular of Saint-Saëns' orchestral works. It is simple and expressive; the opening chords and the subsequent fugal section lend it a certain impressiveness and dignity, in keeping with the nature of the subject. The prelude was scored originally for string orchestra.

Overture, The Yellow Princess (*La Princesse Jaune*): *The Yellow Princess* was the second of Saint-Saëns' operas, but the first to be performed. The première took place in Paris in 1872, with a very moderate success. Saint-Saëns received no encouragement to continue writing opera as a result of it. Possibly due to the lack of dramatic force in his music, the operas of Saint-Saëns are best known only by certain excerpts, such as the prelude to *The Deluge* and this overture to *The Yellow Princess.*

Selections from *Samson and Delilah: Saint-Saëns* had many difficulties in getting his operatic works performed; his masterpiece, *Samson and Delilah,* was refused by the directors of the Paris Opera, and only received its initial hearing through the good offices of Franz Liszt, who produced it at Weimar in 1877. The work was not given in France until 1890, and in America (New Orleans) until 1893.

The opera follows the Biblical story with fair fidelity, but it has not maintained a permanent place in the repertory. The music is more familiar in concert form than it is on the stage. The air, *My Heart at Thy Sweet Voice,* is familiar to all, as is the ballet music. The score has the grace and fluency characteristic of Saint-Saëns, together with a warmth not always found in his other works.

Bacchanale from *Samson and Delilah:* Saint-Saëns' most famous opera follows the familiar Biblical story with little deviation. The third act shows Samson, shorn of his locks, chained to a grinding-mill. He sings the well-known air, *See*

My Distress!, as the Philistines taunt him. The *Bacchanale* is introduced at that point, as an expression of the exultation of the Philistines over the downfall of their enemies. The music is Oriental in coloring, marked by strong rhythms and the climax is brilliant, full of a fierce animation and triumphant energy. At the conclusion of this *Bacchanale* Samson is infuriated; he asks to be led to the pillars of the Temple, and prays for strength to destroy it and his enemies.

Ballet Music from *Henry VIII:*
I. Introduction
II. Entry of the Clans
III. Scotch Idyll
IV. Gypsy Dance
V. Gigue and Finale

After his election to the Institute in 1881, Saint-Saëns was considerably more successful than he had been in gaining access to the operatic stage. In 1883 his opera *Henry VIII* was produced. The libretto dealt with the English King and Anne Boleyn. The composer, with more conscience than his librettists, spent some time in research and study before setting down any of the music, to which he wished to give some air of authenticity. In the ballet music he incorporated a number of well-known Scotch and English melodies.

Marche Héroique (*Heroic March*): The *Heroic March* was originally written for two pianos, and was later arranged for orchestra by the composer. Written during the Franco-Prussian War, it expressed the patriotic sentiments of Saint-Saëns, aroused by the heroic resistance of his countrymen. The march is broad and dignified in character. The main subject (alla breve) is vigorous and striking; the noble second theme (3/4 time) offers splendid contrast. After the return of the first subject, a bold coda concludes the work. The *Heroic March* was dedicated to the painter Régnault, killed in action in 1871.

Ballet Music from *Ascanio: Ascanio,* the eighth of Saint-Saëns' operas, was produced at the Paris Opera in 1890. Little of the music is remembered today, with the exception of the picturesque and pleasing Ballet Suite.

Franz Xaver Scharwenka

BORN Samter, E. Prussia, January 6, 1850
DIED Berlin, December 8, 1924

ARRANGED FOR BAND:

POLISH DANCE (No.: 1. (F; D; CB; AMP
2. (D
5. (AMP

XAVER SCHARWENKA enjoyed wide renown as pianist and teacher. He made many tours as a virtuoso and spent seven years in New York where he founded a conservatory. He composed an impressive number of large compositions, including an opera, a symphony and four piano concertos, but his reputation rests almost exclusively on these famous dances which were originally composed for pianoforte solo.

The Polish dances, with their brilliant energy and marked rhythms, have become universally known and have been arranged in many forms.

Franz Peter Schubert

BORN Vienna, January 31, 1797
DIED Vienna, November 19, 1828

WORKS ARRANGED FOR BAND:

SYMPHONY IN B MINOR ("Unfinished") (B&H; F
ROSAMUNDE: *Overture* (F; B&H
Three Entr'Actes (C
Ballet Music (F
Overture: ALPHONSE AND ESTRELLA (B&H
Overture: FIERRABRAS (D
MARCHES MILITAIRES, Op. 51 (F; B&H; Ru; J
MOMENTS MUSICAUX (F; J
AVE MARIA and Other Songs (Various Eds.)

SCHUBERT was one of the greatest melodists who ever lived, a genius whose extraordinary gifts revealed themselves in hundreds of wonderful songs, as well as in many larger works. In his short life he gave evidence of a creative facility rivalling that of Mozart whom, of all composers, he most resembled. Schubert's music has the Mozartean naturalness and apparent spontaneity, as well as its purity and perfection of form. No music of the masters is more readily understandable or more universally loved.

Schubert's life was one of hardship and poverty. His publishers took advantage of his good nature, and the public never had the chance to become sufficiently acquainted with his greatest works. Musicians recognized his genius, but few contributed to his support. Had it not been for the kindness of two or three friends, Schubert might have starved in a garret. Yet it is recorded that despite his troubles, his disposition remained genial; certainly his music bears no traces of bitterness or tragedy, nor does his productivity seem to have suffered. The amount of creative work Schubert accomplished is almost incredibly great, just as the level of artistic merit is almost invariably high.

His symphonies and chamber music have a character entirely their own. They are not profound like Beethoven's, nor thoroughly romantic like Schumann's, though they possess perhaps more warmth than the works of Mozart. Schubert's songs stand by themselves; masterpiece follows masterpiece in his volumes of *lieder*. For beauty of melody, fidelity to poetry, and exquisiteness of finish they have never been approached.

Schubert's influence was slight, but his position is secure. Following his death, the German school entered whole-heartedly into romanticism. Many of his works were forgotten until their discovery and revival many years later. Schubert was a "natural" musician; he belonged to no school and influenced no disciples. But for sheer beauty of musical expression he had few equals.

"Unfinished" Symphony (B minor):

I. Allegro Moderato (B Minor—3/4 time)

II. Andante con moto (E major—3/8 time)

The "Unfinished" Symphony is the eighth of Schubert's ten symphonies. It is unquestionably the best-known; possibly even the best-known of all symphonies. It was written in 1822 as Schubert's acknowledgment to the Musical Society of Gratz, which had just made him an honorary member. The work is not, as its popular title suggests, unfinished; there is reason to believe that it was designed as it stands; in any case, Schubert lived long enough to have completed it had he so desired. The work remained in manuscript until 1867, when it was published in Vienna.

It is superfluous to attempt to explain this music in any terms other than its own beauty. The principal theme of the first movement is as famous as that of any song. What is really remarkable about the "Unfinished" Symphony (and indeed about many of Schubert's other large works) is the manner in which Schubert was able to adapt song-like melodies to use in the symphonic medium.

Music from *Rosamunde:* Schubert wrote some of his finest numbers as incidental music to the drama *Rosamunde, Princess of Cyprus,* by Wilhelmine von Chezy, the authoress who was also responsible for Weber's *Euryanthe.* The estimable lady seems to have been more fortunate in her composers than her dramatic talents warranted, for her literary works were, to put it charitably, inept. *Rosamunde,* as a play, had two performances; Schubert's music has had thousands.

(a) The overture now called *Rosamunde* was originally written for *The Magic Harp,* a play by Hofmann. This overture is in C. The overture which was actually written for the drama *Rosamunde* is, however, in D; it was later published as *Alfonso and Estrella.* Questions of nomenclature aside, the *Rosamunde* overture is one of the finest single compositions Schubert ever produced.

(b) Sir George Grove characterized the B minor Entr'Acte as one of the "finest pieces of music existing." The other entr'actes are not far below this level. The ballet music is perhaps more familiar; it too has the unfailing charm and beauty which we associate with the name of the composer.

Rosamunde was produced at the Theater-an-der-Wien, Vienna, in 1823. The music was enormously applauded and Schubert was called to take bows. After the failure of the play, however, the music remained hidden until its discovery in 1867 by Sir George Grove and Sir Arthur Sullivan.

Overture, Alfonso and Estrella (see note to *Rosamunde*): This overture in D was originally written for the drama

Rosamunde, but published under its present title. It has, therefore, no organic connection with the opera *Alfonso and Estrella* which Schubert composed in 1821-22. This opera, with a fantastic libretto and beautiful music, was never performed during Schubert's life. The accompaniments were too difficult for the opera orchestras, and the style of the airs was too dissimilar to that of Rossini and the other operatic idols of the day. Liszt gave *Alfonso and Estrella* its first performance in 1854 at Weimar. It was revised and shortened by the Kapellmeister of the Vienna Opera, and produced with much success in 1880.

Overture, Fierrabras: Schubert had no success with his operas. He began the composition of *Fierrabras* with great enthusiasm and completed the score inside of five months. The libretto was extremely bad, a conglomeration of improbabilities without value even as fantasy. Schubert did not seem to be troubled by it, but he never saw the opera performed. The Vienna opera refused to accept it, on the grounds of its weak libretto. The work as a whole was not performed until 1870. The overture was brought out a few years after Schubert's death, and introduced by Mendelssohn into England. Since that time it has held its own in popularity with Schubert's other overtures.

Marches Militaires, Opus 51: Schubert was extremely fond of writing pianoforte duets. Of these, the three *Military Marches, Opus 51,* are by far the best known. They are delightfully informal in character, far from pompous, but full of spirited swing. The first is played more frequently than the others.

Moments Musicaux: The six *Musical Moments* which Schubert composed for pianoforte solo are among his most widely played and well-known compositions. It is safe to say that nearly every piano student has learned at least one of them. The gracefulness and charm of these miniatures have never been duplicated by would-be imitators.

(*Songs:* Many of Schubert's songs, including the *Serenade*, the *Ave Maria* and others, have been arranged either for band or for solo instruments with band. It is impossible to attempt to provide a note for each of these. The reader is referred to the general comments on Schubert's songs in the short sketch of the composer's life and works.)

Robert Alexander Schumann

BORN Zwickau, Saxony, June 8, 1810
DIED near Bonn, Germany, July 29, 1856

WORKS ARRANGED FOR BAND:

Romanza and *Finale* from FOURTH SYMPHONY (C
FESTIVAL OVERTURE (F
REVERIE ("Träumerei") (F; J
ARABESQUE, SLUMBER SONG, and ORIENTAL PICTURE (B&H
EVENING SONG (F; J

SCHUMANN did not begin a serious study of music until his twentieth year, although as a boy he had learned to play the piano and had composed a good deal without instruction. He matriculated at the University of Leipzig as a law-student, but was more interested in music and in literature than in the legal profession; his literary and philosophical studies, however, exercised a great influence over his subsequent career. Greatly attracted to the works of Byron and Jean Paul Richter, it was only natural that he should express in his music the same type of generous and warm romanticism.

The pianoforte was from the beginning the instrument which held the greatest attraction for Schumann. Disappointed in his hopes of becoming a great virtuoso, he wrote exclusively for that instrument until about 1840; these early works include everything up to Opus 23. At the same time, having definitely taken up the cause of "liberalism" in music, he helped found the *Neue Zeitschrift für Musik* in 1834, and became its sole editor in 1835. This journal exercised tremendous influence in the middle of the century; in it were the famous articles in which Schumann hailed the genius of Chopin and of Brahms. Schumann had much of the crusader's fibre in him. He attacked the shallowness of the Italian opera and the speciousness of much contemporary music.

The University of Jena conferred the degree of Doctor of Philosophy on him in 1840. In that same year he married Clara Wieck, the daughter of his teacher, and herself a splendid pianist. From that time dates his emergence as a composer of songs, chamber music and symphonies. He held positions in Dresden and Düsseldorf, toured but little, and devoted himself almost exclusively to composition. He wrote in every form and for every medium, expressing in all his works the same warmth of feeling, the same romantic individualism and the same earnestness of emotion.

Symphony #4 in D Minor (*Romanza and Finale*): *The D Minor Symphony*, which is known as Schumann's fourth, was really the second in order of composition. It was first performed in 1841, but the composer was quite dissatisfied with it, and withdrew it from circulation. He revised the work thoroughly in 1851; in its new form it was performed in 1853. In the interim Schumann had composed what are known as his second and third symphonies.

The Fourth Symphony was conceived as a "symphonic fantasia" in one long movement; the original edition, in fact, bore the title "Introduction, Allegro, Romanza, Scherzo and Finale in one movement." The work, therefore, is a modification of the classical form, by means of which Schumann hoped that a greater unity could be obtained. To emphasize this idea of unity still further, there is a recurrent use of the same thematic material in different movements.

The movements themselves are rather free in form. The *Romanza* (rather slow, in three quarter time) opens with a plaintive melody played on the oboe, over an accompaniment which lends strength to the supposition that Schumann had intended to write a guitar part in the score. The movement gains in brightness as it proceeds, modulating from A minor to D major and ultimately to A major.

The *Finale* commences with a slow introduction in which the main theme of the first movement is heard. The principal portion of the *Finale* is lively and also contains reminiscences of other movements. The coda is rather lengthy and more rapid in tempo, and brings the symphony to a bright and joyous close.

Festival Overture: Schumann wrote few concert overtures, most of his shorter symphonic works being definitely connected with a drama or opera. The *Festival Overture* is an exception. It is founded on the *Rheinweinlied*, a popular German drinking song. Full of spirit, and worked out with exceptional cleverness, it deserves to rank with Schumann's creative best. It was first performed, with chorus and soloists, at the Lower Rhine Festival in Düsseldorf in 1853.

Piano Pieces (Arabesque, Träumerei, Evening Song, etc.): Schumann's piano music has a peculiarly personal touch, as though each piece were illustrative of some incident in his life or of some mood in which he found himself. Almost all of them have a spontaneous, song-like character, although there is a great range of expression among them. The dreamy and the vigorous pieces are about equally divided. Schumann often used descriptive titles to make more explicit the sentimental or picturesque content of the music; at other times he was content, like Chopin, to use more general titles such as "Arabesque," "Novelette" and so forth. The definite intention to *express* something is, however, always apparent; it is this that stamps Schumann as a romantic in every sense of the word, and which sets his piano music so sharply apart from that, say, of Mozart or of Schubert. It is personalized, intimate, emotional. Schumann's success in conveying delicate shades of "poetic" meaning is perhaps the measure of his greatness as an artist.

Benedetto Secchi

BORN Mondovi, Italy, January 28, 1831
DIED Rome, May 31, 1883

ARRANGED FOR BAND:

Overture, THE MAID OF ASTURIA (F

SECCHI was a minor composer of church music and opera whose work was apparently well regarded in his lifetime. His fame rests on two operas, *The Maid of Asturia*, and *Il Trovatore*, which were produced in 1856 and 1847 respectively.

The overture to *The Maid of Asturia* is very effective. The following summary is taken from the note printed in the score: The opening movement (16 measures of *Allegro vivo*) for clarinets and basses is one of exuberance and leads into a short period of festive choral nature for the full band. After a short pause, the *Andante* (12/8) begins with sustained and *arpeggio* wood-winds accompanying the beautiful aria assigned to the baritone. Another slight pause, and the recurrence of the *Allegro* theme, now elaborate and developed to a greater extent, leads into a slightly slower movement, consisting of figuration in the wood-winds and a charming sustained counter-melody in the alto and baritone voices. Another form of the festive motive for the full band closes the work with a successful climax.

Jan Sibelius

BORN Tavastehus, Finland, December 8, 1865

WORKS ARRANGED FOR BAND:

Tone Poem, FINLANDIA (B&H; D
VALSE TRISTE (F; B&H*
VALSE LYRIQUE (B&H
TANZ INTERMEZZO (F
TWO MARCHES (AMP

SIBELIUS is unquestionably the greatest composer Finland has ever produced. He is a musician who has never courted popular acclaim, yet whose works have made their way throughout the world and whose reputation is growing almost daily. His art is firmly rooted in Finnish national tradition; it is intensely patriotic in conception but universal in its appeal. A great individuality pervades all of the music of Sibelius; the list of his works is long and varied. Sibelius is best known in this country by lighter works with an immediate popular appeal, but appreciation of his symphonies is steadily growing.

The enormous services which Sibelius rendered to the art of Finland have been many times recognized by the Finnish government. The composer is, indeed, a national figure of the first importance, regarded with veneration by a proud people. In 1897, the Finnish government bestowed a life annuity upon him which enabled him to devote himself to an uninterrupted career of composition. His fiftieth and sixtieth birthdays were the occasions of national celebrations.

Sibelius has left Finland but seldom, coming to the United States in 1914 for a short time to teach at the New England Conservatory in Boston.

✓ ✓ ✓

* In U. S. A.—(M

Tone Poem, Finlandia: Finlandia was the first work to bring Sibelius extensive recognition outside of his own country. It is still the most widely known of his compositions. Much easier to grasp, more simple and forthright, it has a far greater popular appeal than his symphonies. The composition has become a symbol of Finland; the broad melody of the middle section is so close to the spirit of Finnish folksong that it has already become almost traditional. The work opens with a turbulence which characterizes the national aspirations for independence of the Finnish people, for it was written while Finland was still part of Russia. So tremendous was the effect produced by *Finlandia* that performances of it were forbidden by the Russian Tsar.

Valse Triste: This well-known number is taken from the incidental music written by Sibelius for *Kuolema* (*Death*), a drama by his brother-in-law, Arvid Jaernefelt. The composer describes the music in the following note:

"It is night. A young man, who has been watching beside the bedside of his sick mother, has fallen asleep from sheer weariness. Gradually a ruddy light is diffused through the room; there is a sound of distant music. The glow and the music come nearer and nearer until the strains of a waltz melody float distantly to the listening ears. The sleeping mother awakens, rises from her bed, and in her long white garment, which takes on the semblance of a ball-dress, begins to move silently and slowly to and fro. She waves her hands and beckons in time to the music, as though to summon a crowd of invisible guests. Now they appear: strange, visionary couples, turning and gliding to an unearthly waltz rhythm. The dying woman mixes with the dancers; she strives to make them look into her eyes, but the shadowy guests avoid her glance. Then she sinks exhausted on her bed and the music breaks off. She gathers her strength and invokes the dance once more, with increasingly energetic gestures. The shadowy dancers come back, gyrating in a wild, mad rhythm. The weird gaiety reaches a climax; there is a knock at the door. It flies open; the mother utters a despairing cry; the spectral guests vanish; the music dies away. Death stands on the threshold."

Valse Lyrique: The *Valse Lyrique* is the first of a set of three pieces for orchestra, Opus 96. The second and third numbers are entitled, respectively, *Autrefois* (*Times Past*), and *Valse Chevaleresque* (*Knightly Waltz*). The *Valse Lyrique* is an example of the peculiarly personal vehicle Sibelius has made out of the concert waltz form. His works in this idiom are hardly dance numbers, but are filled with a crepuscular atmosphere, mysterious and strange.

Tanz Intermezzo: The *Dance Intermezzo* is the second of two tone-poems for orchestra, Opus 45, written almost directly after the *Valse Triste*. The *Dance Intermezzo,* indeed, makes an admirable companion piece to the latter, having much of the same character of mystery and darkness. It, too, is in three-quarter time and like the *Valse Triste* partakes but little of the character of a waltz. The introduction is extremely sombre; the principal section is lighter in color, but is restrained and melancholy rather than gay.

Bedrich (Frederick) Smetana

BORN Litomyšl, Bohemia (now Czechoslovakia), March 2, 1824
DIED Prague, May 12, 1884

WORKS ARRANGED FOR BAND:

Overture, THE BARTERED BRIDE (F; B&H
Dances from THE BARTERED BRIDE
1. Polka (S
2. Furiant (S
3. Comedian's Dance (S; F
Symphonic Poem, THE MOLDAU (B&H
Overture, LIBUSSA (F

POSSIBLY no other composer, with the exception of Sibelius, can be identified so completely as Smetana with a "national" school of music. Smetana created the Czech school by his works; Dvořák followed him to a certain extent, but has never taken his place. In his music, as well as in his choice of subjects (for operatic and choral works), Smetana gave expression to the feelings of a people who felt that they were a community although they were at the time divided among various empires. His music expressed their joys and sorrows as well as their aspirations, and provided this expression at the time it was needed most. Hence the position which Smetana holds in the esteem of his countrymen.

The composer's own life was spent in unflagging devotion to his musical ideas. In his later years, like Beethoven, he became deaf; during this period, despite intense suffering, he composed some of his finest music. The centenary of his birth, in 1924, was celebrated throughout Czechoslovakia.

The Bartered Bride: Smetana composed nine operas, of which only *The Bartered Bride* is well-known throughout the world. The gaiety and vivacity of this charming work give it a universal appeal, apart from the special significance it has for the Czech people. The story deals with Czech peasants, emphasizing their humor and resourcefulness in an artful bit of intrigue. Smetana was fortunate in his librettist, Sabina, for the opera avoids the pitfalls which usually bring treatments of rustic subjects to grief. It is natural without being coarse, and agreeable without being preposterous. The music, with its occasional reference to Bohemian (Czech) melodies, is sparkling, and has a superb finish of form.

The Polka and Furiant are dance-forms native to what is now called Czechoslovakia. The Polka is in two-quarter time, the tempo being that of a moderately slow march. The tempo is determined, however, by the steps which are used in the dancing. The Furiant is not, strictly speaking, a dance form, but the name is used to characterize a dance of a frenzied bacchanalian character. The term was first used in serious music by Smetana, and later popularized by Dvořák.

Symphonic Poem, The Moldau (Vltava): *The Moldau* is the second of six symphonic poems which are grouped together under the title of *My Country* (*Má Vlast*). These were written between 1874 and 1879, and form but a small part of the work which Smetana dedicated to the glory of his country. The composer's intentions are expressed in the following note which is prefaced to the score of *The Moldau:*

"Two springs pour forth their streams in the shade of the Bohemian forest, the one warm and gushing, the other cold and tranquil. Their waves, joyfully flowing over their rocky beds, unite and sparkle in the morning sun. The forest brook, rushing on, becomes the River Moldau, with its waters speeding through dense woods in which are heard the joyous sounds of the hunt, and the notes of the hunter's horn ever nearer and nearer.

"It flows through emerald meadows and lowlands where there is being celebrated with song and dancing a wedding feast. At night, in its shining waves, wood and water nymphs hold their revels, and in these waves are reflected many a fortress and castle—witnesses of bygone splendor and chivalry and the vanishing martial fame of days that are no more. At the rapids of Saint John the stream speeds on, winding its way through the cataracts and hewing a path for its foaming waters through the rocky chasm into the broad river bed in which it flows on in majestic calm toward Prague, welcomed by time-honored Vyšehrad, to disappear in the far distance from the poet's gaze." (Translation by W. H. Humiston, from the original.)

Overture, Libussa: Libussa was the fourth of Smetana's epoch-making Czech operas. Extraordinary significance was attached to it by the composer, who desired it to be (as indeed he desired of so many of his works) an inspiring expression of Czech glory and freedom. Founded on a famous legend of Bohemia, the opera was intended for presentation on "festivals which touch the whole Czech people." The legend concerns the marriage of Libussa, foundress of Prague, and Přemysl, a peasant symbolic of the Czech character.

The splendid overture opens with a brilliant fanfare, which recurs in the opera itself. The main portion of the overture is built on the two themes associated with Libussa and Premysl. *Libussa* was composed for the opening of the National Theatre of Prague, and was first performed there on June 11, 1881.

John Philip Sousa

BORN Washington, D. C., November 6, 1856
DIED Reading, Pa., March 6, 1932

ORIGINAL WORKS FOR BAND:

Suites: THE DWELLERS IN THE WESTERN WORLD (C; P
CUBALAND (F
AT THE MOVIES (F
THREE QUOTATIONS (P
TALES OF A TRAVELER (P
LAST DAYS OF POMPEII (P
SHERIDAN'S RIDE (P

Selections from: THE BRIDE ELECT (P
THE FREE LANCE (P

Also numerous famous marches, including:
THE STARS AND STRIPES FOREVER,
THE THUNDERER, HANDS ACROSS
THE SEA, KING COTTON, etc.

Waltzes, Descriptive pieces, etc.

THE career of John Philip Sousa is certainly familiar to every follower of bands and band music in America. No one person ever brought more fame or prestige to American bands, or so endeared himself to a public which included the entire world. His name is an inspiration to bandmasters everywhere.

Sousa studied the violin as well as various band instruments, and at the age of seventeen made his debut as conductor. He was associated for many years with traveling theatrical companies both as violinist and conductor. When Offenbach made his tour of America in 1877, Sousa played under him. Not long after that he made his own first venture into the field of comic-opera composition. His marches enjoyed great popularity from the start, and in 1880 he was sufficiently well known to receive the appointment as conductor of the United States Marine Band. His work with this organization was outstanding; he remained at its head until 1892 and during this time made it the leading band of the nation. In 1892 he formed his own famous band, giving his first concert at Plainfield, N. J., on September 26 of that year. There followed concerts throughout the United States and Canada, four tours through Europe and one around the world. The Sousa Band played before royalty, and its conductor received many decorations and other expressions of approval and admiration. The triumphs recorded by the Sousa Band are a matter of history. It was a European critic who first gave Sousa the soubriquet of "The March King."

As long as the Sousa Band was active, it was the standard to which all other bands had to be compared. Men trained under Sousa are today among the leading bandmasters in the country. Just as Sousa's Band was a standard, so were his marches, of which he wrote almost one hundred. These are classics in their field, and represent an accomplishment of which any composer might well be proud.

Sousa was an extremely versatile man. Besides his conducting and composing, he wrote several novels, an autobiography, and the libretto of one of his comic-operas. He also wrote a Method for the Violin and a number of other instructive works. The respect and esteem in which he was held by all music-lovers is legendary. One of the first actions of the American Bandmasters' Association, directly after its formation, was to ask him to be its Honorary Life President; this was but one of the many tributes to him as a man and as a musician.

ᐟ ᐟ ᐟ

Suite, At the Movies:

I. The Serenaders
II. The Crafty Villain and the Timid Maid
III. Balance All and Swing Partners

This suite is full of humor and will recall the good old days of the movies when the finer points of drama were conspicuous by their absence. The first part of the suite, *The Serenaders,* opens with a *Marcia Brillante* in 6/8 time. The middle-section of the movement introduces a *Tempo di Redowa* (similar to the Mazurka) and an old-fashioned Polka. The march returns to end the movement.

The Crafty Villain enters the scene by means of menacing sounds from the lower instruments. The Timid Maid plays an oboe solo, a rather naive tune. The Villain pursues—the Maid plays on—and the movement ends with a bang.

The final movement is an old-fashioned dance with plenty of gusto and humor. The suite was published in 1922.

Suite, Dwellers of the Western World:

I. The Red Man
II. The White Man
III. The Black Man

This suite gives characteristic music of the three races inhabiting the New World. The Red Man, first to be established, is pictured in the rhythms and melodies associated with him. This movement is in common time, *moderato.* The music of the White Man is descriptive of his spirit of adventure and energy. The tempo shifts several times, as does the character of the music. The third movement, devoted to the Black Man, emphasizes the happier aspects of the Negro—his dances and good humor. This movement is an *allegro brillante,* the rhythm being that of the old plantation dance. The suite was published in 1906.

Suite, Three Quotations:

I. "The King of France with 20,000 men
Marched up the hill and then marched down again."
II. I Too was Born in Arcadia
III. In Darkest Africa

As the titles indicate, these numbers are fantasies evolving about the random quotations chosen. Like many of Sousa's compositions, these numbers show not only expert musicianship, but also a subtle sense of humor. The first number, dealing with the King of France and his famed exploit, is in *tempo marziale,* which becomes, as the adventure nears its end, *grandioso.* The second number is pastoral in character, as befits suggestions of Arcadia, while the third is an *allegretto* in dance rhythm. This suite is one of Sousa's early works, having been published in 1896.

Suite, Tales of a Traveler:

I. The Kaffir in the Karoo
II. In the Land of the Golden Fleece
III. The Grand Promenade at the White House

This suite was first published in 1914, sometime after Sousa's band had returned from a tour around the world. In these short numbers, Sousa may be said to have imaginatively recorded the trip, ending up with a return to Washington and the pomp of the White House. The first number is exotic in character, as befits its somewhat mysterious character. The second is a *Valse brillante,* while the third is full of dignity and pageantry.

Suite, The Last Days of Pompeii:

I. In the House of Burbo and Stratonice
II. Nydia
III. The Destruction of Pompeii and Nydia's Death

Sousa's suite, inspired by the famous novel of Bulwer-Lytton, was first published in 1912. The movements are prefixed by appropriate quotations from the book, and are very straightforward in their descriptiveness. The theme associated with Nydia is easily recognizable by its lyricism. The last movement opens *moderato,* as if to suggest the quiet of the city, not in the least expecting its doom; an *allegro con fuoco* follows, depicting the terrors of the destruction, while at the end an *andante tranquillo* recalls the sad fate of the fair heroine.

Johann Strauss (The Younger)

BORN Vienna, October 25, 1825
DIED Vienna, June 3, 1899

WORKS ARRANGED FOR BAND:

Selections from: THE BAT (F; B&H
THE GYPSY BARON (F
THE QUEEN'S LACE HANDKERCHIEF (F
RITTER PASMAN (AMP
and others

PERSIAN MARCH (SF; F
EGYPTIAN MARCH (F
PIZZICATO POLKA (F; CB; J
PERPETUUM MOBILE (F; B&H
Waltzes—including:
THE BEAUTIFUL BLUE DANUBE (F; D; B&H; Ru; Ba; CB
ARTIST'S LIFE (D; B&H; F
WINE, WOMEN & SONG (B&H; F
WIENERBLUT (F
FLEDERMAUS (F; S
and many others. . . .

THE ELDER JOHANN STRAUSS did not wish his son to be a musician, but young Johann, before reaching the age of nineteen, emerged as a conductor at a Viennese restaurant, scoring an instantaneous success. Soon Strauss Senior saw his own fame as a composer of waltzes and other dances eclipsed by that of his son. At the death of his father, Johann the Second combined their two orchestras. He toured Austria, Poland and Germany, and in 1855 was given a ten years' engagement to conduct the summer concerts in St. Petersburg.

He was conductor of the court balls in Vienna for a time, but eventually resigned to devote more time to composition. From 1870 on, he achieved many successes in the field of operetta. Altogether he composed almost five-hundred pieces of dance-music and more than fifteen operettas. His career was a decided artistic and popular success. "One of Strauss' waltzes," said Wagner, "as far surpasses in charm, finish and real musical worth the artificial compositions of his contemporaries, as the tower of St. Stephen's surpasses the advertising columns on the Paris Boulevards."

✓ ✓ ✓

Selections from *The Bat* (*Die Fledermaus*): Strauss' success in operetta rivalled that of Suppé. *The Bat* was one of the earliest and greatest triumphs, written in 1874 and produced at the Theatre An-der-Wien. It includes many well-known melodies, including the delightful waltz, *Du und Du* (You and You).

✓

Selections from *The Gypsy Baron* (*Zigeunerbaron*): *The Gypsy Baron* was first performed at the Theatre An-der-Wien in 1885, scoring a marked success. Like many of Strauss' other operettas, *The Gypsy Baron* soon was known and sung throughout the world.

✓

The Beautiful Blue Danube: Strauss' most famous waltz was not a success when it was first played, but it has since become the greatest favorite in the world, and practically a national anthem in Vienna. Strauss conceived it for orchestra and chorus, and it was first given in that form. Later, Strauss eliminated the vocal portions.

It is related that the great Brahms, when asked by Mme. Strauss to autograph her fan, jotted down the opening bars of this waltz and wrote under them: "Unfortunately not by me, Johannes Brahms."

✓

Perpetuum Mobile: This characteristic number is one of many written by "The Waltz King" during his long and distinguished career. It is sub-titled "A Musical Joke." Solo passages for almost every instrument, while showing off the instruments to best advantage, are comic in conception, as is the sudden and marked alternation of fortissimi and pianissimi. The transferring of the theme from one instrument to another, and the agitated character of the theme itself, suffice to explain the title, *Perpetual Motion*. The piece ends abruptly, as if it were simply interrupted in the course of its movement.

Josef Strauss

BORN Vienna, April 25, 1827
DIED Vienna, July 22, 1870

WORKS ARRANGED FOR BAND:

Numerous waltzes, including:
WEDDING FESTIVAL (F; S
and polkas, etc., including:
WOMAN'S HEART (F

JOSEF STRAUSS was the brother of the famous "Waltz King," and was almost equally gifted as a composer of elegant dance music. Like his brother, he was not encouraged by his parents to become a musician; during an illness of Johann's, however, he conducted the orchestra and launched himself upon a successful career. He later formed his own orchestra and made a number of tours, acquiring a reputation second only to that of his brother. In his short career he wrote almost three hundred numbers, many of which attained the greatest popularity. His health was delicate, and his death was directly caused by the action of a group of Russian officers in Warsaw, who routed him out of bed in the early morning with demands that he provide music for them. Upon his refusal, the drunken officers mistreated the composer severely. He was able to return to Vienna, but succumbed soon afterwards.

Richard Strauss

BORN Munich, Germany, June 11, 1864

WORKS ARRANGED FOR BAND:

Waltzes from DER ROSENKAVALIER (C

Selections from DER ROSENKAVALIER (C

AT THE beginning of this century, storms of criticism raged about the music of Strauss. His works were called brutal, incomprehensible and a variety of other unflattering things; while on the other hand a number of staunch supporters saw in these compositions the ultimate goal toward which Wagner and Liszt had been striving. Today we are able to view Strauss' art in somewhat better perspective. Developments in music since the war make it seem clear that Strauss represents the end of a certain tradition; that is, rather than pointing out paths for the future, Strauss brought the opera of Wagner and the tone-poem of Liszt to points beyond which no one will desire to develop them.

Strauss' most important works are his operas and his symphonic tone-poems. The early operas, such as *Salomé* and *Elektra,* show much power, although they are rather unvocal. The tone-poems, such as *Don Juan, Till Eulenspiegel* and *A Hero's Life,* are extremely programmatic in character and sensational in effect. They require a considerable amount of concentration on the part of the audience in order to follow them. Both the operas and the tone-poems are characterized by an almost unparalleled brilliance of orchestration.

Strauss was conductor of the Berlin opera from 1898 to 1910. He had toured widely, and appeared several times in America as conductor. Numbers of his songs have become great favorites on concert programs. His recent compositions show an unfortunate decline of his powers and have been greeted with very indifferent success.

✓ ✓ ✓

Der Rosenkavalier (*Waltzes* and *Selections*): *Der Rosenkavalier* is the most tuneful, popular and likely to endure of Strauss' operas. Written directly after *Elektra,* it exhibited a startling change of style, substituting a melodious and lyrical expression for the violent mannerisms of its predecessor. For the turbulent drama of *Salomé* and *Elektra, Der Rosenkavalier* presents sprightly comedy. The librettist was Hugo von Hofmannsthal, who collaborated with Strauss in many of the latter's operas.

It may be said that in *Der Rosenkavalier,* Strauss exhibits all of his technical mastery, all of his brilliant orchestration and all of his best melodic invention, without marring the unity or charm of the whole by striving after sensational effects. There is a spontaneity in the airs and concerted pieces which, unfortunately, is often lacking in Strauss' other work. The waltzes are the best examples of this; they are frankly in the popular Viennese style, although they are much richer harmonically and developed with more freedom.

(Sir) Arthur Seymour Sullivan

BORN London, May 3, 1842
DIED London, November 22, 1900

WORKS ARRANGED FOR BAND:

Selections from: THE MIKADO (C; F; Ru
H. M. S. PINAFORE (C; F; Ru
IOLANTHE (F; C
THE PIRATES OF PENZANCE (F; C
PATIENCE (F
THE GONDOLIERS (C
THE SORCERER (C
THE YEOMEN OF THE GUARD (C; F
THE CHIEFTAIN (B&H
IVANHOE (B&H
THE PRODIGAL SON (B&H

Overtures: IOLANTHE (F
IN MEMORIAM (N

Entrance & *March of the Peers* from IOLANTHE (F; B&H

Incidental Music to HENRY VIII (C

O Gladsome Light from THE GOLDEN LEGEND (N

Suite, MASCARADE (B&H

Suite, THE MERCHANT OF VENICE (B&H

SULLIVAN, of course, is best known by the inimitable comic-operas which he wrote in collaboration with W. S. Gilbert. It is sometimes forgotten that these works, so genial in their content, could have been written only by a musician of the very first rank. Such a musician Sullivan was; indeed, he is one of the chief glories of nineteenth-century English music. His orchestral and choral works are excellent by any standards, the works not only of a skilled and thoroughly trained composer, but of a genuinely gifted artist.

Sullivan's father was a bandmaster and a Professor of Clarinet at Kneller Hall. The future Sir Arthur began his studies at an early age. He conducted his own works in public when he was but eighteen years old. His reputation grew rapidly and many honors were allotted to him. He was made a Doctor of Music by both Oxford and Cambridge, received the Legion of Honor from France, and was knighted by Queen Victoria in 1883. His comic-operas enjoyed (and still enjoy) enormous success, as did his cantatas and oratorios. His one symphony, in E, is a splendid work, and shows what he might have accomplished in that form had he so desired.

Selections from *The Sorcerer:* In 1876 a London impressario by the name of Richard D'Oyly Carte conceived the happy idea of leasing a theatre and forming a syndicate for the express purpose of producing operas by Gilbert and Sullivan. The writer and the composer had already given proof of the excellence of their work together in *Thespis* (1871) and *Trial by Jury* (1875). Under the management of D'Oyly Carte, however, the two men proceeded to write the marvelous series of comic-operas with which their names are forever associated. The first of these was *The Sorcerer,* which had its première at the Opera Comique Theatre on November 17, 1877. It ran for almost six months and securely established the fame of the collaborators.

While not as familiar as, for example, *The Mikado, The Sorcerer* nevertheless contains many sparkling gems. Gilbert's libretti do not lend themselves to summarizing; his plots are extremely ingenious and are developed with a wit which is all too rare in so-called comic-opera. His clever versification and mastery of metrical forms give much added zest to his books. All of these characteristics of Gilbert are already to be found in *The Sorcerer,* just as in it the musical idiom of Sullivan seems to be completely developed.

Selections from *H. M. S. Pinafore: Pinafore* was the second of the comic-operas Gilbert and Sullivan wrote for the D'Oyly Carte management. It was first performed at the Opera Comique Theatre on May 25, 1878. Its success was unprecedented; it ran for over 700 consecutive performances in London and was played at the same time throughout England. The composer and author may have felt that their success was too great, for American companies took possession of the opera and gave hundreds of "pirate" performances. To protect themselves, Gilbert and Sullivan visited New York in 1879, putting on an authorized version at the Fifth Avenue Theatre.

The music and verses of *Pinafore* are second to none of the Gilbert and Sullivan creations in popularity. The songs sung by the Admiral and by "poor little Buttercup" are known to almost everyone. The opera is still performed frequently by professionals and amateurs in all the English speaking countries.

Selections from *The Pirates of Penzance:* Following the success of *Pinafore,* Gilbert and Sullivan brought out *The Pirates of Penzance* at the Opera Comique Theatre on April 3, 1880. To avoid a repetition of the "pirating" of *Pinafore* in America, the work had its actual première in New York, at the Fifth Avenue Theatre. *The Pirates* was again a prodigious success in both countries. The freshness of the tunes and the lively wit of the book placed the work on the same high level as its predecessors. *The Pirates of Penzance* would be remembered if only because it introduced the tune now known as *Hail, Hail, The Gang's All Here,* but that is only one of its well-known melodies.

Selections from *Patience:* On April 25, 1881, the sixth of the operas Gilbert and Sullivan wrote together was produced at the Opera Comique Theatre in London. *Patience* was a devastating satire on the "aestheticism" of the times, directed in particular at Oscar Wilde and his followers. To Gilbert's clever libretto, Sullivan matched sparkling tunes; the success of the work was immediate and overwhelming. It enjoyed a run of 408 performances, in the middle of which it was transferred from the Opera Comique to the Savoy Theatre, newly built by D'Oyly Carte. It thus became the first of "the Savoy operas," although even the earlier works are now often referred to by that name.

The years have not dulled Sullivan's music; Gilbert's libretto in this one instance seems a bit remote, but the work is still performed continually in all parts of the English-speaking world.

Selections from Iolanthe: Iolanthe had its première at D'Oyly Carte's Savoy Theatre on November 25, 1882, following the conclusion of the triumphant run of *Patience*. *Iolanthe* was an even greater success than its predecessor; it ran more than a year, during the course of which the composer was knighted by Queen Victoria. The music represents a great advance over *Patience* and most of the earlier works. In many respects it is the most brilliant example of Sullivan's comic-opera music, not only being replete with delightful melodies, but possessing a fullness beyond most of his other endeavors.

The libretto is a gay and often satirical fantasy, dealing with the misadventures of a group of dignified English peers among a band of attractive fairies. Sullivan's music provides a superb contrast of pompous and stirring tunes for the Lords, and light and tripping ones for the fairies. The ensembles are wonderful examples of his musicianly skill and theatrical sense. It is safe to say that there is more good music in

Iolanthe than there is in half of the "grand" operas ever written.

March of the Peers from *Iolanthe:* As a concert number, the *March of the Peers* is both grand in style and stirring in effect. It occurs in the first act of *Iolanthe,* sung by the Lords of Parliament as they make their entrance. The pomposity of the Peers is, in Gilbert's expert hands, a mock-pomposity of course; the music Sullivan wrote for the scene is, however, worthy of a much more serious occasion.

Selections from *The Mikado: The Mikado* is probably the most popular of all the Gilbert and Sullivan operettas. It was the ninth produced by the collaboration of the two men, and was first produced at D'Oyly Carte's Savoy Theatre on March 14, 1885. It ran continuously for 672 performances, a not unenviable record, and has been played thousands of times since. Gilbert's witty libretto inspired Sullivan to write some of his best music; nowhere in their joint works did the partners succeed better in achieving a perfect unity between play and score. Nowhere did Gilbert exhibit a more delightful fantasy than in the characters and plot of *The Mikado;* nowhere did Sullivan write more solid and appropriate settings. Possibly no opera or play has ever given pleasure to as many thousands of people as this work.

Selections from *The Yeomen of the Guard:* Sullivan is said to have considered *The Yeomen of the Guard* the best of the series he wrote in collaboration with Gilbert. It was the eleventh of their joint productions, and received its first performance at the Savoy Theatre of D'Oyly Carte on October 3, 1888. Sullivan had a great desire to do a grand opera with Gilbert. The plan did not materialize, but *The Yeomen of the Guard* represented a step in that direction. Both libretto and music are lacking in that fantasy and humor which characterized their other works. *The Yeomen of the Guard* has never had, probably for that reason, the popularity of *The Mikado* or of *Pinafore*. It is revived occasionally, however, and is always well received. Much of the music shows Sullivan in a broader, more serious vein, but there are not lacking numerous suggestions of the more familiar Sullivan.

Selections from *The Gondoliers: The Gondoliers* received its first performance on December 7, 1889, at the Savoy Theatre in London. It was the twelfth of the great series Gilbert and Sullivan wrote for D'Oyly Carte's Theatre. Coming directly after *The Yeomen of the Guard,* in which composer and author had attempted a slightly more serious type of work, *The Gondoliers* reverted to the manner of their earlier and more successful operettas and scored a like success. Queen Victoria had a command performance given for her at Windsor Castle during the course of the operetta's long run.

The plot is a typically Gilbertian fantasy dressed up in his usual clever rhymes and dialogue. Sullivan's music makes the perfect foil for it. There are many famous airs in *The Gondoliers,* including the sparkling Bolero which occurs at the end.

Selections from *The Chieftain:* Following the termination of his collaboration with Gilbert, Sullivan turned to one of his old operettas and remodelled it into *The Chieftain.* It was performed at the Savoy, scene of the Gilbert and Sullivan triumphs in December 12, 1895. The librettist was F. C. Burnand, one time editor of *Punch.* In spite of some excellent music, the operetta has never enjoyed the popularity of the ones written with the gifted Gilbert.

Selections from *Ivanhoe:* Sullivan's ambition to write a grand opera was of long standing. Indeed he often expressed the hope that Gilbert would provide him with a suitable libretto. Gilbert, however, declined, and Sullivan turned to Julian Sturgis, who provided a book based on Sir Walter Scott's famous novel, *Ivanhoe.* The opera was completed in 1890 and first performed on January 31, 1891. A new opera house had been specially constructed by Richard D'Oyly Carte in anticipation of the event. Unfortunately, the opera was by no means a complete success. It enjoyed a considerable run but eventually had to be taken off. Musically, however, *Ivanhoe* shows Sullivan at a high level, comparable to that exhibited in his oratorios and cantatas. Portions of the work rank with his very best.

Selections from *The Prodigal Son:* Sullivan's fame rests principally on the sparkling comic-operas which he wrote with W. S. Gilbert, but his creative activity was by no means confined to these. He wrote many choral and orchestral works of the highest worth. Among these are several oratorios. *The Prodigal Son* was his first venture in this type of composition and one of the most successful. It was first performed at the Worcester Festival on September 8, 1869.

Incidental Music to *Henry VIII:* In 1878, although burdened with work and saddened by the death of his brother, Sullivan accepted a commission to write incidental music for a new production of Shakespeare's *Henry VIII,* to be staged at Manchester by Charles Calvert. The music he provided did much to add to his reputation as an orchestral composer.

Arranged in the form of a concert suite, the music exhibits Sullivan's typical melodic vein, his sense of form and proportion and his originality and finesse in orchestration.

Suite from *The Merchant of Venice:*

I. Introduction
II. Barcarolle
III. Bourrée
IV. Danse Grotesque
V. Valse
VI. Melodrama
VII. Finale

In 1871, Sullivan, already well known as a composer, was commissioned to write new music for a revival of Shakespeare's *Merchant of Venice* to be given at Prince's Theatre in Manchester. The music he composed for that ranks with his very best in inspiration and execution. His use of traditional dance forms showed considerable originality. The suite as a whole is ample evidence of Sullivan's talent for writing orchestral music.

Franz Von Suppé
(Francesco Ezechiele Ermenegilde Cavaliere Suppé-Demelli)

BORN Spalato, Dalmatia (Now Jugoslavia), April 18, 1820
DIED Vienna, May 22, 1895

WORKS ARRANGED FOR BAND:

Overtures: POET AND PEASANT (F; B&H; D; CB; Fil; Ru
BEAUTIFUL GALATEA (F; B&H; D
LIGHT CAVALRY (D; B&H; F; CB; Fil; Ru; J
MORNING, NOON & NIGHT IN VIENNA (D; F; B&H; CB; Fil
FRANZ SCHUBERT (B&H; F; P
TANTALUSQUALEN (B&H; F
THE JOLLY ROBBERS (F; B&H
and many others seldom performed (various eds.)

Selections from: BOCCACCIO (F; B&H
FATINITZA (F
and others—as above

SUPPÉ AND JOHANN STRAUSS (q. v.) were the uncrowned rulers of Viennese operetta in the late decades of the last century. Suppé began his career as conductor of a theatre in Vienna, without salary; he soon showed his worth, however, and moved on to better positions. The greater part of his life he was associated with the Leopoldstädter Theatre, where many of his sixty or seventy operettas were produced. Suppé's success in his day was prodigious, although only two of his works, *Boccaccio* and *Fatinitza*—became internationally known. A great number of the operettas, however, are still known by their overtures, which are frequently played. These works are light and pleasing, full of the gaiety and elegance for which Viennese music is noted.

Overture, Poet and Peasant: The most popular of all Suppé's overtures and indeed, one that is second only to

William Tell in popularity, was strangely enough not written for an operetta, but as a separate composition. The work is known to everyone; it is played all over the world.

Overture, Franz Schubert: The operetta *Franz Schubert,* founded on the life of the great composer, was produced in Vienna in 1864. In the work, Suppé introduced five Schubert melodies.

Johan Severin Svendsen

BORN Christiania (Oslo), Norway, September 30, 1840
DIED Copenhagen, Denmark, June 14, 1911

WORKS ARRANGED FOR BAND:

NORWEGIAN RHAPSODY NO. 1 (B&H
NORWEGIAN RHAPSODY NO. 2 (B&H
NORWEGIAN RHAPSODY NO. 3 (F
Tone Poem, CARNIVAL IN PARIS (C
NORWEGIAN ARTISTS' FESTIVAL (F
SWEDISH CORONATION MARCH (F

SVENDSEN'S father was a bandmaster in the Norwegian army. The young composer started his own career by following in his father's footsteps, but soon tired of army life and started off on his own to travel through Sweden and Germany. Having never seriously studied composition, he attended the Conservatory in Leipzig, made extremely rapid progress, and soon was off again on his travels. He lived in Paris until the outbreak of the war of 1870, returned to Leipzig, and then made a short trip to America. While in this country he married an American lady whom he had met in Paris.

From 1872 to 1877, he conducted an orchestra in Christiania. For his services to Norwegian music, he was decorated by the king and received a pension from the *Storthing,* or Parliament. He went abroad once more, visiting Rome, London and Paris, and eventually became court conductor at Copenhagen.

Svendsen's music is far less "national" in character than that of his contemporary, Grieg. It is more or less classical in structure, but at the same time bears the marks of a strong individuality.

Norwegian Rhapsodies: Svendsen composed four Norwegian rhapsodies for orchestra during the five years he was conductor of the Christiania Musical Association. That period (1872-1877) was the only one in which the composer seemed to take a serious interest in the music of his own country. These rhapsodies are based on traditional tunes, but the treatment of them is more classical than national.

Swedish Coronation March: In 1872 Svendsen was commissioned to write a march for the funeral of King Charles XV of Sweden and Norway, and in the same year a coronation march for his successor, King Oscar II. This coronation march is today probably Svendsen's best-known work. It is a splendid example of dignified and inspiring march writing.

Tone Poem, Carnival in Paris: Svendsen composed this work in 1873, during a short sojourn in Bayreuth. While there is no definite program associated with the composition, the title suggests that it is a portrayal of the festivities connected with the celebration of Mardi Gras in the French capital. The spirit and colorful bustle of the music are very striking. Svendsen lived in Paris for several years, and doubtless participated in a number of similar carnivals.

Sergei Ivanovich Taneiev

BORN Government of Vladimir, Russia, November 13, 1850
DIED Moscow, June, 1915

ARRANGED FOR BAND:

Entr'Acte from ORESTES (F

TANEIEV was a student at the Moscow Conservatory under Tchaikovsky and Nicholas Rubinstein, gaining the first gold medal ever given by that institution. He was one of the outstanding Russian pianists of his day, and was a great force in the musical life of the country. He succeeded Tchaikovsky as Professor of Instrumentation at the Conservatory, and became its director in 1885. Taneiev was one of Tchaikovsky's most valued friends; the latter esteemed his pupil's criticisms more than those of any one else.

Taneiev's own compositions include several symphonies, much chamber music, choral works and the operatic trilogy, *Orestes,* founded on the tragic cycle of Aeschylus. It received its first performance at the Mariinsky Theatre in St. Petersburg in 1895, meeting with only moderate success. The score, however, has passages of great beauty and impressiveness, and like most of Taneiev's work, shows admirable craftsmanship and sensitive taste. This entr'acte, the first music of Taneiev to be arranged for band, is the introduction to the second tableau of the trilogy. The curtain rises during the performance of the music, revealing the Temple of Apollo: "The smoke of sacrifices fills the background of the sanctuary and golden beams shine through the haze."

Peter Ilyitch Tchaikovsky

BORN Kamsko-Votkinsk, Russia, April 25, 1840
DIED St. Petersburg, November 16, 1893

WORKS ARRANGED FOR BAND:

Symphonies: NO. 4 (Canzona & Scherzo: B&H); (Finale: F. C
NO. 5 Andante (B&H, F; Valse (B&H
NO. 6 (B&H); 3rd & 4th Mvts (F
Overtures: *1812* (F; B&H
DANISH FESTIVAL (F
ITALIAN CAPRICE (F; B&H
NUTCRACKER SUITE (F; C
MARCHE SLAVE (F; C; B&H
MARCHE SOLENNELLE (C
Selections from: EUGENE ONEGIN (F; B&H
CATHERINE (B&H
THE OPRITCHNIK (Overture & Ballet) (C
Suite from Ballet THE SWAN LAKE (C; Lud
Russian Dance from THE SWAN LAKE (EV
Rustic Suite from PIQUE DAME (C
HUMORESQUE (F; B&H; J
CHANT SANS PAROLES (F; B&H
ANDANTE CANTABILE (Op. 11) (B&H
CHANSON TRISTE (B&H; J
TROIKA EN TRAINEAUX (W
Air and Variations from SUITE IN G (B&H
Many smaller pieces in various editions, especially B&H

THE CAREER OF TCHAIKOVSKY is one of the strangest in the history of music. The composer came of a moderately well-to-do family; he received the usual musical instruction during his childhood, but it was never thought that he would make music his career. He attended the School of Jurisprudence and after completing the course obtained a position in the Ministry of Justice. The attraction of music was too strong, however. He gave up his position in order to study at the St. Petersburg Conservatory just founded by Anton Rubinstein. This was in 1862. His family had lost most of its means and Tchaikovsky endured real poverty as a result of his choice.

In 1866 Nicholas Rubinstein offered the composer the position of Professor of Harmony at the Moscow Conservatory. Tchaikovsky accepted and remained until 1877. Meanwhile he composed steadily. The strain of teaching and the slow acceptance of his works brought on during these years the first of those periods of depression and nervous collapse which were to mark his subsequent career. Extraordinarily sensitive and predisposed to melancholy, the whole history of Tchaikovsky's creative life is one of struggle against his own nature. An unfortunate marriage added greatly to his spiritual troubles. The same year, however, marked the beginning of a friendship which is one of the strangest ever known, and which was to release the composer from most of his pecuniary cares as well as act as a powerful inspiration upon him. This friendship between Tchaikovsky and Nadiedja von Meck lasted almost to the end of the composer's life. The two never met, although they exchanged many letters testifying to an exceptional sympathy. Several of the composer's greatest works were dedicated to his "best friend."

From about 1880 there was an increasing recognition of Tchaikovsky's status as a composer. His works were performed with greater frequency throughout Russia and Western Europe. In England particularly there was great acclaim for the symphonies and tone-poems. During the last years of his life Tchaikovsky toured widely, conducting concerts largely given over to his own compositions. He visited New York in April and May of 1891 for the dedication of the new Carnegie Hall and met with tremendous success. A few months before his death Cambridge University conferred the honorary degree of Doctor of Music upon him.

No Russian composer has achieved greater popularity than Tchaikovsky among music-lovers throughout the world. There are a number of apparent reasons for this. Tchaikovsky's music is considerably less full of the spirit of Russian folk song than the music of Moussorgsky or Rimsky-Korsakov; his musical enthusiasms ran to Italian lyricism and emotionalism rather than to the sometimes austere modal traditions of his own country's folk tunes. Around 1868 Tchaikovsky came into contact with the "radical" group of Balakirev and his followers, but their influence on him was momentary. Later he expressed his strong disapproval of their ideas. Yet a certain native influence and use of traditional material is evident in many of his works. Where Tchaikovsky used a folk tune, however, he set it in a European context. There is, for example, a world of difference between Tchaikovsky's Russian operas and the *Boris Goudounov* of Moussorgsky or the *Prince Igor* of Borodin.

The intense gloom and melancholy of much of Tchaikovsky's music is often explained in terms of the composer's nationality. The justice of this is open to question; an examination of Russian folk music will do much to shake the foundation of the claim. Tchaikovsky's character, his pessimism and moods of despair, are much more to the point; his expression of these in music, moreover, is tinged with as much of general romantic luxuriousness as of specifically Russian gloominess.

His most popular compositions aside from the three last symphonies have been his tone-poems and other programmatic works. In this connection, another Tchaikovskian contradiction is interesting. He preferred the "classic" forms and wrote that: "When I write a program-symphony I always feel that I am not paying in sterling coin, but in worthless paper money." A remarkable statement from the composer of "1812"!

✓ ✓ ✓

Symphony No. 4, in F Minor:

I. Andante Sostenuto. Moderato con Anima (not arranged for band)
II. Andantino in Modo di Canzona (B&H
III. Scherzo. Pizzicato Ostinato (B&H
IV. Finale. Allegro con fuoco (F; C

Tchaikovsky's Fourth Symphony was composed during the year 1877-1878, a period of terrific stress, both emotional and financial, for the composer. He was enabled to carry on largely through the intervention of his generous benefactress, Mme. von Meck. The symphony was consequently dedicated to her as an expression of gratitude, with the inscription, "To My Best Friend."

The work met with a cool reception at its first performance in Moscow, but the public in Petrograd acclaimed it enthusiastically when it was given there late in the same year. It has since become one of the favorite works of the composer, many people preferring it to any of his other symphonic compositions.

The first movement opens with what is known as the "Fate" theme, sonorously stated by the brass section. The movement is full of pulsating energy, sudden changes from the mood of despair to that of hope. The "Fate" theme recurs throughout.

The second movement is in song-form. The principal melody, one of the most appealing Tchaikovsky ever wrote, is hardly modified throughout except with respect to accompaniment and instrumentation. The middle section offers a strong contrast.

The principal section of the *Scherzo* is remarkable for the pizzicato accompaniment which continues through it. The trio affords a contrast, after which the pizzicato movement returns.

A powerful, swirling theme opens the *Finale.* Passages in the full band lead to the next theme, based on a popular Russian folk tune, *In the Field There Stood a Birch-Tree.* A march-like motive completes the thematic content of the movement, which is energetically developed. Toward the end the "Fate" theme of the first movement is heard again, sounded *fortissimo* by the brasses.

Symphony No. 5, in E Minor:

I. Andante, Allegro con Anima (not arranged for band)
II. Andante Cantabile (B&H; F
III. Valse (B&H
IV. Finale (not arranged for band)

Ten years elapsed between Tchaikovsky's Fourth and Fifth Symphonies. The latter was first played at St. Petersburg in 1888, under the direction of the composer. Its reception at first was not over-enthusiastic, but with the passage of time both composer and public began to hold the work in high favor.

The Fifth Symphony, like the Fourth, opens with what has come to be known as a "Fate" theme. This is repeated in each of the movements in different guises. The two movements arranged for band have both become very popular as independent pieces. The *Andante Cantabile* is constructed around a beautiful flowing melody first played by the solo horn. The movement is twice interrupted by the sombre "Fate" theme, sounded by the full band. It closes quietly, in a mood of wistfulness.

The introduction of a *Waltz* into a symphony was much criticized in Tchaikovsky's day. The *Waltz* in this composition, however, is linked with the other movements by the "Fate" theme, which is heard at the end, and which gives a mysterious character to the movement in spite of the dance-form in which it is cast.

Symphony No. 6, in B Minor (*Pathétique*):

I. Adagio. Allegro non troppo (B&H
II. Allegro con Grazia (not arranged for band)
III. Allegro molto vivace (F; B&H
IV. Finale. Adagio lamentoso (F; B&H

The Sixth Symphony, or "Pathétique," was completed by Tchaikovsky while he was laboring under a pre-occupation with death, and was performed only a few days before he breathed his last. The work made little impression at its first hearing, but the composer maintained his opinion that it was the best thing he had ever composed.

This symphony, more than any other of his works, has caused the name of Tchaikovsky to be linked with the expression of profound despair and passionate melancholy in music. Yet in actuality it is only the last movement which gives full scope to such expression. The *Adagio lamentoso* has been called "suicide music"; certainly there is nothing in symphonic literature to which it can be compared. Coming as it does at the very end of the symphony, it has suggested many interpretations, but about its essential spirit there can be little difference of opinion.

The other movements of the symphony are of another character. The first movement (B minor, 4/4 time) contrasts an energetic first theme with a tender song-like second subject in D major. The development is largely taken up with the agitated material of the first theme, but the recapitulation and coda bring the movement to a quiet close. The second movement is one of the most remarkable Tchaikovsky ever composed. It is in 5/4 time throughout, the principal subject being an ascending motive of peculiar grace. The middle section introduces a plaintive theme played over an organ-point which continues for forty bars. The entire movement is notable for a restrained delicacy and lightness. The third movement is well known and is often played separately. It is introduced by a lively figure in triplets which leads into a march-like theme ingeniously built on a two-bar motive. The music is worked up into a brilliant climax in which the march-like theme predominates.

When performed after Tchaikovsky's death, the symphony created a sensation. It has since become the work which has contributed perhaps more than any other to the composer's fame.

Overture "1812": The *1812* Overture was written in 1880 for a musical festival organized in Moscow by Nicholas Rubinstein. The work is descriptive of the events of 1812, when Napoleon, after his victory at Borodino, marched on Moscow with his armies. The Russians, setting fire to the city, forced Napoleon to retreat and shortly after freed the country of invaders. The overture opens with an introduction based on a Russian hymn, *God Preserve Thy People.* The main section which follows is devoted to the "battle music." The French arms are symbolized by the *Marseillaise;* the Russian by a folk song (*I Was Sitting at the Window*) from the Government of Novgorod. At first the French theme predominates, but in the course of the struggle it gradually gives way to the Russian tune. The famous bells of Moscow chime triumphantly in honor of the victory, while the Russian national hymn is thundered out.

Overture, Danish Festival: This early work, which is also known as a *"Triumphal" Overture,* and more properly as a *Festival Overture on the Danish National Hymn,* was written shortly after Tchaikovsky had become Professor of Harmony at the Moscow Conservatory in 1877. In many ways it anticipates the more famous *1812* Overture, for the Danish National Anthem ("King Christian,")* is used in it much as the Russian hymn in the latter work.

Italian Caprice: Tchaikovsky composed this popular piece during one of his periodic visits to Italy. It reflects the happier feelings the composer enjoyed in the sunny atmosphere of the southern country, and is entirely devoid of that gloominess so characteristic of his music. The opening strains are those of a bugle call which Tchaikovsky heard each evening while stopping at a hotel near the barracks of the Royal Italian Cuirassiers. There are indications throughout the work that Tchaikovsky wished to recreate the spirit of the Italian popular song. The *Italian Caprice* was dedicated to Karl Davidoff, the 'cellist, and had its first performance in Moscow in 1889.

Marche Slave: This impressive and popular march was composed in 1876 as Tchaikovsky's contribution to a concert organized by Nicholas Rubinstein for the benefit of soldiers wounded in the war between Serbia and Turkey. The war aroused tremendous Pan-Slavic enthusiasm in Russia, and Tchaikovsky's march, which expressed these feelings completely, met with tremendous success.

The march is both dignified and stirring in character. Four bars of introduction lead to a theme of unmistakable Slavic inspiration, which in turn gives way to the Russian national hymn. In the coda, the solemnity of the march is transformed into a victorious brilliance, symbolic of the ultimate victory of the Slavic cause.

Marche Solenelle: (*Lawyer's March*): This march was

* This tune was composed by Johann Ernst Hartmann (1726-1793), and occurs in one of his operas, "Die Fischer" (1780).

composed in honor of the School of Jurisprudence of St. Petersburg, which Tchaikovsky attended from 1850 to 1859. It was not published until after the composer's death, and bears no opus number. Although it is not as well-known as the *Marche Slave,* to which it is in some respects comparable, it is a worthy composition and possesses great dignity and impressiveness.

Selections from *Eugene Onegin:* Tchaikovsky's operas are not very well-known in this country, yet they form a major part of his work. He composed eight operas in all, the most successful and most popular being *Eugene Onegin* and *Pique Dame,* both founded on works of Pushkin. *Eugene Onegin* was completed in 1878, and first presented by students of the Moscow Conservatory in 1879. The opera was not too well received at that time, but at its first performance in St. Petersburg met with great popular success, which it subsequently maintained.

Overture and *Ballet* from *The Opritschnik: The Opritschnik* (*The Guardsman*) was composed in 1874 and first performed in St. Petersburg. It has seldom been heard outside of Russia, and even there has not held its place alongside of *Eugene Onegin* and *Pique Dame.* The subject of the opera is historical, based on events which occurred during the time of Tsar Ivan II (Ivan the Terrible), who reigned from 1533 to 1584. The "Opritschniks" were a special corps which constituted the secret police and storm troops of the period. They wore little brooms on their caps as a symbol of their function, which was to "clean out" the opposition to Tsar Ivan.

Rustic Suite from *Pique Dame:* Tchaikovsky went to Florence in 1890 in order to complete the opera *Pique Dame*

(*The Queen of Spades*). The libretto had been adapted by his brother Modeste from the famous short-story of Pushkin. The first performance of the opera, on December 19, 1890, was mildly successful. Later it became one of the most popular of Tchaikovsky's operas and has had considerable success abroad.

Nutcracker Suite (*Casse-Noisette*):

I. Overture
II. March
III. Danse de la Fée Dragée (Dance of the Sugar-Plum Fairy)
IV. Trepak
V. Danse Russe (Russian Dance)
VI. Danse Arabe (Arabian Dance)
VII. Danse Chinoise (Chinese Dance)
VIII. Danse des Mirlitons (Dance of the Reed-pipes)
IX. Valse des Fleurs (Flower Waltz)

The ever-popular *Nutcracker Suite* consists of numbers arranged by Tchaikovsky from a ballet written in 1891 for the Imperial Opera of St. Petersburg. Like many of the Russian ballets, the *Nutcracker* ballet was based on a fairy-tale; in this case the famous story by E. T. A. Hoffmann of the little girl who dreams on Christmas Night that she sees the toys and dolls holding a revel, led by "Prince Nutcracker of Fairyland." Tchaikovsky's music is extremely bright and delicate, full of clever effects, and totally lacking in that melancholy spirit so often found in his other works. The first performance of the ballet met with prodigious success; many of the numbers had to be repeated, much to the composer's delight. All of the numbers are skillfully constructed and beautifully scored and reveal the deft touch of a master.

Ballet Suite from *The Swan Lake* (*Le Lac des Cygnes*):
I. A Scene (Lud B. Waltz (C
II. Dance of the Swans (C; Lud
III. Hungarian Dance (C; Lud

Tchaikovsky's first ballet was commissioned by the Imperial Opera of Moscow. It was produced in 1877. Although the work does not reveal as great an inspiration as some of the composer's later ballets, notably the *Nutcracker* ballet, the suite which was arranged from it retains its popularity as concert music. The subject of the ballet is of a fairy-tale nature.

Andante Cantabile (from *String Quartet, Opus 11*): This movement from Tchaikovsky's first string quartet, in D, has become most popular in independent orchestral arrangements. The principal melody is that of a Russian folk tune (*Johnny Seated on the Divan*), said to have been heard by the composer from a workman at his house. The striking tune is reprinted in Rimsky-Korsakov's collection of Russian folk songs, Volume I.

Air and Variations from *Third Suite for Orchestra:*

Tchaikovsky's *Third Suite for Orchestra,* in G major, Opus 55, was written in 1883, shortly after the production of the opera *Mazeppa.* That the suite was dear to the composer's heart is proven by the fact that he included it on the programs of many of his concerts in England and America, where he was anxious to appear with his most favored works. The *Air and Variations* which concludes the suite was (and is) often played separately, and has achieved a quite independent popularity.

Tchaikovsky's brilliant sense of instrumentation is nowhere better shown than in the orchestral suites. One might say of this *Air and Variations* that the interest is sustained as much or more by the instrumental color than by any startling developments of the theme. In the band version several of the variations have been omitted for this reason. The seven variations included are as follows:

Theme: *Andante* 4/8

I. Theme in Bass: Andante 4/8
II. Andante 4/8
III. Andante 4/8—
IV. Moderato 2/4
V. Largo 3/4
VI. Allegro Molto Vivace 2/4
VII. Finale alla Polacca 3/4

Chanson Triste *Humoresque* *Chant sans Paroles* *etc.*	Tchaikovsky wrote many sets of short piano pieces, among which are to be found some of his most charming melodies.

Ambroise Thomas
(Charles Louis Ambroise Thomas)

BORN Metz, France, August 5, 1811
DIED Paris, February 12, 1896

WORKS ARRANGED FOR BAND:

Overtures: MIGNON (F; B&H
RAYMOND (B&H; F; D
THE CARNIVAL OF VENICE (F
JACK AND JILL (D
LE CAÏD (F

Entr'acte and *Gavotte* from MIGNON (F; B&H
Selections from the above (various eds.) and from HAMLET (B&H
Ballet Music from HAMLET (C

THOMAS was one of the most representative dramatic composers of France during the last half of the past century. His music has the grace and elegance characteristic of the French school. He was in every sense of the word a traditional artist, following in the footsteps of Boieldieu, Hérold and Auber, and succeeding in civil life to their distinctions. He started his career well by winning the Grand Prix de Rome in 1832. Following a tour of Europe he returned to Paris, where he produced nine operas in seven years. His works were moderately successful, but not until after the production of *Mignon,* in 1866, did he achieve a great reputation. He succeeded Auber as Director of the Conservatory in 1871, and was created successively Chevalier, Officer and Commander of the Legion of Honor.

✓ ✓ ✓

Mignon: Mignon, produced in 1866, was the most successful of Thomas' many operas. The work is founded on an episode from Goethe's *Wilhelm Meister;* several of Goethe's poems, which occur in the book, are set as arias in the opera.

The story deals with the adventures of Wilhelm, a young man wandering in search of knowledge, and Mignon, a girl stolen by gypsies from her home in Italy. Following a troupe of actors from place to place, Wilhelm and Mignon meet with many adventures until, at the happy end, Mignon is restored to her father and Wilhelm realizes that he loves her. The overture opens with a short pastoral movement, leading directly into the well-known melody *Know'st thou the Land,* which is sung by Mignon in the first act. The overture concludes with the spirited Polacca, a colorful dance which takes place at the end of Act II.

Selections from *Hamlet: Hamlet* was produced at the Paris Opera in 1868, and was the composer's first work after *Mignon.* It scored a great success and helped to consolidate the enviable position Thomas had already won for himself with his previous opera. The libretto is taken from Shakespeare's play, which, in the course of this libertarian adaptation, becomes so altered that Shakespeare himself would not recognize it; the principal similarity of the libretto to the play is the title.

The *Hamlet* of Thomas contains some well-known scenes and melodies, particularly the *Brindisi,* or drinking-song, which Hamlet sings to the players in Act II.

Overture, Raymond: The overture to Thomas' three-act opera *Raymond* ranks in popularity with Rossini's *William Tell* and other favorites. The opera itself, although moderately successful when first performed, is seldom given nowadays. The première took place at the Opéra Comique in Paris on June 5, 1851. The overture is melodious and sparkling, and has a slow movement which is the equal of any written by Thomas.

Overture, The Caïd: Up to the year 1843, Thomas had composed a number of operas and ballets. The last of these met with little success, and the composer became overly discouraged. He abandoned dramatic composition for five years, finally making a brilliant come-back with the two-act satire, *Le Caïd.* This was produced at the Opéra Comique in Paris on January 3, 1849, with considerable success. Berlioz wrote an article praising it. The overture, in the composer's characteristically elegant and tuneful manner, continues to be a favorite.

Overture, The Carnival of Venice: Thomas' three-act opera, *The Carnival of Venice,* achieved only moderate success when produced at the Opéra Comique of Paris on December 9, 1857. As a whole, it does not compare to such a work as *Mignon* for sustained inspiration, but the overture ranks with the best of Thomas' compositions in that form. It is based on the famous Italian song from which it derives its title. *The Carnival of Venice* has been used as a basis for variations probably as often as any other single tune in the world, but nowhere to better effect than in this work of Thomas. The overture opens with the theme in the full band. Variations then follow for two clarinets and for oboe solo. The brasses then take up the theme, first in the lower range and then the upper. A delicate variation for flute comes next, and is followed by a brilliant passage for two cornets. The overture ends with a sparkling climax.

Overture, Jack and Jill (Gille et Gillotin): Jack and Jill was the title of a one-act comedy composed by Thomas in 1861. It was not produced, however, until 1874. The overture reveals the composer in a light and sparkling vein.

Giuseppe Verdi
(Fortunio Giuseppe Francesco Verdi)

BORN Le Roncole, Italy, October 9, 1813
DIED near Busseto, Italy, January 27, 1901

WORKS ARRANGED FOR BAND:

AIDA: *Selection* (F; B&H; Fil
March (F; D; Ru; CB; J
Moorish Dance (F
Fantasia (D

ARALDO: *Overture* (F

ATTILA: *Selection* (F
Terzetta & Finale (F

DON CARLOS: *Selection* (F

ERNANI: *Selection* (F; D; B&H

FORZA DEL DESTINO: *Selection* (F
Overture (F

I LOMBARDI: *Selection* (F; D
Pilgrim's Chorus (F

IL TROVATORE: *Selection* (F; D; B&H; Ba; CB; Fil
Anvil Chorus (F
Miserere (F

JOAN OF ARC: *Overture* (F; D

MACBETH: *Selection* (F

MASKED BALL: *Selection* (F

NEBUCHADNEZZAR: *Overture* (F; CB
Selection (F
Cavatina (F

RIGOLETTO: *Selection* (F; B&H
Quartet (F; B&H; CB

SICILIAN VESPERS: *Overture* (F
Selection (F
Bolero (F; J
Duet (F

TRAVIATA: *Selection* (F; C; CB

Note: The Italian catalogue of Ricordi contains a large variety of selections from the above and nearly all the other operas of Verdi. Any one sufficiently interested would do well to investigate, despite the differences in instrumentation. The notable thing in the above listing is, of course, that Verdi's two greatest operas (*Otello* and *Falstaff*) are not represented.

GIUSEPPE VERDI was born of a poor family in a small Italian village. His musical talent was evident in childhood, but there were many difficulties in the way of its development. The friendly interest of neighbors and nearby townspeople, however, was not lacking, and in spite of obstacles young Verdi was enabled to study. He became the organist of the church in Le Roncole when he was but ten years of age; soon afterwards he went to nearby Busseto to attend school and to learn more of music. When he reached the age of sixteen the people of Busseto saw to it that he was sent to Milan.

The young composer was refused a scholarship at the Milan Conservatory, but studied with private teachers, among whom the most important was one Lavigna. In 1833 Verdi returned to Busseto, where he spent the next years composing, conducting and playing the organ for the town cathedral. He wrote his first opera during these years, and returned to Milan for its production in 1839.

Merelli, impressario of several opera houses, was friendly to Verdi and commissioned him to compose three more operas. Despite personal troubles, Verdi completed the commission, writing *Un Giorno di Regno, Nabucco* and *I Lombardi. Un Giorno di Regno* was a complete failure. Verdi lost his young wife and two sons in 1840, and was naturally unable to write a comic opera. *Nabucco* (1842) and *I Lombardi* were, however, great successes. With them Verdi was launched upon his glorious career.

Thenceforward his operas were in great demand. Between 1844 and 1850 he composed twelve works for the stages of Venice, Milan, Naples and other musical centers; among these were *Ernani, Macbeth, Luisa Miller* and several less successful works. The period in which he wrote his most famous operas begins around 1850. *Rigoletto, Il Trovatore* and *La Traviata* were produced within two years, and Verdi's position as the greatest contemporary composer of Italian opera was incontestably established.

Many more operas came from his pen in the ensuing years, but none was particularly noteworthy. A fresh triumph was recorded only with the production of *Aïda,* given for the first time in Italy in 1872, after its première in Egypt. Following this event Verdi devoted himself to the completion of his famous *Requiem* dedicated to the memory of Alessandro Manzoni (1785-1873), the founder of the Italian romantic school in literature and the author of *I Promessi Sposi.*

In his late years Verdi composed his two greatest operas, works full of vigor and invention. He was seventy-three years of age when *Otello* was performed at La Scala, and not quite eighty when *Falstaff* had its first hearing. These operas revealed entirely new aspects of the composer's genius, and were, in fact, based on a new conception of Italian opera style.

Outside of the realm of opera, Verdi's most famous work is the *Manzoni Requiem,* a work of great power and beauty. He wrote occasional songs, some church music and a string quartet which are infrequently heard. His early compositions, including marches for military band, have not survived.

Verdi's early operas are not very different in style or quality from those of Bellini or Donizetti. His melodic gifts were always marked and his sense of the dramatic was perhaps more evident than that of his predecessors, but he never made any sort of a break with the Italian tradition, and even in his later works continued to treat the vocal line as the foremost medium of expression. The melodies of his later operas have more distinction and originality, and the orchestral accompaniments are more full and elaborate, yet his advances kept strictly in line with the Italian tradition. Only in *Otello* and *Falstaff* are there passages which show a fuller development and a richer texture. These works are still essentially melodic, but they make use of a far greater range of musical and dramatic device than had ever before been considered possible in the Italian opera.

/ / /

Aïda (*Selections*): *Aïda* was written at the request of the Egyptian government for the inauguration of the new opera house in Cairo, where it was first performed on December 24, 1871. The success of the opera was phenomenal, and marked one of the high points of Verdi's career. It was immediately recognized that in *Aïda* the composer had given a new breadth and distinction to the Italian opera. The work is on a far grander scale than any of Verdi's earlier operas, although it follows the same general outlines. No opera of the Italian master is more popular today, with the possible exception of *Il Trovatore*.

The story was suggested by Marietta Bey, a famed Egyptologist. The action takes place in the time of Egypt's historic grandeur; it is full of splendid pageantry and color. Musically, the opera is a succession of airs and concerted pieces, one as famous and as inspired as another. The effect of sustained melodic invention and dramatic power entitles *Aïda* to rank as one of Verdi's greatest accomplishments.

March: The well-known *Triumphal March* occurs in the second scene of the second act of the opera, and is played as the conquering Egyptian army, under the leadership of Rhadames, returns to Thebes. The colorful pageantry of this scene is one of the high spots of the opera. Before the King, seated on his throne, passes a procession of trumpeters, warchariots, statues of the gods, dancing-girls and victorious soldiers, the procession reaching its end when Rhadames makes his appearance under a canopy borne by twelve slaves.

Araldo, Overture: In 1850 Verdi composed his sixteenth opera, known as *Stiffelio.* It was produced at Trieste on November 16 of that year, and was one of the few complete failures in the career of the composer. The work was completely rewritten, and produced seven years later at Rimini with the present title, *Araldo.* Even in its revised version the opera was not greatly successful. It contains some fine passages, and these, with the overture, are about all that has survived of the work. The music is typical of Verdi at the period of *Rigoletto* and *La Traviata.*

Attila (Selections): Attila was one of the most successful of Verdi's early operas, ranking with *Ernani* in the acclaim it received. It was first performed at the Fenice Theatre in Venice on March 17, 1846. According to the records of the event, the audience was roused to a perfect frenzy of enthusiasm, no less by the music than by the allusions to Austrian despotism. Political manifestations were very much on the order of the day, and even opera composers were anxious to express their nationalistic feelings. Police intervention was not uncommon during operatic performances. *Attila* did not long survive the appositeness of its libretto. The opera today is seldom heard, although it is on a level with Verdi's other early works in melodiousness and spontaneity.

Don Carlos (Selections): Don Carlos was Verdi's last opera before the change in his style represented by *Aïda.* It was written for the Paris Opera, and had its first production there on March 11, 1867. The libretto was adapted from a drama by Schiller (1759-1805), the great German romantic poet and playwright. The story tells of the unhappy love of Don Carlos, son of Philip II of Spain, for his step-mother, and his eventual tragic end. The opera contains some of Verdi's most dramatic writing, and although it is seldom performed today, is also notable for the number of fine arias which occur in it.

Ernani (*Selections*): *Ernani* was the fifth opera composed by Verdi, and by far the most successful of his early works. It was first performed at the Fenice Theatre in Venice on March 9, 1844, with such considerable success that performances on fifteen different operatic stages followed within the year. The libretto is founded on the drama by Victor Hugo (1802-1885), who apparently was not over-enthusiastic about the adaptation, since he asked that the name be changed when the work was produced in Paris. The story deals with the love between the bandit Ernani (really Prince John of Aragon) and the beautiful Elvira, betrothed to an elderly and repulsive Grandee. The plot becomes quite involved and ends with the suicide of Ernani. The stormy drama, however, gave Verdi opportunity to compose a number of exceedingly effective airs, ranking with his best and most expressive. The opera was produced in America as early as 1846, but is seldom heard nowadays.

La Forza del Destino (*The Force of Destiny*) (*Selections*): The plot of Verdi's twenty-fourth opera reminds one of those ancient ballads in which everyone dies violently, but the tinsel horrors of the libretto are hardly enough to destroy the effectiveness of Verdi's music. *La Forza del Destino* contains some of the composer's most impressive melodies. The work was first performed at St. Petersburg in 1862, where it achieved only a moderate success. Verdi later revised the opera and it was received with greater favor. It is still occasionally revived for the beauty of its music.

Overture: Unlike many of Verdi's operas, *La Forza del Destino* contains a comparatively well-developed overture. It opens with an ominous warning note of the trumpet, introducing a dramatic theme in a minor key. The second theme, taken from the Prayer to the Virgin in Act II, is a noble melody in B major. A gentle pastoral melody forms a contrast to this, and the material of the three principal themes is worked up into a brilliant climax.

I Lombardi (*The Lombards*), *Selections: I Lombardi* was the third of the operas which Verdi wrote for the friendly impressario Merelli at the very beginning of his career. Produced at La Scala in Milan on February 11, 1843, it was the most successful of the composer's efforts up to that time. As usual at that time, the censorship caused difficulties in regard to having the opera produced; although the action of the story concerned the First Crusade, it was feared that the Austrian government would find suggestions of rebellion in it. The work was finally given in its original form, and was cordially received. It is still performed occasionally. There are a number of powerful and effective scenes in it, especially the *Crusaders' Chorus* and the *Trio* in Act III.

Chorus of Crusaders: The *Crusaders' Chorus* (*Signor, dal tetto natio*) provoked tremendous enthusiasm at the first performance of *I Lombardi,* and had to be repeated three times. It remains one of the most popular portions of the work by reason of its forceful and dramatic character.

Il Trovatore (*The Troubadour*) *Selections: Il Trovatore* is probably the most popular of Verdi's many operas. It was first performed in Rome on January 19, 1853, less than two months before the première of *La Traviata. Il Trovatore* was a success from the start. Its many fine melodies gave it an immediate appeal which it still holds. After its first production it was heard in almost all of the world's leading opera houses. The first American performance took place in New York in 1855. The story, a compound of witchcraft and horror, gave Verdi ample opportunity to write dramatic music; no opera is more replete with melodrama, and possibly none has given a more varied number of popular airs to the world.

Anvil Chorus: The famous *Anvil Chorus* is heard at the beginning of the second act of the opera, sung by the gypsies as they busy themselves with their hammers.

Miserere: The *Miserere* is heard early in the Fourth Act of *Il Trovatore.* Manrico, the hero, and Azucena, the gypsy, have been confined to prison, and as Leonora arrives to be near her lover, she hears the tolling of a bell and the chant of the priests announcing the doom of a prisoner. The scene is one of the most famous in operatic literature, and is the musical climax of *Il Trovatore.*

Overture, Giovanna d'Arco (*Joan of Arc*): *Joan of Arc* is one of the earlier operas of Verdi of which little survives. It was first performed at Milan on February 15, 1845. Today the work is known almost entirely by the overture, which is written in the melodious vein associated with the composer.

Macbeth (*Selections*): Verdi's opera, with libretto adapted from Shakespeare by Piave and Maffei, was first performed at the Pergola of Florence in 1847. Its one claim to distinction was that it had no tenor part, but that claim to distinction robbed it of all chances of success. The opera must be considered one of Verdi's failures despite a number of fine passages which it contains.

A Masked Ball (*Un Ballo in Maschera*) (*Selections*): The première of *A Masked Ball* was one of Verdi's greatest triumphs, but the event took place only after numerous difficulties. Originally entitled *Gustavus III,* the work incurred the disfavor of the police of Naples, on the lookout for political implications. The work had to be withdrawn from Naples altogether; the title and characters were changed, and the first performance finally took place in Rome on February 17, 1859. It is said that the banning of the work almost caused a revolution in Naples! The opera contains some of Verdi's most admired arias and concerted pieces and has held its place on many opera stages.

Nabucco (*Nebuchadnezzar*) (*Selections*): *Nabucco* really started Verdi on his successful career. It was written as one of the three operas commissioned by Merelli, the Milanese impressario, and produced at La Scala on March 9, 1842. Prior to its composition the composer had suffered the loss of his wife and children, and had little heart to begin work on an opera. The libretto, however, impressed him tremendously, and little by little the music began to take shape. The work was altogether successful when first performed, and portions of it have maintained their popularity.

Rigoletto (*Selections*): *Rigoletto* was produced with triumphant success in Venice on March 11, 1851, but due to the usual complications with the strict censorship, the performance narrowly missed not taking place at all. Verdi's usual librettist, Piave, had made an adaptation of Victor Hugo's melodrama, *Le Roi S'Amuse* (*The King Amuses Himself*) but the Venetian police stated in no uncertain terms that an opera in which a monarch was shown in an unfavorable light could not possibly be produced. Verdi refused to have changes made, but a compromise was finally effected by substituting "A Duke of Mantua" for King Francis I, and altering the title of the opera to *Rigoletto.*

The libretto is by no means one of literature's bright gems, but it served Verdi admirably as a vehicle for some of his finest and most popular music. The opera abounds in famous airs, and includes, of course, the celebrated *Quartet. Rigoletto* has had thousands of performances, in all countries and in all languages.

The Quartet from *Rigoletto:* This famous number occurs in the last act of the opera, where it is sung by the Duke, Gilda, Maddalena and the assassin. It is considered one of Verdi's greatest accomplishments that he was able in a concerted piece of this nature to embody sentiments and characters of the various personalities so successfully.

La Traviata (*Selections*): Verdi's famous opera is founded on Alexander Dumas' equally famous play, *The Lady of the Camellias,* better known as *Camille.* The opera was first produced in Venice on March 6, 1853. Its complete failure was entirely due to the singers; several of them had bad colds, and the heroine, supposed to impersonate a young and beautiful girl dying of consumption, was so extraordinarily stout that the audience burst into laughter. At the Paris production, when Christine Nilsson made her début, and at other subsequent productions of the opera, *Traviata* won immediate favor. It has been in the repertories of almost all opera companies ever since. One of Verdi's most genial creations, it includes a number of airs and ensembles that never grow old. The first American production took place in 1856.

The Sicilian Vespers (*Selections*): *The Sicilian Vespers* was written almost directly after *La Traviata,* and was produced in Paris on June 13, 1855. The libretto, by Scribe and Duveyrier, dealt with the uprising of the Sicilians in 1282 against the tyrannous rule of Charles I of Anjou. (The revolt broke out at the hour of Vespers on Easter Tuesday of 1282, and has become known as *The Sicilian Vespers.*) Despite the anti-French nature of the subject, a peculiar choice for the Paris opera, the work was well received. While the opera has never attained the popularity of many of Verdi's other works of this period, it is not forgotten, and excerpts from it are frequently heard in the concert hall.

Richard Wagner
(Wilhelm Richard Wagner)

BORN Leipzig, Germany, May 22, 1813
DIED Venice, Italy, February 13, 1883

WORKS ARRANGED FOR BAND:

RIENZI: *Overture* (F; B&H; C; Ba
March (F; B&H
Selection (B&H; D
War March & Battle Hymn (F; D

FLYING DUTCHMAN: *Overture* (F
Selection (F; B&H; D
Sailors' Chorus (F
Spinning Song (F

TANNHAUSER: *Overture* (F; B&H; Ru
Selection (F; B&H; Ba; Fil
March (F; B&H; CB
Pilgrims' Chorus (F; Ru; CB; Ba; J
Song to the Evening Star (F; CB; Ba; J

LOHENGRIN: *Prelude* (F; B&H
Selection (F; B&H; D
March & Bridal Chorus (F; B&H; CB
Elsa Entering the Cathedral (F; Rem

RHINEGOLD: *Selection* (B&H
Entry of the Gods into Valhalla (F; B&H

THE VALKYRIES: *Selection* (B&H
Fantasia (F
Ride of the Valkyries (F; B&H
Wotan's Farewell & Fire-Music (B&H

SIEGFRIED: *Selection* (B&H
Fantasia (F

DUSK OF THE GODS: *Siegfried's Death & Funeral March* (F; B&H; C
Selection (B&H
Fantasia (F

TRISTAN AND ISOLDE: *Prelude & Love-Death* (B&H
Love-Death (F
Night-Music (F
Selection (B&H

THE MASTERSINGERS: *Prelude* (F
Selection (B&H
Prize Song (C

PARSIFAL: *Prelude* (C
Selection (B&H
Fantasia (F
Good Friday Music (C
Procession of Knights of the Holy Grail (F

SIEGFRIED IDYLL (B&H

A FAUST OVERTURE (C

NIBELUNGEN MARCH (F; B&H

ALBUM LEAF (F

KAISER MARCH (C

FESTMARSCH (B&H

Note: Almost all of the above selections and many more are available in German editions which can be obtained through the Associated Music Publishers. Of special interest are the following items:

DREAMS (Träume)

THE HOLY SUPPER OF THE APOSTLES

"POLONIA" OVERTURE

"RULE BRITANNIA" OVERTURE

WORKS WRITTEN FOR BAND:

HULDIGUNGSMARSCH (Homage March) (B&H; D

WEBER FUNERAL MARCH on themes from EURYANTHE (AMP

THE career of Wagner was a succession of ups and downs, of defeats and triumphs. As a boy he was devoted to reading, and showed the power of his imagination in many youthful writings. When he first heard the operas of Weber and the symphonies of Beethoven, he was, as he expressed it, "overpowered." He had a good academic education, although his musical training was irregular and procured largely by self-instruction. His first printed compositions date from 1830. In 1833 he started his career as professional musician, becoming chorus-master at the Theatre at Wurzburg. From there he progressed to the conductorship of the Magdeburg Theatre and later of the Koenigsberg Theatre. 1837 saw him installed as conductor of the Opera at Riga.

His first sojourn in Paris included the years 1839-1842.

In spite of friendly aid from Meyerbeer, he was entirely unsuccessful in Paris and had to exist by hack work. He returned to Dresden in 1842 for the première of *Rienzi,* becoming in the next year director of the Dresden Opera. He remained there for six years, leaving only when forced to flee the country after the 1848 revolution. During this period he was constantly composing, lecturing and concertizing, continuing to do so during the succeeding years in Paris, Zurich and other principal cities of Europe. *Tannhäuser* was brought out without overwhelming success; the most abysmal failure of Wagner's career was the performance of that opera in Paris in 1861.

Liszt and other musicians, however, took up his cause and gave him considerable support and prestige. In 1864, King Ludwig II of Bavaria, upon ascending the throne, invited Wagner to Munich. The composer stayed there only a short time, then retired to Triebschen on Lake Lucerne to complete the scores of *The Nibelungen Ring* and *The Mastersingers.* In 1872, the cornerstone of the Bayreuth Theatre was laid, and in August of 1876 the first complete performance of *The Ring* was given there. The next few years were devoted largely to literary work and to the administrative details of the Bayreuth enterprise. Ill-health drove Wagner to spend the winter of 1882-1883 in Italy; it was there, while he was staying in Venice at the Palazzo Piccolomini, that death overtook him.

Wagner's influence in the field of opera and in music generally has been so enormous that it has succeeded in overshadowing the work not only of many composers who held views differing from his, but even that of many of his direct predecessors. Yet during his life-time, as is well known, his works aroused storms of criticism and opposition, the echoes of which have not altogether died down. Today's criticism is based on entirely different premises, but the fact of its existence is proof enough of the composer's weight.

Wagner's contributions lay in several directions, musically and artistically. Primarily they were in the field of opera, where he carried the reforms of Gluck and Weber to their logical conclusion, emphasizing the importance of the drama and its continuity rather than the prettiness of discrete set airs. He gave what is probably the most complete expression to the romantic idea of the fusion of the arts when he sought to combine the plastic, literary and musical media in one art-form. He believed that his conception of opera was, indeed, *the* definitive form, the all-inclusive form beyond which nothing further could be attempted. His technique, embodying comprehensible declamation by the singers and the identifying of ideas and personages by orchestral motifs, is today familiar to all followers of music.

The course of his music was determined by dramatic or literary considerations rather than by the exigencies of musical form. Free in its development, depending greatly on orchestral and harmonic "color," on the strengthening or evocation of pictures and moods, it is entirely different in conception from the music of the classic period.

⸍ ⸍ ⸍

Overture to Rienzi: The idea of composing a spectacular opera on the subject of Bulwer-Lytton's popular novel, *Rienzi, The Last of the Roman Tribunes,* occurred to Wagner as early as 1837. He began work on the text and music while in Riga the following year. Having decided, however, that Paris was the logical place to have the opera produced, he left for France in the Spring of 1839. Meyerbeer was extremely generous in assisting the composer, but no amount of solicitation succeeded in opening the doors of the Paris Opera to him. The score was completed in 1840, and through the renewed intervention of Meyerbeer was finally accepted for performance in Dresden. The première took place on October 20, 1842, and was a triumphant success. Although the opera lasted six hours, its grandiose and spectacular qualities were fully appreciated, and the audience remained to the end to applaud.

Rienzi was written with an eye to popular success, being modelled on the theatrical style made fashionable by Meyerbeer.

The overture includes almost all the principal themes of the opera. It opens with a sustained *A* played by the trumpet, this being the trumpet call heard in the third act. Rienzi's *Prayer* is introduced, followed by the *Chorus of Roman Citizens* and the *Battle Hymn.* The development and recapitulation make use of these themes and the coda is founded on the *Battle Hymn* alone.

The Flying Dutchman: While on his trip from Riga to Paris to try his fortunes with *Rienzi,* Wagner first conceived the idea of an opera based on the legend of the Dutchman doomed to rove the seas until he should find a woman faithful unto death. The opera was completed in 1841, but it was not until after the success of *Rienzi* at the Dresden Opera in 1842, that a performance was secured. The première took place on January 3, 1843, at Dresden. The audience was indifferent to the work, finding, quite justly, that it did not resemble *Rienzi.*

The overture is based on two principal themes: one representing the Curse on the Flying Dutchman and the other derived from the Ballad sung by Senta in the second act. The first part of the overture is a portrayal of a tempestuous storm. The Senta theme provides a contrast of breadth and tranquillity. The material is worked into a miniature summation of the drama: portions of the *Sailors' Chorus* are heard, and at the conclusion the theme of Senta is heard, triumphantly sounded by the full orchestra.

Tannhäuser: Tannhäuser was first performed in Dresden on October 19, 1845. Its production aroused much comment, both favorable and unfavorable, but on the whole the reception of the work could not be called hostile. Liszt produced the opera at Weimar a few years later, and performances followed throughout Europe.

The story of *Tannhäuser* is taken from a popular Teutonic legend which is found in many forms. The combination of religion, eroticism and myth apparently exercised a strong hold over Wagner's imagination, for he was indebted to it for the dramatic content of several of his operas beside *Tannhäuser*. In his literary works he has made quite clear the significance he attached to his libretti and the quality of the musical illustration he sought to give them. *Tannhäuser*, briefly stated, is a drama of holy righteousness triumphing over profane love.

Overture: The *Tannhäuser* overture may well be called a miniature version of the opera itself, since it is built on themes which have clearly marked dramatic meanings. Opening with the well-known *Chorus of the Pilgrims* on the road to Rome, which is heard softly at first, then strongly, and finally as if dying away, it is taken over by the music associated with the Venusberg, the temptation of Tannhäuser. This swirling motive dominates the music until the emergence of Tannhäuser's *Hymn to Venus*, after which it again returns and is developed. Toward the end the *Pilgrims' Chorus* returns, to bring the overture to a triumphant close.

March: The *March* occurs in the second act of *Tannhäuser*. It is performed during the arrival of the guests for the Tournament of Song which takes place in the Great Hall of the Wartburg, and in which Tannhäuser is to participate.

Song to the Evening Star: This apostrophe to the Evening Star is sung in Act III of *Tannhäuser* by the noble Wolfram, as he and Elizabeth anxiously await the return of Tannhäuser from Rome, whither he has gone to seek the forgiveness of the Pope.

Pilgrims' Chorus: The *Pilgrims' Chorus* is heard in Act I of *Tannhäuser.* It is sung by the penitents on their way to Rome and heard by Tannhäuser, who asks the holy men to intercede for him.

Lohengrin: Lohengrin was first produced by Franz Liszt at Weimar in 1850. Its reception was very similar to that accorded *Tannhäuser* several years previous. The followers of the Wagner cult were enthusiastic about the work, while the general public and most of the critics expressed mixed but not altogether unfriendly feelings. Performances throughout Europe followed within a few years, but the opera was not performed in America until 1871.

Like its predecessor, *Lohengrin* is based on old legends found in the German *Volksbuch.* The story of the pure Knight of the Grail who arrives in a boat drawn by a swan in order to defend Elsa, and who is forced to return whence he came when she is persuaded to ask his name, is familiar to all. Wagner provided one of his most melodious and transparent scores for the drama; in the music his subsequent use of the *leit-motiv* is foreshadowed.

Prelude: Wagner and Liszt both wrote explanatory programs of this prelude, in which they emphasized the unearthly and radiant character of its content. It is in effect a tonal vision of the Holy Grail itself, marvelously delicate and yet impressive throughout. It is constructed on one single motive, subtly varied in timbre and strength; a climax is reached toward the middle of the prelude when the theme is solemnly intoned by the brass, after which the Vision dies away as quietly as it first appeared.

Elsa Entering the Cathedral: The Fourth Scene of the Second Act of *Lohengrin* closes with music of great splendor, as Elsa, preceded by her attendants, prepares to enter the Minster. Slow processional music begins the scene. As Elsa herself appears, a stirring greeting is sung by the entire chorus, reaching a climax with fanfares on the trumpets. The joyous nature of the scene is abruptly changed when Ortrud, seeking her vengeance on Elsa, reminds the latter that she does not know her hero's name. Elsa's agitation is portrayed in the music, which closes in sombre fashion.

Bridal Chorus: Act III of *Lohengrin* opens with the familiar Wedding March played as a prelude by the orchestra. As the curtain rises the march becomes softer until the bridal party enters. The assembled guests sing the *Bridal Chorus* as Elsa and Lohengrin appear.

The Ring of the Nibelungs: The Ring, Wagner's most grandiose work, occupied the composer well over twenty years, from the time of its first conception, before 1850, to the time *The Dusk of the Gods* was completed, in 1874. During this period Wagner had traveled, written, conducted and tried to promote the appreciation of his work, but had had little time for the completion of his enormous trilogy. Other operas had been composed in the meantime, but the idea of *The Ring* had never ceased to occupy him. It was finally performed for the first time at Bayreuth in August, 1876, Hans Richter conducting.

The Ring of the Nibelungs consists of three music-dramas and a prologue. Wagner, of course, wrote the poems as well as the music, taking his theme from the epic Teuton mythology. The plot is far too complex to be outlined in a short space; the reader is therefore referred to any one of a number of competent summaries which have been made, or to the original. The musical setting of *The Ring* embodies Wagner's mature conception of the music-drama as an art-form. The elimination of the chorus, the "continuous melody" in the orchestra, the use of identifying leit-motivs, the increased reliance on stage effects, the abandonment of the "set piece" —all of these things are found fully realized in the Nibelung Trilogy.

(Probably more descriptive, defensive and exegetical rubbish has been written about *The Ring* than about any other work of art with the possible exception of the *Mona Lisa.* The reader seeking a somewhat acid antidote would do well to investigate a remarkable book by Tolstoi, entitled, *What is Art?* Another interesting interpretation of *The Ring* is that given by George Bernard Shaw in *The Perfect Wagnerite.*)

The Rhinegold: The Rhinegold, although it is as long as the ordinary opera, is actually the prologue to *The Ring of the Nibelungen.* Wagner began work on it in 1853, although the idea had been pre-occupying him long before. The score was completed in 1854, but the work was not performed until 1869, when it was produced at Munich.

Entry of the Gods Into Valhalla: The Rhinegold gives the background of the epic of *The Ring,* and tells the story of the building of the new abode of the Gods, Valhalla. The last scene of the opera shows the completed castle gleaming in the distance. Donner, the God of Thunder, creates a rainbow to serve as passage to it, and the Gods majestically proceed across. As they make their way toward Valhalla, which they have acquired through so much trickery and intrigue, Loge, the God of Fire, watches them with foreboding, while from the Rhine below come the lamentations of the Rhine-Maidens who have been robbed of their treasure. The music includes the motives of all of these characters, as well as those for the Gold and for Valhalla.

The Valkyries: The first opera of the *Ring* trilogy takes its name from the daughters of Wotan, the Valkyries, who carry to Valhalla the bodies of heroes fallen in battle. Wagner began work on this opera immediately after completing *The Rhinegold,* and finished the score in 1856. It received its first performance at Munich in 1870.

Wotan's Farewell and Fire-Music: The Valkyries closes with the impressive scene in which Wotan, enraged at Brünnhilde for her disobedience to his commands, causes the Valkyrie to fall into a deep sleep from which only a great hero can wake her. Wotan's fatherly feelings are stirred, and he bids his favorite daughter farewell in this solemn music. At the conclusion of his farewell, he places Brünnhilde on a high and lonely rock and summons Loge to surround the rock with a ring of fire. The Fire-Music which follows is one of the most remarkable passages of descriptive music ever penned. As the flames mount higher, Wotan gazes tenderly at Brünnhilde until he finally disappears in the fire.

The Ride of the Valkyries: The Third Act of *The Valkyries* opens with this most popular of all excerpts from *The Ring.* The scene is the summit of a rocky mountain, the gathering place of the nine Valkyries, or daughters of Wotan. As these warlike demi-goddesses arrive on their winged horses, they greet each other with their battle-cry. The music which accompanies this scene hardly needs description, since it is in itself admirably descriptive of the character of the scene and its protagonists.

Siegfried: The first sketches for the music of *Siegfried,* the second of the *Ring* trilogy, were made by Wagner in 1854, but the opera remained incomplete until 1869, when favorable conditions enabled the composer to resume his work. The first production of *Siegfried* took place at Bayreuth in 1876, when Hans Richter directed the complete *Ring* cycle.

Siegfried tells the story of the youth of the hero, from his forging of the sword of Wotan and his slaying of the dragon to his rescue of Brünnhilde, the Valkyrie who has been awaiting her deliverance at the hands of a great hero. The music of this part of *The Ring* is for the most part less sombre than that of the other portions. The youth and strength of *Siegfried*, and his heroic exploits, give a noble and buoyant character to the score. The passage known as "Forest Murmurs," and the scene in which the hero breaks through the ring of fire to discover Brünnhilde have always been great favorites among Wagnerians.

The Dusk of the Gods: The last part of the *Ring* trilogy was composed somewhat later than the preceding operas. Due to the unsettled conditions of Wagner's life, and the worries to which he was subjected, the composition of *The Ring* was repeatedly interrupted. The composer did not begin actual work on *The Dusk of the Gods* until late in 1869, thirteen years after the completion of *The Valkyries.* The first performance took place in 1876 at Bayreuth, as part of the first complete production of *The Ring.*

The Dusk of the Gods tells of the death of Siegfried and the doom of the Gods and heroes. The musical material is for the most part that which is introduced in the earlier portions of *The Ring,* although new characters and new situations bring with them new motives as well as mutations of the old ones. The most famous portions of the opera are *Siegfried's Rhine Journey,* which occurs in the First Act, and *Siegfried's Death.* This latter scene takes place in Act III as the hero, slain by the treachery of Hagen and Gunther, is borne back to the Hall. The Funeral March which accompanies the scene is unrivalled in all of Wagner's music for intensity of expression. Almost all of the motives connected with Siegfried's life are woven together in the music, but in deeply tragic guise. The closing notes of this epic passage recall the fateful motive of *The Curse of the Ring*, the motivating force of the entire drama.

Tristan and Isolde: The most intensely passionate of Wagner's music-dramas was written under the direct inspiration of Mathilde Wesendonck. There is some question, too, as to the extent of the influence brought to bear on the composer by the philosophy of Schopenhauer. In any case, *Tristan* is a creation embodying the idea of the identity of Love and Death. Wagner began work on the opera in 1857, completing it in 1859. As usual, Wagner found it difficult to obtain a hearing for the work. Fifty-seven rehearsals in Vienna were found to be insufficient, and the project of performing it there was abandoned. Finally, in 1865, the opera was performed in Munich. The first American performance took place in 1886.

The legend of Tristan has been treated by many poets. Wagner based his version on the medieval poem of Godfrey of Strasbourg, but introduced a number of changes to suit his own purposes. It is said that Wagner regarded *Tristan* as a supplement to *The Ring*, since the legends involved are closely related.

The opera is constructed on the same basic principles which Wagner adhered to in *The Ring*. Yet the simpler dramatic content and the more natural emotional quality of the work give the music a more direct and immediately moving quality. From the opening notes of the *Prelude* to the closing notes of the *Love-Death* there is little material which is not germane to the central ideas of Love and Death. The emotional approach to both ideas is that of passionate yearning.

The *Prelude* and *Love-Death* are generally performed together in concert. The *Prelude,* properly speaking, has no formal ending, and the arrangement of the *Love-Death* as a closing is Wagner's own.

The Mastersingers: Wagner's sole comic-opera was first sketched as early as 1845. The book was completed in 1852; the music was begun in the same year and finished in 1867. *The Mastersingers* was first performed at Munich, under the direction of Hans von Bülow, on June 21, 1868. The first American performance took place in 1886.

The material of the opera is partly historic, partly romantic and partly satiric. The scene is Nuremberg in the sixteenth century, when the Guilds of Mastersingers still existed. Hans Sachs, a character in the opera, was actually one of the leading musicians of the time (1494-1576). Wagner's opera was presumably intended, at least in part, as an answer to the critics who claimed he was incapable of writing a melody. The Contest of Song is, in that sense, an allegorical bout between Wagner and his detractors. The satire in *The Mastersingers* is often a bit heavy-handed, but the music has a spirit quite different from any of Wagner's other operas. It is, as one would expect, considerably more blithe and hearty, and at the same time reveals a clearness of contrapuntal line which deserves to rank as one of Wagner's greatest musical achievements.

The Prelude is based on some of the principal themes of the opera, beginning with the dignified and rhythmic theme of the Mastersingers and including a tender love theme and Walter's *Prize Song*. The *Prelude* has the character of a gay and colorful procession, in which the various motives are skillfully intertwined. It is one of the liveliest examples of Wagner's art.

The Prize Song is sung by Walter, the hero of the opera, to win the *Mastersingers* contest which he had to enter in order to win the hand of his beloved Eva. Walter's success is due in large part to the friendly aid of old Hans Sachs, who takes a beneficent interest in the lovers.

Parsifal: Parsifal, called by Wagner a *Bühnenweihfestspiel* (*Holy-Festival-Stage-Play*), was the composer's last major work, occupying him during the years 1878 and 1879. The poem had been published previously. The basic idea of the work had been in his mind for many years, and, in fact, he had at one time commenced work on an opera to be known as *Jesus of Nazareth.* The subject of a religious drama was finally found in the legends of the Holy Grail and the Knights who guarded it. The first performance of *Parsifal* took place at Bayreuth on July 28, 1882.

The *Prelude* leads directly into the opening scene of the opera. The first motive to be heard in the *Prelude* is that of the Eucharist. This is repeated in different aspects, and is followed by the motive of the Grail. Other motives which occur are those of Faith and the Sacred Lance. The entire *Prelude* moves with great solemnity and is confined to the purely religious elements of the drama.

Good Friday Music: For concert use some of the music of Act III of *Parsifal* has been extracted and re-arranged. This music, known as the *Good Friday Spell,* accompanies the scene in the drama where Parsifal once again meets the aged Gurnemanz. Gurnemanz this time is certain that Parsifal is the appointed hero, and anoints him as Prince and King of the Holy Grail. Parsifal is struck by the beauty of the surroundings, and in response to his question Gurnemanz explains that the supernatural beauty is caused by the spell of Good Friday. The motives which are heard during this passage include the two Parsifal motives (Parsifal the Victorious and Parsifal the Guileless Fool), Faith and Atonement. The motive of the Lance is also momentarily heard.

Procession of the Knights of the Holy Grail: After Parsifal has been anointed Prince and King of the Grail, he and Gurnemanz return to the Temple, where the funeral of Titurel is about to take place. The Knights file into the Hall in solemn procession, while this music, which includes the motives of the Grail and of the Chimes of the Temple, is heard.

Siegfried Idyll: The *Siegfried Idyll* was composed by Wagner in 1871 as an expression of happiness at the birth of a son. It is based on four motives from the opera *Siegfried* and an old German cradle-song. Wagner conducted the first performance of the work as an *aubade* for his wife, the orchestra gathering in the early morning outside of the Wagner villa at Triebschen. The *Siegfried Idyll* was written for small orchestra, but has been often transcribed.

A Faust Overture: This composition was originally intended to be the first movement of a program symphony dealing with Goethe's *Faust.* The scheme was never carried out, and the peculiar emotional character of the *Faust Overture* is explained in Wagner's own words, by the fact that it deals with only one aspect of the hero, that of his loneliness and despair. The *Faust Overture* was written in 1840, but revised in 1855. It opens with a lengthy introduction, in the course of which most of the principal themes are suggested. The principal theme is of a sombre and melancholy character, but the second theme provides the necessary contrast of mood. The development is quite lengthy, but dramatic and agitated throughout.

Album Leaf: This popular selection was originally written for pianoforte, although it achieved greater fame in the violin arrangement made by Wilhelmj. It was written about 1860 and dedicated to Princess Metternich.

Dreams: This composition is one of a set of songs written by Wagner in 1857 to words of Mathilde Wesendonck. *Dreams* was published as a *Study for Tristan and Isolde.* The material in it was used by the composer for the love-duet in the second act of the opera.

The Holy Supper of the Apostles: This comparatively little known work of Wagner was composed in 1843 for the Men's Song Festival in Dresden, at which the composer was to conduct. The work originally called for three separate choirs and full orchestra. It is subtitled, *A Biblical Scene.*

Huldigungsmarsch: When Wagner was invited to Munich by the young King Ludwig II of Bavaria, he desired to show his respect for that amiable monarch by the composition of a suitable occasional piece. The *Homage March* was written in 1864, the year of his arrival in Munich, and scored for military band. It was never published in that form. Wagner himself began the orchestral version but due to the pressure of other activities never finished it. This task was later accomplished by Raff. The composition is not in the usual march form, but retains the characteristics of a ceremonial march.

Kaisermarsch: The *Kaisermarsch* was written to celebrate the Prussian victory over France in 1870. The work is very elaborate in conception and strictly German in character. Wagner originally intended to have a chorus sing words to it, but abandoned the plan. The Chorale of Martin Luther, *Ein'Feste Burg,* is introduced. The *Kaisermarsch* is really more of a tone-poem than a march, replete with fanfares, battle music and hymns.

Festival March: This march was composed for the Philadelphia Centennial Exposition in 1876. Like Wagner's other "Marches," the *Festmarsch* departs from the conventional form, but retains the swinging spirit and movement of the true march.

Weber Funeral March (*Trauermarsch zur Besetzung C. M. von Webers*): Eighteen years after the death in London of Carl Maria von Weber, a patriotic movement in Germany resulted in the transference of his remains to his native land. In that year (1844) an impressive ceremony took place at Dresden, in which Wagner took a leading part. Besides reading the funeral oration, Wagner composed the march for the procession. This march, now known as the *Weber Funeral March,* or sometimes as *By Weber's Grave,* was based on two themes from Weber's *Euryanthe,* and was scored for large wind band. The work is marked *andante maestoso* and is in the key of B flat, minor and major.

Wagner's score calls for 5 flutes, 4 first obes, 3 second oboes, 5 first B♭ clarinets, 5 second, 5 third and 5 fourth B♭ clarinets, 5 first bassoons, 5 second bassoons, 4 first horns, 4 second horns, 3 first B♭ horns, 3 second B♭ horns, 6 trumpets in F, 3 alto trombones, 3 tenor trombones, 3 bass trombones, 4 tubas in C and 6 muffled side drums. The score was not published until 1926.

William Vincent Wallace

BORN Waterford, Ireland, June 1, 1814
DIED Chateau de Bages (Pyrenees), October 12, 1865

WORKS ARRANGED FOR BAND:

Overtures: MARITANA (B&H; F
LURLINE (F

Selections: MARITANA (F; B&H; D
LURLINE (F

PROBABLY no other composer has ever had such extensive travels to his credit as the composer of *Maritana* and *Lurline.* Wallace visited every continent, concertizing with enormous success. He was a violinist of considerable attainments. Aside from his popular operas, his compositions for the pianoforte had a great vogue.

✓ ✓ ✓

Maritana was first performed at the Drury Lane Theatre in London in 1845, scoring a great success. The overture introduces the famous melody *Scenes That Are Brightest,* which occurs in the opera. Brilliant in character, this overture includes a splendid fugue which places it far above the level of most light-opera overtures.

✓

Lurline was an even greater triumph for Wallace than was *Maritana.* It was first played at Covent Garden in 1860. Although the opera is outmoded and seldom revived, many of the melodies which occur in it are still popular. Notable among these is the song, *Sweet Spirit Hear My Prayer,* which has been a universal favorite for many years.

Carl Maria von Weber

BORN Eutin, Germany, December 18, 1786
DIED London, June 5, 1826

WORKS ARRANGED FOR BAND:

Overtures: DER FREISCHÜTZ (B&H; F
OBERON (B&H; F; C
EURYANTHE (F; C
JUBEL (B&H; F
PRECIOSA (F
ABU HASSAN (D
PETER SCHMOLL (D
Selections from: DER FREISCHÜTZ (F; B&H; C
INVITATION TO THE WALTZ (B&H; F

WEBER'S father was conductor of the town orchestra at Eutin and had as his fondest ambition that his son should become a great composer. A fortunate father indeed! Carl Maria's childhood was passed with his family, traveling with a dramatic company. His musical studies were irregular but thorough, Michael Haydn and the Abbé Vogler being among his teachers. His first opera was written when he was eleven years of age; it was never performed and the manuscript was destroyed. It was not long, however, before the talented young man had an opera produced, the first of many prodigious successes.

His reputation thus early established, Weber traveled from one opera house to another as conductor, giving piano recitals in between times, and composing steadily. In 1816 he was called upon to reorganize the Royal Opera at Dresden. The success of his later great operas caused him to give up this position in order to travel again. In his last years he was almost a national hero in German-speaking countries.

Weber was the founder of the German romantic opera. An extremely original talent, he succeeded in upsetting the

Italian domination of the opera stage and in substituting for it something genuinely national, warmer in feeling and of greater musical depth. His vein of melody was vivid and sensitive, his dramatic sense pronounced. His influence on later German composers was enormous; on Schumann and on Marschner it is quite evident, but it is not generally realized to how great an extent Wagner was also indebted to him.

Der Freischütz (*The Freeshooters*): While in Dresden, Weber conceived the idea of writing an opera on a national subject. A friend, one Friedrich Kind, arranged the libretto from a popular novel by Apel, and in 1817 Weber began work on *Der Freischütz*. The composition took him three years. The first production took place in Berlin in 1821 and was a triumph for the composer. The opera took hold immediately on all German and Austrian stages, and has been a fixture to this day.

Der Freischütz is based on a popular tale of the woods; hunters and woodsmen are its characters. The music is full of the freshness and calm of the setting and the robust vigor of the characters. It is deeply and completely German in character, full of those simple but lovely melodies which are almost indistinguishable from true folk-songs. The instrumentation is brilliant; the dramatic quality inspired. The opera created almost at one stroke a new operatic school, totally different in feeling from the prevailing Italian style, and paving the way for Schumann and Wagner.

Overture, Euryanthe: Following the triumph of *Der Freischütz,* Weber began the composition of *Euryanthe* to a miserable libretto by Wilhelmine von Chezy. It was brought out at Vienna in 1823, and despite its extraordinarily beautiful music, was not overwhelmingly successful. It fared better in Berlin, but has never attained the popularity of *Der Frei-*

schütz. The story of *Euryanthe* is taken from a medieval legend which recurs many times in literature—notably in Boccaccio and in Shakespeare (*Cymbeline*). The overture is based on themes from the opera; it has always maintained its place as a concert piece, although the opera itself is seldom performed.

Overture, Oberon: Weber was commissioned to write an English opera for Covent Garden in London after he had achieved European fame as a result of *Der Freischütz.* Although plagued by ill-health, the composer commenced work on *Oberon* in 1825. The libretto was by J. R. Planche and was based on a fairy tale by Wieland. Weber went to London to supervise the first performances in March, 1826. The effort entailed in conducting the rehearsals and in giving concerts exhausted him and he died eight weeks after the first performance of the opera.

The overture to *Oberon* is Weber at his best. The opening *adagio* is marvelous in coloring; the three notes played by the horn, with the reply by the clarinets, create a haunting atmosphere. Weber's skill in writing for horns and woodwinds is evident throughout. The horn motif is heard again in the *Allegro,* just before the introduction of the second subject. The *Allegro* is fresh and vigorous, full of the delicate shading which was the particular secret of Weber.

Overture, Preciosa: The *Preciosa Overture* is part of the incidental music which Weber wrote in 1820 for a play by P. A. Wolff, adapted from a novel by Cervantes. It takes high rank among Weber's compositions in this form. The composer is said to have been greatly taken by the character of the play. In any case, it gave him an opportunity to write music full of the "local color" which he so dearly loved. Spanish and gypsy tunes abound in the dances and vocal pieces which he wrote for *Preciosa;* some of these are, indeed, discernible in the overture. Weber's talent for illustrating and underlining dramatic situations was nowhere better shown than in this music; it abounds in contrasts and is forceful without being over-emphatic.

Jubel Overture: Weber wrote this famous overture for the celebration of the fiftieth anniversary of the accession to the throne of King Friedrich August of Saxony. Along with other music he had composed for the occasion, it was performed in Dresden in 1818. Weber was extremely conscientious about the "occasional" music he was called upon to write, and invariably put his best efforts into it. The *Jubel Overture* reveals Weber's dramatic instincts, for although a concert overture, it is full of surprising contrasts. It is developed with Weber's characteristic polish and scored with his usual brilliance.

Overture, Abu Hassan: The one-act *singspiel, Abu Hassan,* belongs to the middle period of Weber's artistic life. It was the last stage work he composed before the three great operas *Der Freischütz, Euryanthe* and *Oberon.* The libretto, which is full of real comedy, was adapted from an Arabian tale. The music consisted originally of the overture and eight vocal pieces. It shows much ingenuity and originality. The little opera was first performed on June 4, 1811, at Munich.

The overture is full of the contrast and color for which Weber is famous. It is built on themes from the opera itself, but is developed as an independent unit.

Overture, Peter Schmoll: Peter Schmoll was Weber's second attempt in the field of opera, undertaken at the age of fourteen. Although a remarkable production for one of such tender years, the work was far from a great one, and it has not survived. The story was based on a romance of knights and robbers, set during the period of the French Revolution. The libretto had little worth, but its romanticism evidently attracted the young composer.

The overture was remodelled and published in 1807 as a separate number, bearing the legend: "Grand Overture for Several Instruments." It is slight in substance, but full of excellent and charming melodies which suggest Weber's future development in that they are much closer in spirit to German folk-song than to the operatic style which prevailed at the time.

Invitation to the Waltz (Weber-Weingartner): This ever-popular number was originally written for the pianoforte, and later arranged for orchestra by Berlioz. Felix Weingartner, the eminent German composer and conductor, evidently felt that in this case Berlioz had overlooked many possibilities for elaboration, and accordingly made a new orchestral arrangement which has become a classic. Weingartner's arrangement is extremely ingenious. He used the first subject of the waltz as a counter-melody in the trio, and introduced a number of further contrapuntal effects which greatly enrich the original.

Weber was one of the great piano virtuosi of his day. He composed much fine music for the instrument, including four sonatas and ten sets of variations.

Jaromir Weinberger

BORN Prague, Czechoslovakia, 1896

ARRANGED FOR BAND:

Polka and *Fugue* from SCHWANDA, THE BAGPIPE PLAYER (AMP

WEINBERGER'S reputation in this country rests almost entirely on his brilliant opera, *Schwanda, the Bagpipe Player,* although the opera itself was not produced until after the *Polka* and *Fugue* and several other excerpts had scored great successes as concert pieces. The première of *Schwanda* took place at Prague in 1928; in the same year the *Polka* and *Fugue* were played at a concert of the Philharmonic Society in New York under Erich Kleiber. The Metropolitan Opera House performed the work in the following year.

The opera itself is a delightfully gay fantasy, which involves its hero in many bizarre adventures. The score is complex and masterly; the composer, even in the most elaborate pages, did not lose the lightness of touch which makes the work so vigorously gay. The *Polka* has a magnificent swing; it is, of course, patterned after the traditional Czech dance. The *Fugue* has an extraordinarily long subject, which is worked out freely and with great skill. The melody of the *Polka* is worked into it as a counter-theme. The score calls for a large orchestra and organ.

Weinberger studied at the Prague Conservatory and under Max Reger in Leipzig. For a brief period, beginning with 1922, he was Professor of Theory at the Ithaca Conservatory, at Ithaca, N. Y.

Ernest S. Williams

BORN Wayne County, Indiana, 1881

WRITTEN FOR BAND:

SYMPHONY NO. 1 IN C MINOR (Wil
(Also many marches, cornet solos, trios, etc.)

ERNEST S. WILLIAMS is one of the most celebrated cornetists America has ever produced. From his sixteenth year he enjoyed phenomenal success as soloist, playing with the bands of Gilmore, Sousa and Goldman, and also with his own organization. In 1913-14, Mr. Williams toured the world as soloist, gaining wide acclaim. In addition to his solo work with bands, he performed as first trumpeter and soloist under Nahan Franko, Victor Herbert and other celebrities, and finally went to the Philadelphia Orchestra, where he remained for six years as solo trumpeter under Stokowski, Richard Strauss, Georges Enesco and other noted conductors.

In 1922 Mr. Williams founded the Ernest Williams School of Music in Brooklyn, N. Y., and since that time has devoted most of his energies to teaching and composing. Many of his pupils have had great success. Mr. Williams has written a Cornet Method and several Concerti for the instrument, as well as many solos and ensemble pieces.

Symphony in C Minor

Andante. Allegro Moderato
Larghetto
Allegro Vivace

This symphony, probably the first written for band by an American composer, was completed by Mr. Williams early in 1938 and received its first public performance at the annual festival of the Ernest Williams School in Town Hall, New York, in May of that year.

The introduction is based on the principal theme of the first movement, and strikes a note of mystery and expectation. The *Allegro* itself is vigorous and strong, though the second theme, in the major, is of a more lyrical character. The movement ends in the minor, in a stern and almost defiant mood.

The *Larghetto*, in A flat major, is deeply serene. Agitated passages provide contrast, but the movement ends, after an outburst of ardor, with the peace which marks its opening.

The finale is full of vigorous and ingenious cross-rhythms, relieved by the song-like character of the subordinate theme. The movement builds up to a victorious fortissimo, and is brought to a close by the first theme transformed into a brilliant major.

Ralph Vaughan Williams

BORN Gloucestershire, England, October 12, 1872

ORIGINAL WORKS FOR BAND:

ENGLISH FOLK SONG SUITE (B&H
TOCCATA MARZIALE (B&H

VAUGHAN WILLIAMS is one of the most eminent of contemporary English composers, known throughout the world for his splendid choral and orchestral works. He completed his musical studies with Max Bruch and Maurice Ravel. Like many modern English composers, especially Holst (q. v.), he has found great inspiration in the study of folk music and of the early English masters such as Purcell. He has made his own the modal harmonies and striking rhythms found in the traditional songs and dances of Norfolk and Somerset, but has formed an entirely individual style out of these elements.

✓ ✓ ✓

English Folk Song Suite:

I. I'm Seventeen Come Sunday
II. My Bonnie Boy
III. Folk Songs from Somerset

Vaughan Williams' interest in the wind band has nowhere found more satisfactory expression than in this characteristic suite. The score is remarkable for its originality and for the subtle touches in it. The musical subjects are all traditional, and reflect the composer's lifelong studies in the field of folk music.

✓

Toccata Marziale: Vaughan Williams' *Toccata Marziale* is one of the great contributions to the original band repertory made by a distinguished contemporary composer. The work is scored for full band and is exceedingly impressive and stirring. The form chosen by the composer, that of the Toccata, is of fairly ancient origin, having first been used in the early part of the seventeenth century. It is a rather free form, varying in its treatment from century to century. Its principal characteristics are a flowing movement in notes of approximately the same length, with an accompaniment of marked chords. The name is derived from the Italian *toccare*, to touch, and the Toccata seems to have been originally a composition designed to display the touch of a performer on a keyed instrument.

Ermanno Wolf-Ferrari

BORN Venice, January 12, 1876

ARRANGED FOR BAND:

Two *Intermezzi* from THE JEWELS OF THE MADONNA (S; B&H

WOLF-FERRARI has written several successful operas, of which the best-known are *The Jewels of the Madonna* and *The Secret of Suzanne.* The composer studied in Germany, but although he greatly admired Wagner, traces of German influence are not marked in his work. His chamber-music is distinguished, but is not very well known in America.

The Jewels of the Madonna was first performed at Berlin in 1911. It is on the order of *Cavalleria Rusticana* in its "realism" and melodrama. The story concerns the truly amazing doings of a group of Camorrists during the preparations for the celebration in honor of the Virgin. The two intermezzi yield in popularity only to the intermezzo from *Cavalleria.* The waltz intermezzo occurs between the second and third acts; the other is played just before the beginning of the second act.

Haydn Wood

BORN Slaithwaite, England (Yorkshire), 1882

ORIGINAL WORKS FOR BAND:

MANNIN VEEN (B&H
Overture, APOLLO (B&H

WORKS ARRANGED FOR BAND:

A Southern Rhapsody, VIRGINIA (C
Overture, A MAY DAY (B&H
Suite, HARVEST TIME (B&H
Suite, FRESCOES (B&H
A MANX RHAPSODY (C

ALTHOUGH Haydn Wood is fast achieving fame as one of the world's foremost composers of band music, he first gained prominence as a violinist. He studied that instrument at the Royal College of Music in London under Arbos and later in Brussels under César Thomson. For many years he toured as a concert violinist, appearing in nearly every part of the world.

While at the Royal College of Music he pursued studies in composition under Sir Charles Villiers Stanford. Prior to entering that institution, he had won the Morley Scholarship, being then but fifteen years of age.

Before the attention of the band world was attracted to his compositions, Haydn Wood was best known as a writer of ballads. Many of these, such as *Roses of Picardy, A Brown Bird Singing* and others have achieved very great popularity. Their pleasing vein of melody is developed on a larger scale in Wood's band compositions; these latter show, in addition, a finished workmanship, a harmonic richness, and a thorough understanding of the band.

Mannin Veen (*Dear Isle of Man*): Haydn Wood spent much of his early childhood on the Isle of Man, situated in the Irish Sea between England and Ireland. Steeped in the tradition of the Island, with its abundant folklore and wealth of native music, the composer has turned his knowledge to good musical account in many of his works. His tone-poem, *Mannin Veen,* is based on four Manx folk tunes: *The Good Old Way, The Manx Fiddler, Sweet Water In The Common,* and a hymn, *The Harvest of the Sea.* The simple beauty and expressiveness of these modal tunes are admirably brought out in this work.

Overture, Apollo: The *Apollo Overture* was written directly for band and appeared in 1936. The composer has given no indication of a program for the overture, which is simple in structure and pleasing in its melodic content. It opens with four bars of introduction, after which the first theme, in A minor, is given out by the clarinets. At the twenty-fifth bar of the *Allegro,* a transitional theme, derived from the first, is heard in G major. The second theme proper, in F major, is announced a few bars later by the alto saxophone. These themes are developed with skill and clarity, and with an abundance of the rich harmony which characterizes the composer's scores. The recapitulation begins with a repetition of the introductory bars and follows the usual pattern.

A Southern Rhapsody, Virginia: The *Southern Rhapsody* was one of the first of Wood's works to become popular with American bands, possibly because it is distinctly American in flavor. The composer, although an Englishman, succeeded admirably in capturing the spirit of the musical South. *Swanee River* is heard in various guises throughout the Rhapsody, which is characterized by rich flowing harmonies and frequent modulations. An *Allegro* theme in the style of a Plantation Dance provides a contrast to the languorous mood of the sections based on *Swanee River*. The composition was originally written for orchestra.

Overture, A May Day: This overture is one of the early orchestral compositions of Haydn Wood. It is smoothly written and pleasing in its melodic content, suggesting perhaps more than Wood's other large compositions the ballad-style which first made him famous. The overture opens with a languorous *andante* in which the principal themes are heard. The first theme is given out as a horn solo. At the fifty-fifth bar the tempo changes to *vivace,* and the themes are heard in brighter colors. The overture builds up to a heavy climax in which most of the thematic material is heard in strong accents.

Suite, Frescoes:

I. Vienna, 1913
II. Sea Chanties
III. The Bandstand, Hyde Park

The numbers of this suite are intended as musical companion-pieces to a set of decorative panels in the offices of Boosey and Hawkes, Ltd., in London. All are written in the melodious and pleasing style which has brought popularity to the work of the composer. The first is in waltz time, and suggests the atmosphere of pre-war Vienna. The second is based on two melodies, the first broad and flowing, the second spirited and jolly. The third is full of animation and movement.

Date Due

15 Mar 41			
16 Apr 41			
3-23-57			